Mount Rogers
National Recreation Area
Guidebook

Other Books by Johnny Molloy

Visit the author's Web site: www.johnnymolloy.com

Mount Rogers
National Recreation Area
Guidebook

A Complete Resource for Outdoor Enthusiasts

Second Edition

Johnny Molloy

The University of Tennessee Press / Knoxville

Copyright © 2008 by The University of Tennessee Press / Knoxville.
All Rights Reserved. Manufactured in the United States of America.
First Edition.

Unless otherwise noted, photographs are by the author.

A previous edition of this book was published in 2001 by Menasha Ridge Press.

This book is printed on acid-free paper.

Library of Congress Cataloging-in-Publication Data

Molloy, Johnny, 1961–
    [Mount Rogers outdoor recreation handbook]
    Mount Rogers National Recreation Area guidebook : a complete resource for
outdoor enthusiasts / Johnny Molloy. — 2nd ed.
    p. cm.
    First published in 2001 by Menasha Ridge Press under the title Mount Rogers outdoor
recreation handbook.
    Includes index.
    ISBN-13: 978-1-57233-628-5 (pbk. : alk. paper)
    ISBN-10: 1-57233-628-5
1. Outdoor recreation—Virginia—Guidebooks.
2. Mount Rogers National Recreation Area (Va.)—Guidebooks.
I. Title.
    GV191.42.V8M65 2008
    917.55'723–dc22   2007047848

Contents

Suggested Trail Loops

Illustrations

Maps follow page xxxiii.

Acknowledgments

Researching and writing a book of this scope takes a lot of time and a lot of help. So many friends, old and new, helped me make this project happen. I would like to thank Bud Zehmer, as he backed the initial idea for this book.

Traveling the trails of Mount Rogers was made more enjoyable by the presence of Bryan Delay, Kim Berney, Chris Phillips, Bob Phillips, Bernadette Pedagno, Kevin Thomas, and John D. Bland. Thanks to John Cox for making numerous backpacking trips with me, in cold and rain and when the weather was nice.

Thanks to my old pal Steve Grayson for letting me stay at his Marion home on occasion. Thanks to Lafuma for their fine packs, sleeping bags, and hiking shoes.

All the folks at Mount Rogers National Recreation Headquarters were very helpful. I've got to single out Bob McKinney, who answered too many questions about everything, and Tim Eling, who answered my post-hike trail questions. Also helpful were Tom Blevins, who has a knack for words, and Cookie Patterson, Sue Combs, Deanna Roe, that Vol Doug Byerly, Mike Evans, Beth Merz, Ginny Williams, and Sue Blevins. Thanks to the staffs at Grayson Highlands State Park and New River Rail Trail State Park.

Thanks to Dave Patrick, Jeff Patrick, and Tom Davenport from Mount Rogers Outfitters for their help. Thanks to Tom Horsch at Adventure Damascus for outfitting my mountain bike and to Tim Williams, Marvin and Shirley Phillips, Lynette Barker, and Roy Hacker for their help.

For the second edition, many other people helped. I'm grateful to Scot Danforth and Gene Adair at UT Press for their enthusiasm, to Will Skelton for his suggestions, and to everyone else who made this book possible.

Introduction

Welcome to the second edition of this book. Mount Rogers National Recreation Area in Virginia is the least known great destination in the Southern Appalachians. It is the third crown jewel of these mountains, along with the Great Smoky Mountains National Park in Tennessee and North Carolina and the Shenandoah National Park in Virginia. These highlands offer recreationalists numerous activities in which to indulge: hiking, mountain biking, horseback riding, camping, fishing, swimming, skiing, auto touring, and picnicking.

Around Mount Rogers, the marked and maintained trails in the federal recreation area and Grayson Highlands State Park, along with New River Rail Trail State Park, add up to over 430 miles worth of trails. This includes the Mount Rogers Trail, which heads to the highest point in Virginia at over 5,700 feet, and the Virginia Creeper Trail, a popular rail trail used by hikers, bikers, and equestrians alike. The Virginia Highlands Horse Trail extends for nearly 80 miles, from Elk Garden all the way to the New River. Other paths in the Mount Rogers high country meander atop the grassy balds where wild ponies roam. And the granddaddy of all trails, the Appalachian Trail, courses through the mountains northward past such special areas as Little Wilson Creek Wilderness and Lewis Fork Wilderness. Not to be overlooked, the New River Rail Trail courses for over 50 miles through the New River Valley.

The trails are the stars of the show at Mount Rogers. Starting in the west, near Damascus, which may be the best trail town in America, the west side trail system offers abundant opportunities for mountain bikers. The Iron Mountain Trail, once the route of the Appalachian Trail before it was rerouted through the high country, is the master path of this network, which runs along high ridges and beside tumbling creeks. The central area is less traveled. It offers waterfalls, views, and loop possibilities. The far east is the recreation area's forgotten land. Here, solitude seekers will discover the Little Dry Run Wilderness, a little-used portion of the Iron Mountain Trail and the East Fork area; here you will find yourself wondering why no one else is enjoying the beauty it offers. The Mount Rogers high country is—deservedly— the area's most popular destination. Vast mountain panoramas from meadows that form the highest land mass in the Old Dominion overwhelm first-time visitors. Rare

Appalachian Trail near Damascus.

spruce-fir forests cloak windswept ridges. A plethora of trails offers loops and more for hikers, bikers, and equestrians. And these visitors soon become repeat visitors who bring their friends. The high country is as busy as the far east is deserted. Consider visiting this area during the week or the off-season for the best overall experience. Grayson Highlands State Park adjoins the high country. It offers panoramic trails of its own that connect with the trails of the high country.

The two rail trails, the Virginia Creeper and the New River Rail Trail, attract visitors from all over. These paths are served by outfitters offering shuttle service for bikers and horse rides for trail enthusiasts who seek a more user-friendly outdoor experience. The scenery along these rail trails will fulfill even the most trail-hardened veteran.

Complementing this wonderful trail system is a host of other recreational options at Mount Rogers. Fishing, swimming, picnicking, and scenic driving possibilities are all detailed in this book. Anglers will enjoy the section that reveals the best streams and offers tips that will aid fly and spin-cast fishermen. Favorite area swimming holes, which offer a place to cool off after a mountain excursion, are also described. And since auto touring is a time-honored way to see America's natural beauty, the best roads to view the scenery and wildlife of Mount Rogers are also revealed.

To facilitate one's activities at Mount Rogers, this book also includes information on national forest campgrounds, state park campgrounds, and accommodations

The author backpacking in the Mount Rogers high country.

and services in area towns, including motels, bed-and-breakfasts, outfitters, and stores. This guide will spare readers the tiring and sometimes frustrating research of the Mount Rogers Recreation Area and leave them to enjoy all this swath of southwest Virginia has to offer.

Over the past few years, since the first edition of this book was published, changes in the area have taken place, for better and for worse. For starters, the hemlock wooly adelgid is pushing into southwest Virginia, killing the important evergreen for which the insect is named, though some trees are being treated at developed campgrounds. Despite cutting and grazing, the grassy high country continues to recover. A new wilderness is being considered in the Raccoon Branch area, and other wildernesses may be expanded. Two picnic areas have been closed. More services for visitors have opened in area towns, especially Damascus. But other things have stayed the same, namely the wide array of outdoor activities in a superlative setting that makes Mount Rogers such a marvelous destination for visitors.

Mount Rogers Area History

The richness and beauty of southwest Virginia have attracted humans for untold years. This was the northern edge of Cherokee country, and these Native Americans had established a network of pathways that traversed the mountains and valleys by the time the first white explorers came from eastern Virginia, heading into the New River country as early as 1671. Most settlers to the area followed land speculators down the Shenandoah Valley after the Treaty of Lancaster in 1744, when the Six Nations of Indians renounced their claim to all lands in Virginia. Surveyors began laying out tracts of land, and by 1750 the first settlers were living in Washington County, near the Holston River. These settlements would not last for long, however, as Indians drove the white pioneers back east of the Blue Ridge and down into the Carolinas.

The French and Indian War of the 1760s brought soldiers to Fort Chiswell, northwest of Mount Rogers. These soldiers built the first real road into southwest Virginia. Seeing the fertile lands surrounding the fort, many chose to stay there, populating the valleys of the New and Holston rivers. Others came as miners from Europe to extract the nearby lead, critical for rifle shot. The mining continued in the late 1700s. Interestingly, at one time, Moses Austin, father of Stephen Austin of Texas fame, ran the lead mines at Austinville. During the Civil War, these mines were the chief source of shot for the Confederacy. Well before then, on what is now the east end of the recreation area, on the banks of the New River, was a shot operation. Now known as Shot Tower Historical State Park, this site was established in 1807. The tower, 75 feet high and built of stone with walls 2 ½ feet thick, held a pouring kettle at its top. Here, hot lead was poured down through the entire height of the tower and, for another 75 feet, through a shaft in the ground into a water-filled kettle, where the hardened shot was formed. The shot was then accessed via a tunnel located near the New River. The tower fell out of use by the mid-1800s but was briefly revived during the Civil War by the Confederacy. It was first renovated and opened to the public in 1968 and thereafter became the state park we see today. It can be accessed by the New River Trail, detailed in this guidebook.

Meanwhile, a rural agricultural economy thrived until the tumult of the Civil War. In typical southern Appalachian fashion, both Union and Confederate sympathizers, stragglers, and deserters roamed the countryside. Both sides struggled for lead and salt mines. Although no major battles were fought here, troops passed constantly through the valley corridors.

After the war, ambitious men turned their eyes on the area's valuable resources, one of which was iron ore. Some iron extraction had occurred before the war, as attested to by a number of ore furnaces that still stand in the countryside, including the Raven Cliff furnace, believed to have been built in 1810 and now an attraction for visitors to the recreation area. A more concerted effort to extract the ore came in the postwar period. By this time, railroads had begun to crisscross the valleys and were extended into the mountains for resource extraction. Eventually, the discovery of much richer ore in the Iron Range of northern Minnesota all but killed the local iron industry, but there were other resources to exploit. After the massive cutting of the midwestern forests, timber companies looked to the southern Appalachians, and the woodlands of what is now Mount Rogers Recreation Area were not spared.

Narrow-gauge tracks were laid all over the high country and through adjoining hollows and ridges. By 1907 logging was in full swing. The once-dense forest of evergreens was denuded. Farmers followed, and their grazing cattle, ironically, helped to create and preserve the gorgeous open high country we see today. By 1930 the timber harvest was over. Boomtowns like Fairwood, in the shadow of Mount Rogers, became nearly deserted. In the early 1930s the timber companies sold their lands to the federal government for its new national forest system. The forest service took over burned, eroded, and devastated lands and began to manage them for longer-term forest health and recreation as part of the Jefferson National Forest.

Mount Rogers's most significant trail town, Damascus, was once just a trail stop for Daniel Boone as he headed west in 1769 to explore the Kentucky country. A fellow settler from the Yadkin River Valley, Henry Mock, thought the flats beside Laurel Creek were pretty enough for him and decided to stay. The community that grew up around Mock and his grist operation became known as Mocks Mill. Life moved slowly there until 1886, when a speculator named Imboden bought much of the area land. Thinking that the mountains were rich with iron ore, he renamed the town Damascus after the iron-rich Syrian capital. Imboden was wrong about the extensiveness of the iron deposits, but the name stuck. Damascus did reach a heyday when much of what is now the recreation area was logged over. Today the town bases its economy on tourism and recreation.

One of Damascus's premier recreation attractions is the Virginia Creeper Trail. Purportedly, this national recreation trail roughly follows Daniel Boone's route through this part of Virginia. Of course, Boone was following animal and Native American trails. In the early 1900s, a rail line was built between Abingdon and Damascus to haul seemingly endless lumber and what iron there was, along with some passengers and assorted supplies desired by area residents. At one point the line extended 75 miles east to Elkland, North Carolina. It was often difficult for the loaded train to make it up the steep mountain grades; thus, according to one story, the train earned the name Virginia Creeper. Others say that the rail got its name from the vine that grows on area trees. Either way, the name caught on. The rail line stayed in operation into the 1970s, despite its long-term unprofitability and the periodic floods that undercut its numerous trestles. A terrible flood in 1977 undermined much of the railroad and was the final blow. The national forest acquired railroad right-of-way from Damascus to the North Carolina state line, while the cities of Damascus and Abingdon acquired the portion between them. Thus, the Virginia Creeper came into its new incarnation as a multiuse trail, described later in this book.

After the establishment of the Virginia Creeper Trail, the New River Trail came into existence on the eastern end of the national recreation area. In late 1986, the Norfolk Southern Corporation donated a 57-mile tract of abandoned railroad right-of-way to Virginia for the establishment of the New River Trail State Park. Because the bed was in good condition, the trail was easy to establish, and within six months the first four miles of rail trail were established. Over time the full 57 miles have been opened, and the trail, also detailed in this book, is a major asset of the recreation area.

Long ago, the actual Mount Rogers was recognized as the highest point in Virginia. This conclusion was first pointed out by William Rogers in an 1841 report to the Virginia General Assembly. Rogers had a distinguished career. Educated at William and Mary, he became the first state geologist for the Old Dominion before moving north and founding the Massachusetts Institute of Technology (MIT). After his death in 1882, what was then called Balsam Mountain was renamed in his honor.

Over the past several decades, nature has restored the beauty of the area, and the forest service has purchased additional lands, including the Mount Rogers High Country, where Mount Rogers stands. The entire Jefferson National Forest now has over 714,000 acres. The exceptional beauty and recreation opportunities of the Jefferson between Damascus and the New River were recognized, and the expanse was designated the Mount Rogers National Recreation Area on May 31, 1966. Comprising 140,000 acres of scenic southwest Virginia, the recreation area is managed by the forest service.

A national recreation area is a place of extraordinary beauty, designated by Congress, to be utilized by Americans for various outdoor activities. In 1961 Presi-

The Appalachian Trail was rerouted after the forest service purchased the high country.

dent John F. Kennedy made a speech emphasizing the need for acquiring federal lands for recreation and jump-started the effort to establish national recreation areas. The first result of this movement was the Boulder Dam Recreation Area, later renamed Lake Mead National Recreation Area. At first, national recreation areas were established by interagency memoranda of agreement between the U.S. Bureau of Reclamation and the National Park Service. In 1963 the President's Recreation Advisory Committee issued an executive branch policy that set forth criteria for establishing national recreation areas. The policy also called for all future national recreation areas to be established by acts of the United States Congress. National recreation areas are sometimes managed by the U.S. Forest Service, as Mount Rogers is, or by the National Park Service, which manages most national recreation areas. Today Mount Rogers National Recreation Area lives up to its billing and becomes ever more important as a destination for outdoor enthusiasts.

How to Use This Guidebook

At the top of each trail description is an information box that allows the hiker quick access to pertinent information: trail type, difficulty, length, use, trail connections, and highlights. Here is an example:

Dickey Knob Trail

Type:	Foot, bicycle
Length:	2.3 miles
Difficulty:	Difficult
Condition:	Good
Use:	Moderate
Highlights:	Great views from atop Dickey Knob
Book Map #:	8
USGS Topo:	Trout Dale
Connections:	Raccoon Branch Trail, Virginia Highlands Horse Trail, Raccoon Branch Nature Trail

From this information box, the reader can see that the trail is suitable for foot and bicycle travel; it can be any combination of foot, horse, or bicycle. The Dickey Knob Trail is rated "difficult," which means that it is rocky and rough or steep; other ratings used in this book are "easy" or "moderate." The Dickey Knob Trail is 2.3 miles in length and moderately used. Trail use, defined as how frequently the path is traveled, can be low, moderate, or high. This trail is in good condition, and its primary highlight is the view from the top of Dickey Knob. The number following "Book Map #" tells which map you can find this trail on in the series of maps found in the book following this introduction. The designation "USGS Topo" refers to the United States Geographical Survey maps. These rectangular "quad maps" cover every parcel of land in this country and are very detailed. Each quad has a name, usually based on a physical feature located within it. In this case the hike traverses one quad map, named "Trout Dale." Quad maps can be obtained online at www. usgs.gov. "Connections" tells readers the names of the other trails that connect to the trail described. The Dickey Knob Trail connects to the Raccoon Branch Nature Trail and the Virginia Highlands Horse Trail. With this information, the reader can look up these other trails for potential loops or extended one-way trips.

Following each box is a detailed, running narrative of the hike; it notes the various trail junctions, stream crossings, and trailside features with their distance from the trailhead. These accounts will help keep hikers apprised of their whereabouts and ensure that they don't miss the features noted. At the end of each narrative, under the subhead "Access," are detailed directions for reaching the trailhead.

The trails have been divided by type and the areas they cover. The "Long Trails" section covers the Appalachian Trail, the Virginia Highlands Horse Trail, and the Iron Mountain Trail. The "Rail Trails" section covers the Virginia Creeper Rail Trail and the New River Rail Trail. The "West Side Trails" section covers Feathercamp Ridge, Straight Mountain, and the Whitetop Laurel Valley. The "Central Area Trails" section covers the Flat Top and Hurricane Mountain areas. The "Far East" section covers the Dry Creek and Dry Run watersheds and east across Ewing Mountain all the way to the New River. The "High Country" section covers the unique high-elevation areas around Mount Rogers. "Trails of Grayson Highlands State Park" covers the mountain lands within the boundaries of that preserve, which is adjacent to the High Country and centers on Haw Orchard Mountain.

Each section contains a description of every marked and maintained trail within that area. That way, you can flip through the trail descriptions of each section and see which trails appeal to you. And if you don't feel like developing a trip of your own, following the trail descriptions is a section of suggested loops for hikers, bikers, and equestrians covering each section of the national recreation area. Flip through the book and find the hikes most appealing to you; then get out there and hit the trail!

Following the trail sections are sections on various other activities you can enjoy at Mount Rogers, such as fishing, swimming, cross-country skiing, scenic driving, picnicking, and camping. The best and most popular fishing streams and lakes are detailed, with each description covering fishing pressure, fishing quality, a stream overview, and how to access the trail. The swimming holes section includes an overview of the swimming hole, what it is like, and directions for accessing it.

The scenic drives section details some great auto touring trips of the recreation area. There are not only paved auto tours but also forest drives that traverse some of the lesser-used gravel roads of Mount Rogers. Each description includes the type of road, the length of the auto tour, highlights to be seen, and amenities to be found along the tour, such as stores and restaurants. Picnic areas are also described with an overview of what each area is like, along with directions on how to reach it and information on nearby activities.

The "Places to Lay Your Head" section give details on campgrounds, cabins, area bed-and-breakfasts, cottages, and hostels. Recreation area campgrounds are reviewed, including details on when they are open, the number of campsites, the features of each site, site assignment, facilities, fees, and elevation. A narrative follows, describing the campground setting and area activities, along with access directions. Horseback riding is popular at Mount Rogers, and there are special camps for equestrians. These are also included in the campground section. Mount Rogers also has cabins for rent, and this special opportunity to enjoy a rustic shelter within the recreation area is described. For those who want a more refined overnight experience, area bed-and-breakfasts, cottages, and hostels are described, including important contact information.

I hope that this book will make you appreciate and enjoy Mount Rogers National Recreation Area so much that you will want to volunteer to keep it a great place. In case this happens, contact information is included in the appendix. Also included is an overview of area towns and what facilities they have and resupplying opportunities. Need gear or a shuttle? Just check the "Outfitters" section to see who has what and from whom you can get a ride. A contact list gives information on how to reach the national recreation area and the state parks that are covered in the book.

Wilderness Areas at Mount Rogers

The Virginia Wilderness Act of 1984 established three wilderness areas within the boundaries of Mount Rogers National Recreation Area. Lewis Fork Wilderness, encompassing much of the north side of the Mount Rogers High Country, is easily the busiest—and is the largest at 5,802 acres. Little Wilson Creek Wilderness, also in the High Country, comes in at 3,855 acres. In the eastern section of the recreation area, the Little Dry Run Wilderness covers 3,400 acres and, like the rest of the "Far East," is vastly undervisited and underappreciated. These are special slices of land that are managed differently than other parts of the recreation area. Other wilderness areas are being considered, and some of the established ones are being expanded. Stay tuned as this saga evolves.

Wilderness is not only a remnant of the land before settlement; it is a state of mind. It can be a place of solitude, recreation, contemplation, or challenge, in addition to being a place where nature reigns. The people who enter a wilderness determine what it means to them. The Wilderness Act of 1964, which set the guidelines for establishing federal wilderness areas, determined that wilderness is "untrammeled by man, where man is a visitor who does not remain, and has outstanding opportunities

Mount Rogers and Environs Trail Table

	Type	Difficulty	Length	Use	Condition
Long Trails					
AT, Damascus to Tennessee State Line	F only	M	3.5	H	G
AT, Damascus to Creek Junction	F only	M to D	14.0	H	G
AT, Creek Junction to Elk Garden	F only	M to D	9.1	H	G
AT, Elk Garden to Fox Creek	F only	M to D	17.0	H	G to F
AT, Fairwood Valley to Dickey Gap	F only	M	8.5	M to H	E
AT, Dickey Gap to Jennings Visitor Center	F only	M	15.0	H to M	G
IMT, Damascus to Tennessee State Line	F only	M to D	1.4	L	G
IMT, Damascus to Skulls Gap	F, B, E	M to D	12.8	M	G
IMT, Skulls Gap to Hurricane Mountain	F, B, E	M	9.2	M	G
IMT, Hale Lake to Jones Knob	F, B, E	M	15.6	L	G
VHHT, Elk Garden to Fox Creek	F, E	M to D	12.9	M	G to F
VHHT, Fox Creek to Raccoon Branch	F, B, E	M to D	16.4	L to M	Ex
VHHT, Raccoon Branch to Middle Creek	F, B, E	M	14.7	L to M	G
VHHT, Middle Creek to Upper East Fork	F, B, E	M	19.2	L to M	G
VHHT, Upper East Fork to New River	F, B, E	M to D	16.4	L	G
VCT, Whitetop Station to Damascus	F, B, E	M	17.4	H	G
VCT, Damascus to Abingdon	F, B, E	M	16.0	H	G
NRRT, Galax to Foster Falls	F, B, E	H	27.7	H	Ex
NRRT, Fries to Fries Junction	F,B, E	M to D	5.5	H	Ex
NRRT, Pulaski to Foster Falls	F, B, E	Easy to M	22.0	H	Ex
West Side Trails					
Beartree Gap Trail	F, B	M	3.3	M	G
Beartree Lake Trail	F only	Easy	1.0	H	Ex
Beaver Flats Trail	F only	Easy	0.6	M	G
Beech Grove Trail	F, B, E	M	3.3	L to M	G
Bushwacker Trail	F,B	M	1.2	M	G
Buzzard Den Trail	F, B, E	D	1.6	L	G
Chestnut Ridge Trail	F, B, E	D	1.8	L	G
Clark Mountain Trail	F, B, E	Very D	3.7	Very L	P
Feathercamp Ridge Trail	F, B	M	0.7	M	G
Feathercamp Trail	F only	M	2.2	M	G
Lum Trail	F, B	M	1.0	M	Ex
Rush Trail	F, B, E	D	1.8	L	G
Saunders Trail	F, B	M	2.1	L	G
Sawmill Trail	F, B, E	M	2.8	L	G
Shaw Gap Trail	F, B	M	1.0	M	G
Skulls Gap Trail	F, B, E	M	1.0	L	G
Straight Branch Trail	F, B	M	1.7	M	Ex
Taylors Valley Trail	F, B, E	M	2.6	L	G
Tennessee Trail	F, B, E	M	1.1	L	G
Wright Hollow Trail	F, B, E	D	3.0	Very L	Fair
Yancy Trail	F,B	M	0.3	M	G

	Type	Difficulty	Length	Use	Condition
Central Area Trails					
Barton Gap Trail	F, B, E	M	1.6	L	G
Bobbys Trail	F only	M	0.9	L	G
Comers Creek Falls Trail	F only	E	0.4	L	G
Comers Creek Trail	F, B	Easy	0.7	M	G
Dickey Gap Trail	F only	Easy	0.4	M	G
Dickey Knob Trail	F, B	D	2.3	M	G
Fairwood Valley Trail	F, E	E	1.8	M	G
Flat Top Trail	F, B, E	M	1.7	L	G
Hickory Ridge Trail	F, B	D	0.7	L	Fair
Hurricane Creek Trail	F only	Easy	0.4	L	G
Hurricane Knob Trail	F only	M	1.1	M	G
Hurricane Mountain Trail	F only	Easy	0.4	L	G
Jerry's Creek Trail	F, B, E	M	4.1	L to M	G
Little Laurel Trail	F only	Easy	1.0	Very L	G
Mullins Branch Trail	F only	D	2.9	Very L	Fair
Old 84 Trail	F, B, E	Easy to M	4.6	L to M	G
Raccoon Branch Nature Trail	F only	Easy	0.2	M	G
Rowland Creek Trail	F, B, E	M	3.2	L to M	G
Slabtown Trail	F only	M	2.1	L to M	G
Two Ponds Nature Trail	F only	Easy	0.5	L	G
Far East Trails					
Comers Rock Trail	F only	M	0.4	M	G
Divide Trail	F, B, E	D	0.7	M	Fair
Dry Run Gap Trail	F, B, E	M	1.0	M	G
East Fork Trail	F, B, E	Easy	2.7	M	Fair
Ewing Mountain Trail	F, E	D	2.0	M	G
Hale Lake Trail	F only	Easy	0.7	H	G
Henley Hollow Trail	F, B, E	M	1.6	L to M	G
Horne Knob Trail	F, B, E	Easy	0.4	L	G
Kirk Hollow Trail	F, B, E	M	0.8	L	G
Little Dry Run Trail	F, E	D	4.4	M	Fair
Mike's Gap Trail	F, B, E	M	2.8	L	G
Perkins Knob Spur Trail	F, B, E	M	0.5	L	G
Perkins Knob Trail	F, B, E	M	2.2	L	G
Raven Cliff Trail	F, B, E	Easy	1.2	M	G
Raven Cliff Furnace Trail	F only	Easy	0.5	H	G
Unaka Trail	F only	M	1.0	L	G
High Country Trails					
Bearpen Trail	F, E	M	1.2	M	G
Big Wilson Creek Trail	F, E	D	2.1	L	G
Cliffside Trail	F only	D	1.5	L	G
Crest Trail	F, B, E	M	3.4	H	Ex
Elk Garden Trail	F, B, E	M	1.5	L	Ex

Mount Rogers and Environs Trail Table (cont.)

	Type	Difficulty	Length	Use	Condition
First Peak Trail	F, E	M	3.2	H to M	G
Grassy Branch Trail	F, E	M	3.2	L	G
Helton Creek Spur Trail	F, E	M	1.3	L	Fair
Helton Creek Trail	F, E	M	3.1	L	Fair
Hightree Rock Trail	F, E	M to D	4.7	L	G
Jackie Streets Trail	F, E	M	2.5	H	G
Kabel Trail	F, E	Easy	2.1	L	G
Lewis Fork Spur Trail	F only	M	0.4	M	G
Lewis Fork Trail	F, E	M to D	5.5	M	G
Little Wilson Creek Trail	F only	M to D	1.6	L	Fair
Mount Rogers Spur Trail	F only	M	0.5	H	G
Mount Rogers Trail	F only	D	4.0	H	G
Old Orchard Spur Trail	F, E	M	1.7	L	Fair
Old Orchard Trail	F, E	M	1.7	L	Fair
Pine Mountain Trail	F only	M	1.9	H	G
Rhododendron Gap Trail	F, B, E	M	1.4	M to H	G
Scales Trail	F, B, E	M	1.3	H	G
Springs Trail	F only	Easy	0.5	L	G
Sugar Maple Trail	F, E	M	2.2	L	G
Switchback Trail	F, B, E	M	1.2	L	G
Third Peak Trail	F, B, E	M to D	1.7	M	Fair
Whispering Waters Trail	F only	Easy	0.6	M	G
Wilburn Ridge Trail	F only	M	1.0	H	G
Wilson Creek Trail	F, B, E	M	0.7	H	G
Trails of Grayson Highlands State Park					
Appalachian Spur Trail	F only	M	0.8	H	G
Big Pinnacle Trail	F only	M to D	0.5	H	Ex
Cabin Creek Trail	F only	M	1.9	M to H	Ex
Horse Trail	F, E	M	1.7	H	G
Listening Rock Trail	F only	M	1.6	L	G
Rhododendron Trail	F only	M	0.8	M to H	G
Rock House Ridge Trail	F only	M	1.2	L	G
Seed Orchard Road Trail	F, B, E	Easy	0.7	M	G
Stampers Branch Trail	F only	M	1.7	M	G
Twin Pinnacles Trail	F only	M	1.6	H	G
Upchurch Road Trail	F, B, E	M	2.9	M	G
Virginia Highlands Horse Connector Trail	F, E	M	0.9	M to H	Fair
Wilson Trail	F only	M	1.8	H	G

Key

Type:	F = Foot, B = Bicycle, E = Equestrian
Difficulty:	M = Moderate, D = Difficult
Use:	L = Low, M = Moderate, H = High
Condition:	P = Poor, G = Good, Ex = Excellent

for primitive recreation." With that in mind, the forest service is attempting to manage the three wildernesses here by preserving the wilderness resource. The biggest problem land managers here have are with group size. Please keep your group size to ten or less. The following list will further help you preserve the wilderness areas and the rest of Mount Rogers National Recreation Area:

Principles of Leave No Trace

Plan Ahead and Prepare
Travel and Camp on Durable Surfaces
Dispose of Waste Properly
Leave What You Find
Minimize Campfire Impacts
Respect Wildlife
Be Considerate of Other Visitors

Share the Trail

One of the best aspects of Mount Rogers is how so many different groups can enjoy the same recreation area. These groups include hikers, bikers, and equestrians. They all "share the trail." It works like this: bikers yield to hikers; hikers and bikers yield to horses. Whenever you encounter another user on the path, share the trail. When a horse approaches, try to get on the downside of a hill. This is especially true for backpackers, as horses are often startled by large packs on human backs. Mountain bikers need to keep under a controlled speed and look ahead. There are bicycle speed limits posted on a few trails.

The Virginia Creeper Rail Trail and the New River Rail Trail have numerous trestles that span watercourses below them. When encountering a horse is on a trestle, allow the horse to completely cross the trestle before proceeding. The wooden bases of these bridges can be slippery, and a trestle is no place for a horse to slip and throw a rider off the bridge.

Favorite Sights and Scenes at Mount Rogers

Mount Rogers is full of beauty. However, beauty is in the eye of the beholder, as the saying goes. While one person might desire a far-reaching view, another might seek to encounter a variety of wildflowers. Yet another might want to travel beneath a towering forest. After exploring the entire recreation area, here are some of my favorites:

West Side

Reaching the Tennessee-Virginia state line on the Appalachian Trail
Reeling in a rainbow trout from Whitetop Laurel Creek near Creek Junction
Coasting down from Whitetop Station on the Virginia Creeper Trail
Stopping on the Virginia Creeper Trail and jumping in Whitetop Laurel Creek
Walking the rocky valley of Feathercamp Creek
Seeing the mountain laurel in bloom on the Iron Mountain Trail near Sandy
    Flats
Hanging on for dear life while pedaling the Buzzard Den Trail
Riding past the old homesite on Taylors Valley Trail
Navigating the obscure Clark Mountain Trail
Seeing a deer on the Rush Trail

Central Area

Spending a cool spring night at Cherry Tree trail shelter
Finding wildflowers on the Little Laurel Trail
Basking in the spray of Rowland Creek Falls
Riding the loop connecting Fox Creek and Flat Top
Enjoying the views of Pine Mountain from the Iron Mountain Trail near
    Comers Creek
Making the challenging climb to Dickey Knob and being rewarded with
    a great vista
Cooking out over a campfire at Hurricane Campground
Hearing Comers Creek Falls after a summer storm
Absorbing the fall colors around Barton Gap

Far East

Getting a view at Comers Rock
Feeling the sense of solitude on the Virginia Highlands Horse Trail near
    Kirk Hollow
Riding among rhododendron and vistas of Ewing Mountain
Traveling beneath the towering pines of the East Fork Trail
Walking up Perkins Creek valley
Enjoying a night with fellow equestrians at Hussy Mountain Horse Camp
Looking out on the New River at Fries Junction on the New River Rail
    Trail
Navigating the Little Dry Run Trail
Seeing the old homesite on the most easterly section of the Iron Mountain
    Trail
Relaxing by Hale Lake while hoping a trout takes the bait

High Country

Picking berries near Scales in late August
Riding the Virginia Highlands Horse Trail onto open Brier Ridge and being
    overwhelmed by the views
Rock hopping on the Wilburn Ridge Trail
Standing on the rock atop Mount Rogers, knowing you are at the highest
    point in the state
Watching your buddy huff and puff while ascending the Cabin Ridge Trail
Making a scenic drive that ends near the crest of Whitetop
Sitting under a tarp and wondering if it rains all the time in the High Country
Camping at Grindstone after day hiking the Pine Mountain Trail
Seeing the aspens and old homesites on the Sugar Maple Trail
Winter camping in the Little Wilson Creek Wilderness

Grayson Highlands State Park

Enjoying the view from the Pinnacles
Picnicking near the old homesteads
Reaching the falls of Cabin Creek
Listening at Listening Rock
Enjoying the open meadow at Massie Gap
Having a snowball fight in the visitor center parking area
Watching the wild ponies graze on lower Wilburn Ridge
Fishing Wilson Creek among the huge boulders and riverine scenery
Checking out the Fraser fir seed orchard and being encircled by the tallest
    mountains in Virginia
Escaping the heat of the lowlands at the 4,200-foot campground

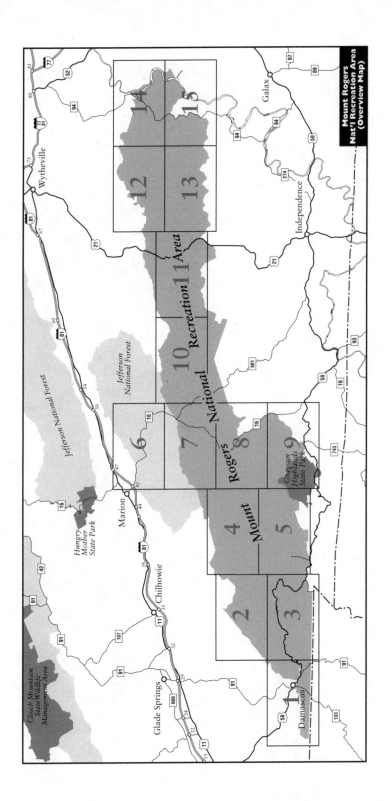

Mount Rogers Nat'l Recreation Area (Overview Map)

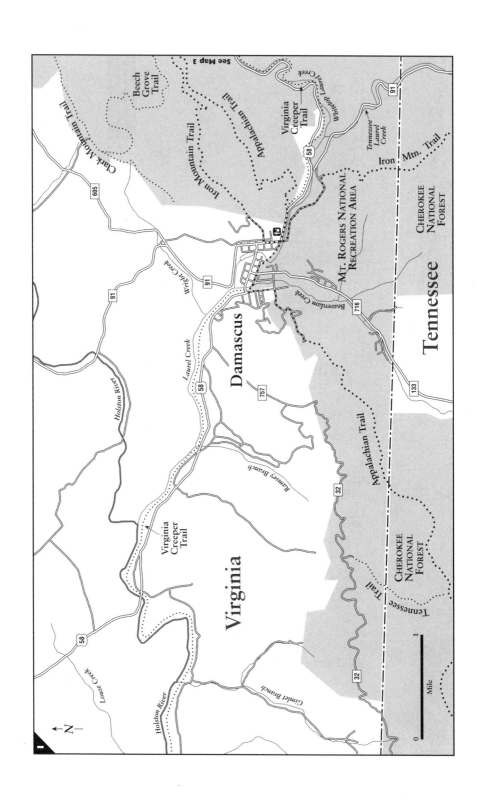

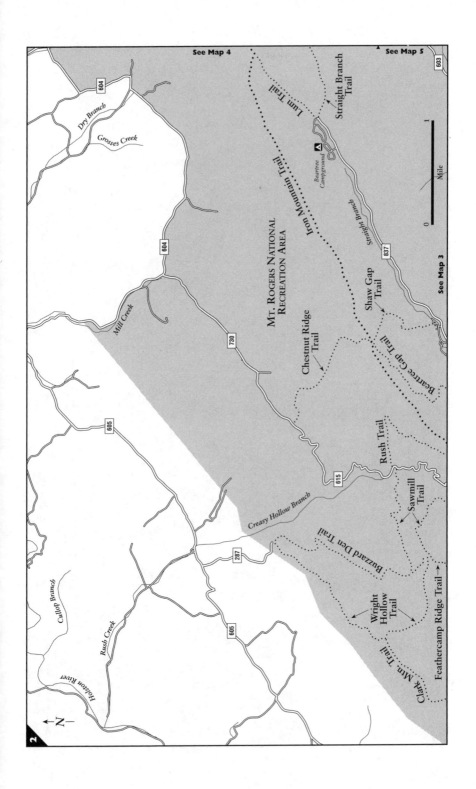

See Map 4
See Map 5
See Map 3

604

Dry Branch

Grosses Creek

604

Mill Creek

730

MT. ROGERS NATIONAL
RECREATION AREA

Iron Mountain Trail

Lum Trail

Straight Branch
Trail

603

Beartree
Campground

Straight Branch

837

Shaw Gap
Trail

Chestnut Ridge
Trail

Beartree Gap Trail

Creasy Hollow Branch

615

605

Rush Trail

Sawmill
Trail

Buzzard Den Trail

287

605

Clark's
Mtn. Trail

Wright
Hollow
Trail

Feathercamp Ridge Trail

Cullop Branch

Rush Creek

Holston River

N

0   1   Mile

2

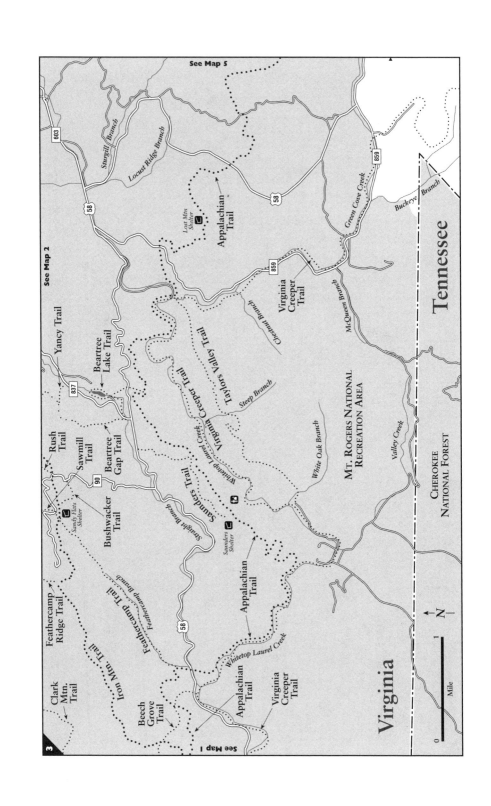

See Map 5

603

Sturgill Branch

Locust Ridge Branch

58

Lost Mtn
Shelter

Appalachian
Trail

859

58

Virginia Creeper
Trail

Green Cove Creek

Buckeye Branch

859

McQueen Branch

Chestnut Branch

Steep Branch

White Oak Branch

Valley Creek

MT. ROGERS NATIONAL
RECREATION AREA

CHEROKEE
NATIONAL FOREST

Tennessee

See Map 2

Yancy Trail

Beartree
Lake Trail

837

Rush
Trail

Sawmill
Trail

Beartree
Gap Trail

90

Bushwacker
Trail

Sandy Flats
Shelter

Featurecamp
Ridge Trail

Clark
Mtn.
Trail

Iron Mtn. Trail

Feathercamp Branch

Feathercamp Trail

Beech
Grove
Trail

Saunders Trail

Straight Branch

Saunders
Shelter

Virginia Creeper Trail

Whitetop Laurel Creek

Taylors Valley Trail

58

Appalachian
Trail

Whitetop Laurel Creek

Appalachian
Trail

Virginia
Creeper
Trail

See Map 1

Virginia

N

0   1
     Mile

3

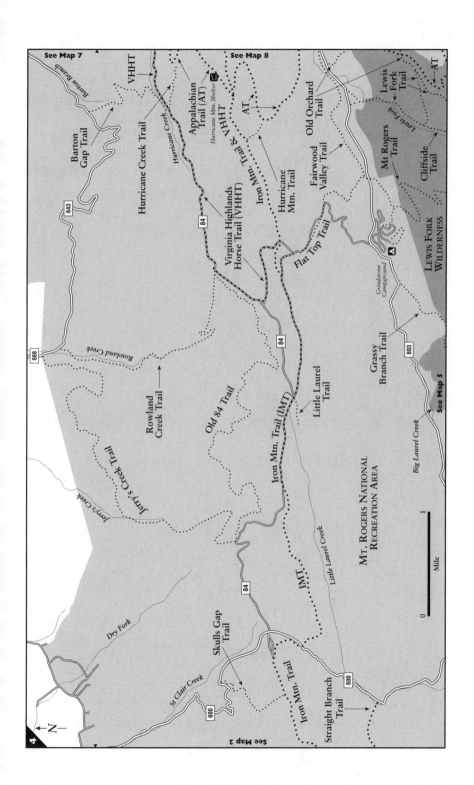

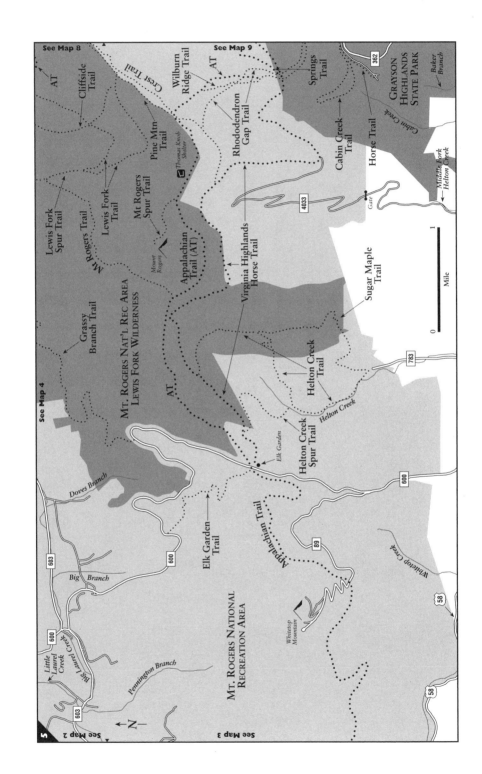

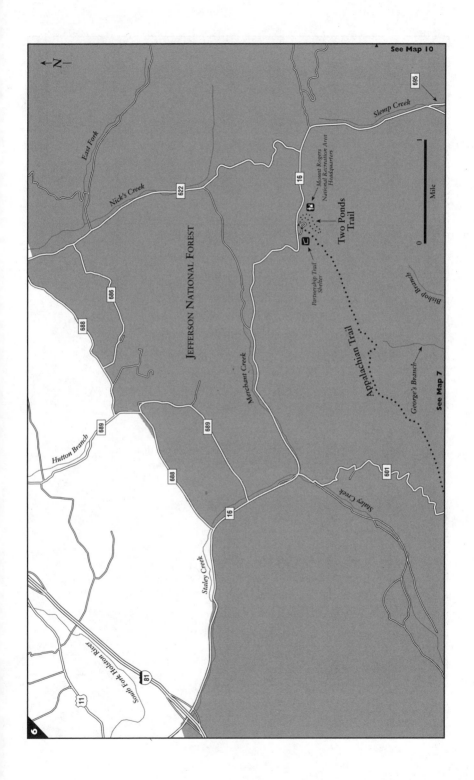

See Map 10

See Map 7

N

695

Slemp Creek

16

Mount Rogers
National Recreation Area
Headquarters

Two Ponds
Trail

Partnership Trail
Shelter

East Fork

Nick's Creek

622

JEFFERSON NATIONAL FOREST

686

688

689

Hutton Branch

Merchant Creek

Appalachian Trail

Bishop Branch

George's Branch

689

688

16

601

Staley Creek

Staley Creek

South Fork Holston River

81

111

0 — Mile — 1

6

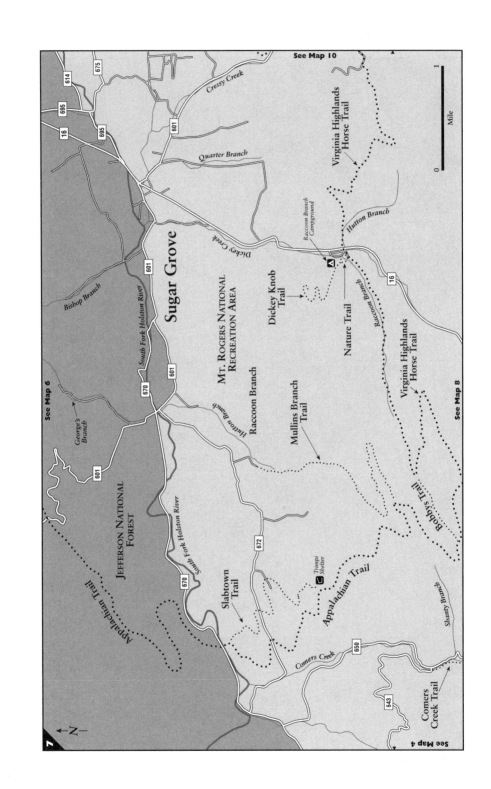

See Map 10

See Map 6

See Map 8

See Map 4

614
675
695
16
695
601

Cressy Creek

Quarter Branch

Virginia Highlands
Horse Trail

Raccoon Branch
Campground

Hutton Branch

0   Mile   1

601

Sugar Grove

Dickey Creek

Bishop Branch

South Fork Holston River

601

Mt. Rogers National
Recreation Area

Dickey Knob
Trail

Nature Trail

Raccoon Branch

16

601

George's
Branch

670

601

Raccoon Branch

Hutton Branch

Virginia Highlands
Horse Trail

Mullins Branch
Trail

Jefferson National
Forest

South Fork Holston River

670

672

Slabtown
Trail

Trimpi
Shelter

Appalachian Trail

Bobby's Trail

Appalachian Trail

Comers Creek

650

Shanty Branch

643

Comers
Creek Trail

N

7

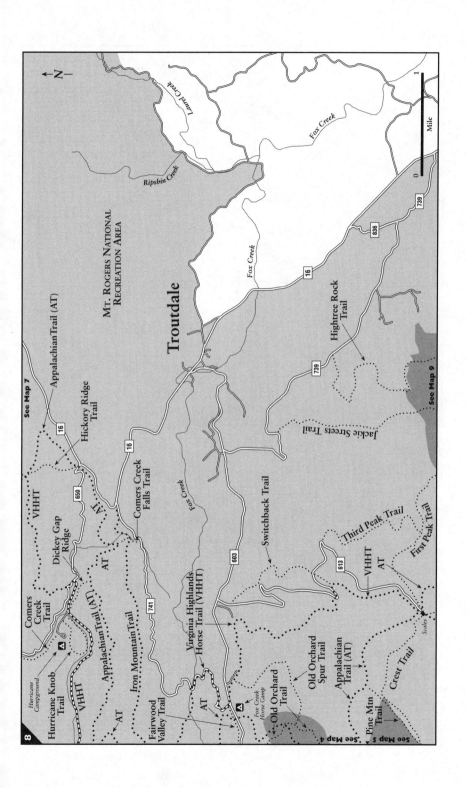

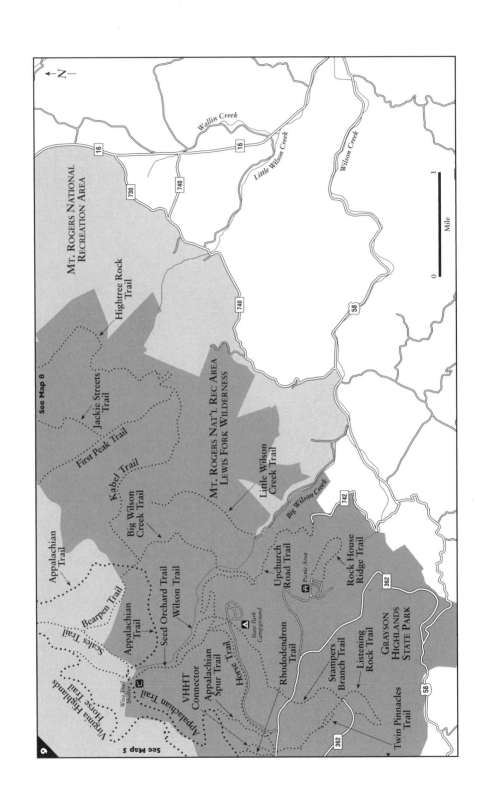

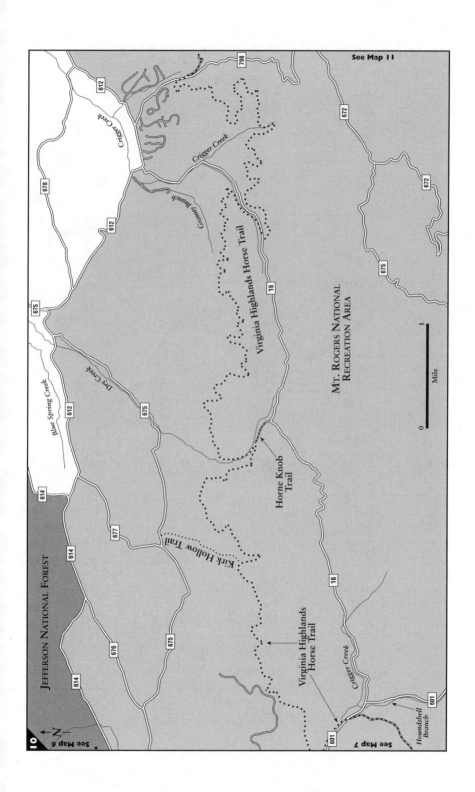

See Map 6

See Map 7

JEFFERSON NATIONAL FOREST

MT. ROGERS NATIONAL RECREATION AREA

Virginia Highlands Horse Trail

Horne Knob Trail

Kirk Hollow Trail

Virginia Highlands Horse Trail

Crigger Creek

Granny Branch

Crigger Creek

Dry Creek

Blue Spring Creek

Crigger Creek

Houndshell Branch

612

612

678

675

612

614

614

614

677

676

675

675

675

672

672

798

16

16

601

601

0 1 Mile

N

10

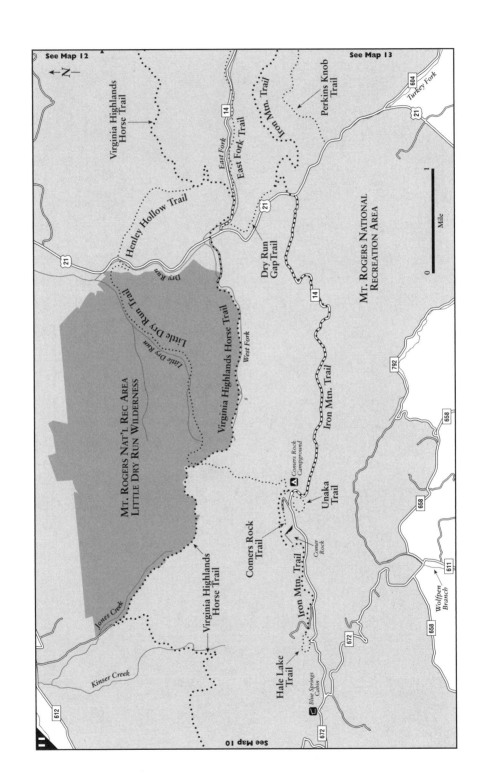

—N—

Virginia Highlands Horse Trail

Henley Hollow Trail

East Fork Trail

East Fork

14

21

Perkins Knob Trail

Horn Mtn. Trail

Turkey Fork

604

21

Dry Run

Little Dry Run Trail

Little Dry Run

Virginia Highlands Horse Trail

West Fork

Dry Run Gap Trail

21

14

MT. ROGERS NAT'L REC AREA
LITTLE DRY RUN WILDERNESS

MT. ROGERS NATIONAL
RECREATION AREA

0   Mile   1

Iron Mtn. Trail

Comers Rock Campground

Unaka Trail

792

658

658

Comers Rock Trail

Comer Rock

Iron Mtn. Trail

Wolffen Branch

611

611

658

Jones Creek

Virginia Highlands Horse Trail

Kinser Creek

Hale Lake Trail

Blue Springs Cabin

672

672

612

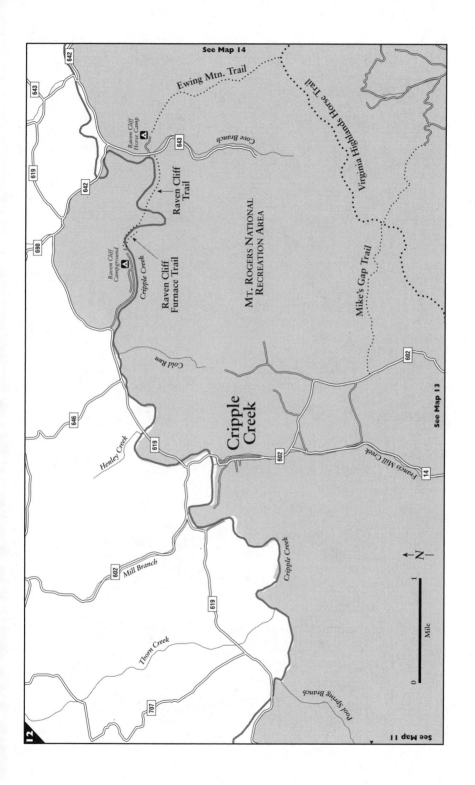

See Map 14

642
643
619
690
642

Ewing Mtn. Trail

Raven Cliff
Horse Camp

643

Cove Branch

Virginia Highlands Horse Trail

Raven Cliff
Trail

Raven Cliff
Campground

Cripple Creek

Raven Cliff
Furnace Trail

Mt. Rogers National
Recreation Area

Mike's Gap Trail

Cold Run

602

See Map 13

646

Henley Creek

619

Cripple
Creek

602

Francis Mill Creek

14

602

Mill Branch

619

Cripple Creek

Thorn Creek

707

N

Pool Spring Branch

See Map 11

0   1
Mile

12

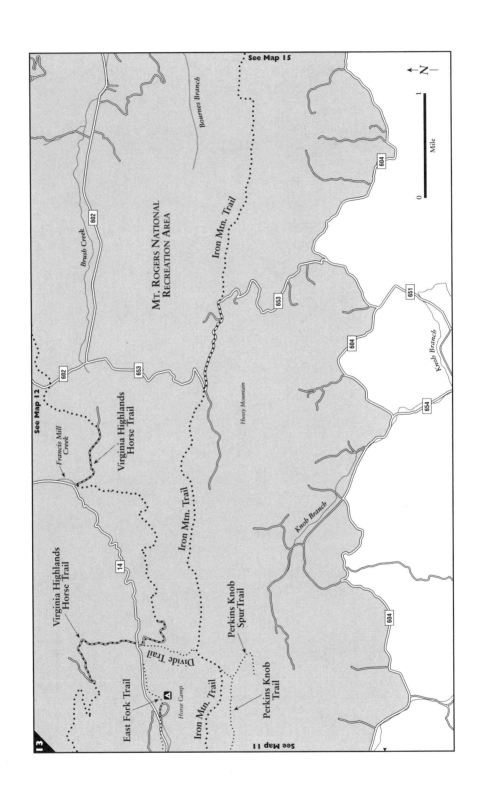

See Map 15

Bournes Branch

Brush Creek

602

MT. ROGERS NATIONAL
RECREATION AREA

Iron Mtn. Trail

604

653

604

651

Hussy Mountain

Knob Branch

654

See Map 12

602

653

Francis Mill
Creek

Virginia Highlands
Horse Trail

Iron Mtn. Trail

Knob Branch

Virginia Highlands
Horse Trail

14

Perkins Knob
Spur Trail

604

East Fork Trail

Divide Trail

Horse Camp

Perkins Knob
Trail

Iron Mtn. Trail

13

See Map 11

N

0   1

Mile

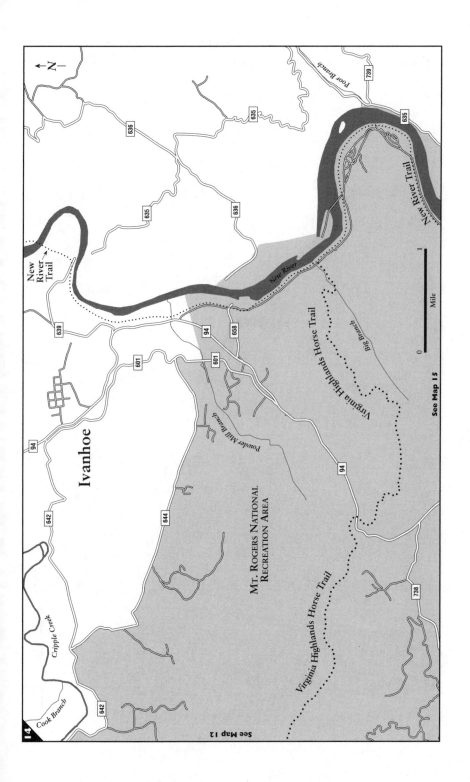

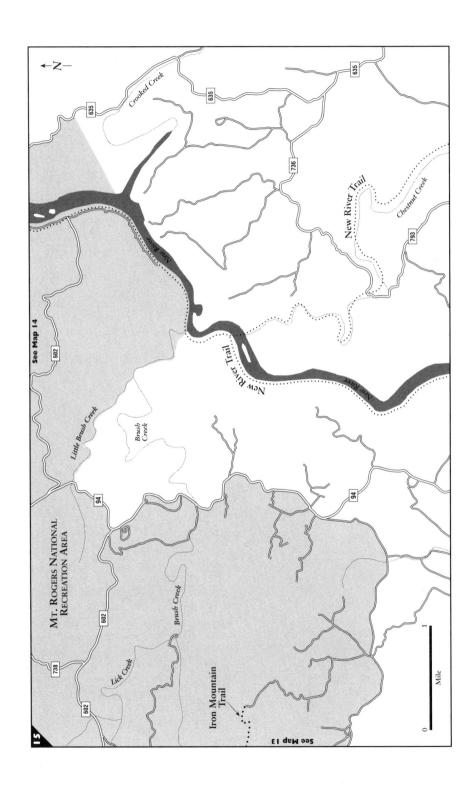

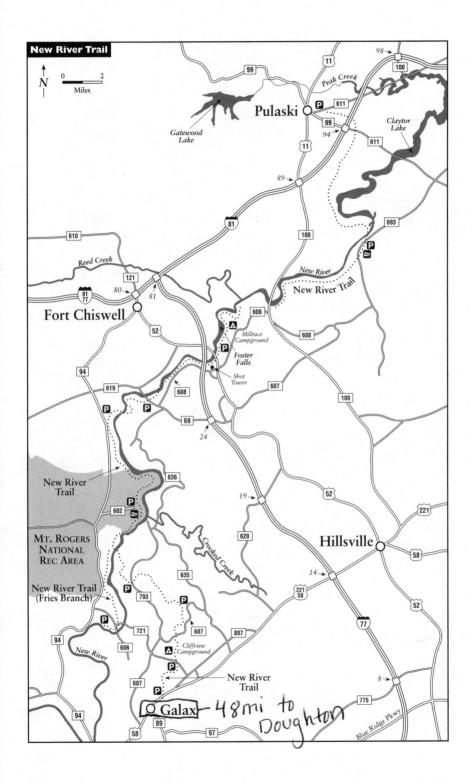

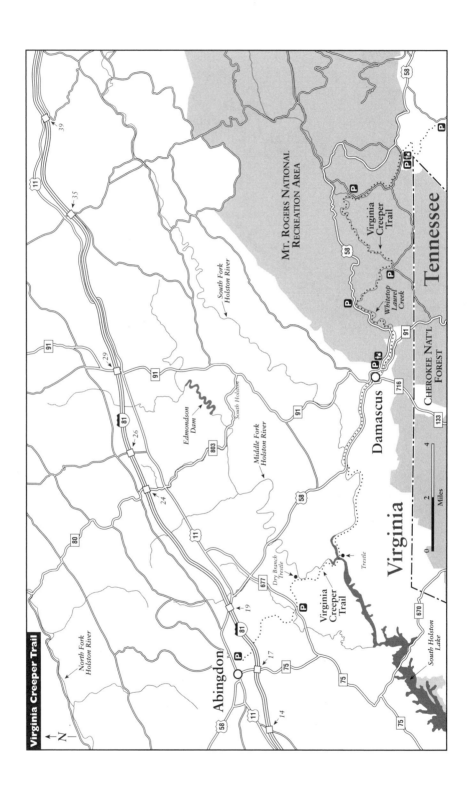

Virginia Creeper Trail

Mount Rogers and Environs Trails

Long Trails

Appalachian Trail

The Appalachian Trail (AT) is the most famous footpath in the United States. It courses from Georgia to Maine along the spine of the Appalachians, passing through the most scenic sections of these mountains. With these parameters, it couldn't miss the Mount Rogers area. Conceived in 1921 by one Benton MacKaye as a retreat to nature for city folk, it began to take shape in the 1930s with help from volunteers, trail clubs, and the Civilian Conservation Corps. The U.S. Forest Service signed on in 1938, protecting many vulnerable sections of the trail. Land disputes resulted in countless reroutes, which continue to this day. (Within the Mount Rogers National Recreation Area, the AT was rerouted from Iron Mountain to different locations

Hiking along Wilburn Ridge on the Appalachian Trail.

in the high country before settling into its current route.) The Appalachian Trail Conference is one of the many driving forces today that keep the world's longest continuously marked footpath a reality; to join, please call (304) 535-6331, or visit www.atconf.org.

Appalachian Trail, Damascus to Tennessee State Line

Type:	Foot only
Length:	3.5 miles
Difficulty:	Moderate
Use:	High
Condition:	Good
Highlights:	Some views
Book Map #:	1
USGS Topo:	Damascus, Laurel Bloomery
Connections:	Appalachian Trail, Damascus to Creek Junction, AT, Tennessee State Line to Georgia

This section of the AT connects the town of Damascus to the Tennessee state line, where it continues through and beyond the Volunteer State to its southern terminus in Georgia. The trail starts out easy, heading south through the Damascus town park and then leaves town, making a steep climb up Holston Mountain. Once on Holston Mountain, the walking is mostly easy again, until one final steady pull to Tennessee, where hikers are greeted by signs marking the state border.

Pick up the Appalachian Trail at the Little Red Caboose and walk south through the park that parallels Beaverdam Road, tracing the white blazes. Pass through an arch; then turn right onto Water Street. Keep going forward, as Water Street turns right and becomes Mock Avenue. Climb steeply up the hill between two houses and pass a trail sign. Immediately pick up an old road. Damascus lies off to your right. At 0.4 mile, make a sharp switchback to your left and ascend steeply through imperiled hemlock and white pine woods.

Pick up another road at 0.6 mile and make a moderate but steady climb to the crest of Holston Mountain. Beyond this point the AT cuts through gaps and around ridgetops, making for easy walking. There are occasional views into the South Fork Holston River valley to your right. At mile 1.9, come to a campsite in a level area. A blue-blazed side trail leads left, east, to water.

Stay primarily in an oak forest, dropping to a sandy gap in a narrow point of the ridge at mile 2.7. Start a steady rise, staying on the east side of the ridge. At mile 3.5, in an area of large oaks, come to the Tennessee state line. A line of rocks crosses the trail, marking the division between the states. There are also signs greeting hikers into both Virginia and Tennessee. Hikers wishing to continue south on the AT will leave Mount Rogers Recreation Area and come to Abingdon Gap shelter 6.5 miles into the Volunteer State.

Access

The segment of the Appalachian Trail starts at the Little Red Caboose on the west side of Damascus at Damascus Community Park.

Appalachian Trail, Damascus to Creek Junction

Type:	Foot only
Length:	14.0 miles
Difficulty:	Moderate to difficult
Use:	High
Condition:	Good to excellent
Highlights:	Some views, good loop possibilities
Book Map #:	1, 3
USGS Topo:	Damascus, Konnarock
Connections:	Virginia Creeper Trail, Iron Mountain Trail, Beech Grove Trail, Feathercamp Trail, Saunders Trail, Beartree Gap Trail, Appalachian Trail, Creek Junction to Elk Garden

This section of the Appalachian Trail takes the hiker from civilized Damascus easterly into the western end of the national recreation area. Along the way it climbs and drops over two significant heights, Feathercamp Ridge and Straight Mountain. There are views up there. Down low, the AT twice follows the Whitetop Laurel Creek valley. All these ups and downs can make this section unsuspectingly challenging. Numerous trail connections allow for great loop hikes, using either the Iron Mountain Trail or the Virginia Creeper Trail. On the AT, leave Damascus and share the path with the Virginia Creeper Trail; then abruptly begin to climb Feathercamp Ridge, gaining over 1,000 feet before the ascent is over. Next, cruise northeasterly down to Feathercamp Branch, to cross US 58. The going is easy beyond 58, in the Whitetop Laurel valley. Then, just as you are really enjoying the walk, climb up the west end of Straight Mountain, once again gaining about 1,000 feet. Pass the Saunders shelter and wind into Beartree Gap. From here, drop back down into Whitetop Laurel Creek and intersect the Virginia Creeper Trail near Creek Junction, site of an old train station, and end this part of the AT.

Start at the Little Red Caboose in Damascus. Follow the white blazes east on US 58, which becomes Laurel Avenue in town, and span Beaver Dam Creek. Keep going through town and at 0.5 mile, veer right at the intersection with VA 91, staying with US 58. Soon, pick up the Virginia Creeper Trail and share the rail trail for a half mile alongside US 58. Turn sharply left, cross US 58, and climb some steps

Long Trails · 5

into the woods. A roadside spring flows to the left of the steps. Start the climb up Feathercamp Ridge, angling upward through pine-oak woods. Make the crest of the ridge; then make a sharp switchback to the right at mile 1.9. Keep climbing for another half mile and then cruise along the ridgeline. There are views off to the south and toward Tennessee. At mile 3.6, intersect a blue-blazed connector trail, leading left 0.2 mile to the Iron Mountain Trail. Continue forward, mostly descending, into moist coves. Span a streamlet on a foot log just before intersecting the Beech Grove Trail at mile 4.9. The Beech Grove Trail leads right 0.3 mile to US 58 and left 0.4 mile to the Iron Mountain Trail.

Continue northbound, jump over a rib ridge, then descend to Feathercamp Branch, and reach the Feathercamp Trail at mile 5.6. At this point, the Feathercamp Trail leads left 2.2 miles to Sandy Flats and the Iron Mountain Trail; the AT curves right and crosses Feathercamp Branch on a plank bridge and then reaches US 58. Take a few steps left, up 58; then look for the AT, dropping right to cross 58 before spanning Straight Branch on a footbridge. Swing around a wide, heavily wooded flat to come alongside Whitetop Laurel Creek at mile 6.1. The Virginia Creeper Trail is visible down by the stream. The next section pushes up the steep-sided valley. Sometimes the Creeper Trail and Whitetop Laurel Creek are in view, sometimes not. At mile 7.0, pick your way through a talus slope to pass a small feeder branch. Keep heading up the valley and come to a trail junction at mile 7.7. A blue-blazed connector trail leads forward a half mile down to the Virginia Creeper Trail and Taylors Valley. The AT, however, turns sharply left and begins the climb up the west slope of Straight Mountain. Start switchbacking up the mountain in pine-oak woods. Count your turns. After 15 switchbacks, at mile 9.4, the path reaches the first spur trail to Saunders shelter. This spur trail drops left down an old logging road to the trail shelter. Another spur trail leading back to the AT is passed just before reaching the structure. Constructed of notched logs, the three-sided Adirondack-style shelter is situated beside a white pine grove and old wildlife clearing. The Saunders Trail comes in from the rear of the shelter, and connects to the AT in 0.7 mile. A spring lies behind the shelter on a blue-blazed spur trail.

Continue on the AT past the side trail to the Saunders Shelter. Soon, come to a cleared overlook to the mountains southeast of Straight Mountain. Intersect the second spur trail to Saunders shelter at mile 9.9. Keep heading northeast along Straight Mountain to intersect the Saunders Trail in a gap. This trail leaves left 0.7 mile, reaching the water trail from the Saunders shelter, then the Sanders shelter itself. The Saunders Trail also leads forward 1.4 miles to US 58. On the AT, briefly share the treadway with the Saunders Trail before splitting right, up Straight Mountain and back into rocky, piney woods on a single-track path. Ascend along the narrow ridgecrest, looking for occasional views. Undulate over Straight Mountain. Cross an intermittent streamed at mile 11.1. Soon, an obscure side trail leads left a short distance back to the Saunders Trail.

Enter a formerly mined area. Notice the planted white pines. At mile 11.7, reach a clearing and a trail junction dotted with autumn olive trees and white pines. Autumn olive, a brushy, exotic species with the silvery green leaves, is planted by the forest service to provide winter food for wildlife. At this junction, the Beartree Gap Trail leaves left and reaches US 58 at 0.3 mile and the Iron Mountain Trail in 3.3 miles.

Keep going forward on the AT, soon passing a pond, also a result of mining, and continue through second-growth forest. Roll down toward Whitetop Laurel valley, reaching the Virginia Creeper Trail at mile 13.8. Stay to the left, once again sharing treadway with the rail trail alongside Whitetop Laurel Creek. Soon, come to another trail junction at mile 14.0. The AT and Creeper Trail split left, and a side trail leads right 0.4 mile to the Creek Junction parking area. From here, the AT heads 9.1 miles north to Elk Garden and VA 600. This section of the AT ends here. To reach the Creek Junction parking area, continue forward on the side trail for 0.4 mile alongside Whitetop Laurel Creek, passing under the Luther Hassinger Memorial Bridge, a wood trestle on the Virginia Creeper Trail.

Access

Southern Access: This section starts at the Little Red Caboose in Damascus.

Northern Access: The north end of this section starts at Creek Junction. To access Creek Junction from the Little Red Caboose in Damascus, head east on US 58 for 11.6 miles to VA 728, Creek Junction Road. Turn acutely right and follow VA 728 for 1.0 mile to dead-end at the spur trail to the Virginia Creeper Trail. Walk the spur for 0.4 mile, passing under the large wooden span above Whitetop Laurel Creek, to the AT.

Appalachian Trail, Creek Junction to Elk Garden

Type:	Foot only
Length:	10.1 miles
Difficulty:	Moderate to difficult
Use:	High to moderate
Condition:	Good
Highlights:	Great views, red spruce woods
Book Map #:	3, 5
USGS Topo:	Konnarock, Whitetop Mountain
Connections:	Virginia Creeper Trail, Taylors Valley Trail, Elk Garden Trail, Virginia Highlands Horse Trail

This section is mostly used by hikers traversing the Appalachian Trail from Damascus to the Mount Rogers high country. There are no trail connections along the way, but there are trail connections at either end of the path. The AT leaves Creek

Junction to join the Virginia Creeper Trail in crossing a large span over White-top Laurel Creek and then heads up the creek valley, leaving the Whitetop Laurel watershed to climb Lost Mountain. On Lost Mountain, ramble through attractive woods to reach the Lost Mountain Trail shelter. Past the shelter, drop down to US 58 and then start ascending toward Beech Mountain, briefly bisecting pastureland availing good views. Gain altitude steadily on Beech Mountain and enter a north-ern hardwood forest. Suddenly, pop out on the lower reaches of Whitetop Mountain and enjoy fantastic views, culminating with the vista from Buzzard Rock at over 5,000 feet; here hikers can see into three states. Ascend the side of Whitetop Moun-tain, enjoying more views; then traverse a high-country red spruce forest. Complete this section with a gradual descent off Whitetop Mountain to Elk Garden.

Start this section of the AT by leaving Creek Junction and heading on a spur trail 0.4 mile under the Luther Hassinger Memorial Bridge, named after a Konna-rock community pioneer, to the actual AT. Turn right on the AT and begin climbing along with the Virginia Creeper Trail. The trail is open to the sky above, in contrast with most of the AT from Damascus. At 0.4 mile, come to the Luther Hassinger Memorial Bridge. This 560-foot span, left over from the Virginia Creeper railroad, offers a treetop view of the Whitetop Laurel valley. Turn abruptly left just past the trestle, splitting from the Virginia Creeper Trail, which leads forward 7.0 miles to Whitetop Station.

The AT drops down to pick up another grade while continuing along Whitetop Laurel Creek. To the left, an unmarked side path works across a flat to access the blue-blazed Taylors Valley Trail. The Taylors Valley Trail leads 2.6 miles back under the trestle to the Virginia Creeper Trail near Taylors Valley. Keep going forward along exposed rock walls and a fern-carpeted forest to reach an unnamed side stream coming in from the right. Turn right up this stream to reach the gravel-surfaced VA 859 at mile 1.1. Continue forward and work up the slope of Lost Mountain, step-ping over a few rivulets. The forest here is rich with straight-trunked tulip trees. Top out on Lost Mountain; then drop into a flat and a trail junction at mile 2.3. Dead ahead is the Lost Mountain trail shelter. This is a three-sided, open-fronted struc-ture of notched logs. A privy is nearby, and a spring is not far down the hill from the shelter.

From the shelter, the AT veers left, undulating easterly in open woods. Drop into the head of a hollow and follow the streambed beneath rhododendron to reach US 58 at mile 3.4, just after spanning Star Hill Branch on a plank footbridge. Cross US 58 and switchback on an old roadbed to climb by a white pine plantation. Leave the roadbed at mile 4.1 and veer left. Clear a walk-through-type fence stile and enter a pasture. There are good views of nearby Beech Mountain. Cruise past an aban-doned house just before reaching gravel-surfaced VA 601 at mile 4.6. Keep heading forward into the woods, passing alongside a pasture to the left and a white pine grove to the right at mile 5.1. Just past this, on the left, is a trail to a spring. On the far side of the spring is the stone foundation of an old pioneer home. The appearance of cherry trees in the woods indicates the rise in elevation and the entry of the trail into a northern hardwood forest. The elevation here is around 3,600 feet.

Begin to angle up the west slope of Beech Mountain. Joining the cherry trees are other components of the northern hardwood forest, such as sugar maple, beech, and finally yellow birch. During summertime, the woods are carpeted with stinging nettle. At mile 6.2, make a sharp switchback to the left. The trail soon emerges into an open canopy and broken woods. Look for hawthorn trees with their thorny branches. Switchback to the right, and the path opens into a large field. Whitetop is visible ahead. Keep going up the field and pass small rock outcrops, reaching Buzzard Rock at mile 7.1. From here, the views are expansive. Beech Mountain is in the foreground to the west. To the north lies Straight Mountain and Iron Mountain. Whitetop is up and to the east. To the south are the mountains of North Carolina and Tennessee.

At the wooden posts, reenter a wind-stunted forest. Intermittent spring branches cross the trail. Open into a field sporadically dotted with trees that flag west to east. Look down to the neat rows and squares of Christmas tree farms. At mile 7.6, pass a spring on trail right. Shortly, cross Forest Road 89 (Whitetop Mountain Road) and reenter the woods again. Spruce trees, much more prevalent in New England and Canada, begin to appear. Begin a very gradual descent. A grassy understory enhances the woodland scenery. Open into Elk Garden and VA 600 at mile 10.1. The Elk Garden Trail comes in from the left and leads 1.5 miles to VA 600. Dead ahead the Appalachian Trail leads 17.0 miles through the high country to Fox Creek and VA 603. The Virginia Highlands Horse Trail leads 12.9 miles through the high country and also to Fox Creek and VA 603.

Access

Southern Access: From the Little Red Caboose in Damascus, head east on US 58 for 11.6 miles to VA 728 (Creek Junction Road). Turn acutely right and follow VA 728 for 1.0 mile to dead-end at the spur trail to the Virginia Creeper Trail at Creek Junction. Walk the spur trail at the far end of the parking area for 0.4 mile, passing under the large wooden span above Whitetop Laurel Creek, to the AT. Turn right on the AT.

Northern Access: From the Little Red Caboose in Damascus, drive 11.0 miles east on US 58. Here, US 58 curves right; keep going forward, now on VA 603 (Konnarock Road). Stay on 603 for 2.6 miles to VA 600 (Whitetop Road). Turn right on VA 600 and follow it for 5.1 miles to the Elk Garden trailhead, where the AT crosses VA 600.

Appalachian Trail, Elk Garden to Fox Creek

Type:	Foot only
Length:	17.0 miles
Difficulty:	Moderate to difficult
Use:	High
Condition:	Good to fair
Highlights:	Unique open landscape, incredible views, spruce-fir forest, berries in summer
Book Map #:	5, 9, 8, 4, 8
USGS Topo:	Whitetop Mountain, Trout Dale
Connections:	Virginia Highlands Horse Trail, Mount Rogers Trail, Mount Rogers Spur Trail, Pine Mountain Trail, Crest Trail, Rhododendron Gap Trail, Wilburn Ridge Trail, Horse Trail, Appalachian Spur Trail, Wilson Creek Trail, Scales Trail, Bearpen Trail, First Peak Trail, Lewis Fork Trail, Old Orchard Trail, Fairwood Valley Trail

This is the most spectacular and the most heavily used section of the Appalachian Trail in the Mount Rogers National Recreation Area. And it may be one of the most spectacular and most heavily used sections of the entire AT. The path offers fine views from the moment it leaves Elk Garden until it drops off Pine Mountain, 13.0 miles later. Along the way it passes though a rare and lofty spruce-fir forest and nears Mount Rogers. Numerous rock outcrops jut above meadows where wild ponies graze and blueberries ripen late in summer. Part of the trail passes through Grayson Highlands State Park.

Sequentially, the trail follows Elk Garden Ridge onto Mount Rogers and passes the side trail for the mountain peak; it then cruises along open meadows to Rhododendron Gap. Next, it veers south along Wilburn Ridge with its many view-laden outcrops and then drops down to the Big Wilson Creek watershed. The trail climbs up to more views and meadows atop Stone Mountain and drops to Scales before ascending to Pine Mountain for one last view. It ends by descending from Pine Mountain into the Fox Creek valley.

Start this section of the Appalachian Trail by leaving VA 600 and Elk Garden to pass through a wide metal gate. The Virginia Highlands Horse Trail heads forward on a dirt path toward Deep Gap. The AT veers left through open country, uphill. Wood posts topped with white blazes mark the trail. Brier Ridge stands off to the right. Views are numerous. Cows and horses may be grazing the fields. Occasional wind-sculpted hawthorn trees break up the landscape. Transition into full woods, clearing a walk-through fence stile and enter the Lewis Fork Wilderness at 0.6 mile. Moderately ascend through a rocky, northern hardwood forest. Top out and descend toward Deep Gap, passing a blue-blazed trail leading right to a campsite before reaching the actual Deep Gap at mile 1.8. Deep Gap is closed to camping. Across the gap, the Virginia Highlands Horse Trail has come 1.7 miles from Elk Garden.

Keep heading forward on the AT, shortly passing a spring. At mile 2.0, intersect the Mount Rogers Trail, which leaves left 5.5 miles down to Fairwood Valley and Grindstone Campground. By mile 2.2, red spruce and Fraser fir trees appear among the northern hardwoods. A clear section of trail allows views back to Elk Garden. At mile 2.9, come to a meadow and fence. Across the fence is the VHHT and Brier Ridge. Stay in woods, ascending the side of Mount Rogers. Numerous streams flow from the mountaintop. Open into a field, broken with spruce, fir, cherry, and hawthorn trees. There are good vistas toward Wilburn Ridge. The Thomas Knob Trail shelter is visible in the foreground. Intersect the Mount Rogers Spur Trail at mile 3.8. It leaves left 0.5 mile to the highest point in the state at 5,729 feet. The AT turns right, drops into a gap, and continues southeast to reach the Thomas Knob shelter at mile 4.2. This is a two-story wooden shelter with a spring behind it and a privy near the AT. No fires are allowed here.

Climb and gain the western slope of Pine Mountain, across mostly open country with myriad views. Span a walk-over-type stile at mile 4.6 and leave the Lewis Fork Wilderness. Rhododendron becomes more apparent as the trail descends toward Rhododendron Gap, which is reached at mile 5.0. A tall rock outcrop lies just to the left. The Pine Mountain Trail continues along the crest of Pine Mountain, intersecting the AT again at 1.9 miles. Just past this, the wide Crest Trail leaves left, also heading along Pine Mountain, reaching Scales in 2.6 miles. The Crest Trail also

Winter at Thomas Knob shelter. Photo courtesy of U.S. Forest Service.

leaves right to intersect the Rhododendron Gap Trail in 0.2 mile. The AT climbs southeasterly toward rocky Wilburn Ridge.

Climb a rocky knob for expansive views from over 5,500 feet. Come to the Wilburn Ridge Trail at mile 5.5. It leaves right and makes a panoramic side trip on the upper reaches of Wilburn Ridge before rejoining the AT in 1.0 mile. Shortly, come to the Fatman Squeeze. Here the trail pinches between a rock wall and a huge boulder; hikers loaded with backpacks will have to twist and turn to get through the squeeze. The trail becomes very rocky beyond the squeeze, slowing progress. Cross the Rhododendron Gap Trail at mile 6.0. Keep heading forward in open country to intersect the south end of the Wilburn Ridge Trail at mile 6.3. Intersect the Virginia Highlands Horse Trail just before crossing a step-over-type stile and entering Grayson Highlands State Park at mile 6.6. The Rhododendron Gap Trail leaves acutely left and reaches Rhododendron Gap via a short section of the Crest Trail in 1.4 miles.

Keep heading forward in the state park, following an old railroad grade through a field. Stay on Wilburn Ridge as it crosses the Virginia Highlands Horse Connector Trail/Rhododendron Trail at mile 7.2. From here it is 0.4 mile right to Massie Gap. The AT continues forward climbing toward a final outcrop on Wilburn Ridge with more phenomenal views. There is also a view down to the Wise trail shelter along Big Wilson Creek. Low-slung trees and bushes grow on the ridge. At mile 7.7, the blue-blazed Appalachian Spur Trail leads right 0.8 mile down to the state park's overnight backpacker parking area.

Shortly beyond this junction, the trail drops through broken woods and brush toward Quebec Branch, which is crossed on a foot log in a rhododendron thicket at mile 8.5. Soon, cross a walk-over-type stile and head east, downstream, along a fence line that parallels Quebec Branch. The trail has left the state park but soon enters it again after passing over a second stile. Numerous streamlets flow over the trail off Wilburn Ridge. Cross a second stile and reenter the state park. Watch for a sudden turn right, off the railroad grade the path has been following. The woods open once again before reaching the Wise trail shelter at mile 9.4. This is a newer, open-fronted wooden structure in a meadow of grass, woods, and many blueberry bushes. There is a privy nearby and a spring reached by blue-blazed side trail. There are vistas of the mountains around the watershed here.

Past the shelter, stay with the white blazes down to cross a stile and reach rhododendron-lined, boulder-laden Big Wilson Creek. Span the stream on a footbridge and leave the state park for the final time. Break out into a large field and intersect the Wilson Creek Trail just before spanning a feeder stream of Big Wilson Creek at mile 9.7. It leaves left 0.6 mile to the Virginia Highlands Horse Trail and right 0.1 mile to the Scales Trail. Cruise along the edge of a meadow and soon intersect the Scales Trail. It leads left 1.2 miles to Scales and right 0.1 mile to the Seed Orchard Road Trail. Veer left, briefly sharing treadway with the Scales Trail before breaking right toward a walk-through-type stile and entering the Little Wilson

Creek Wilderness at mile 9.8. The trail becomes canopied by northern hardwoods here, as it begins to loop around Stone Mountain. Keep going forward on an old logging grade before abruptly turning left, uphill. Spruce becomes more prevalent as the trail rises above 4,400 feet.

At mile 10.9, leave the Little Wilson Creek Wilderness and intersect the Bearpen Trail. The Bearpen Trail leaves left to 0.9 mile to the Scales Trail and right 0.3 mile to the Big Wilson Creek Trail. Beyond the junction, clear a walk-over-type stile and enter the open slopes of Stone Mountain. Follow the blazed wooden posts to incredible views of Wilburn Ridge, Pine Mountain, and forested Mount Rogers. Occasional wind-sculpted cherry trees add a scenic touch to the meadow. Begin to descend off Stone Mountain, toward Scales, which is visible down below. Reach the corral of Scales at mile 12.1. From the right, the First Peak Trail has come 3.2 miles from the east end of the Little Wilson Creek Wilderness. Pass through the corral and intersect the Virginia Highlands Horse Trail and the Scales Trail. The Scales Trail heads south 1.3 miles to intersect the Seed Orchard Road Trail, and the VHHT heads 9.3 miles back to Elk Garden. The Crest Trail leaves left and heads 2.6 miles to Rhododendron Gap. The AT veers right, away from the corral, to enter a field broken by trees.

Mostly climb away from Scales in a forest of northern hardwoods mixed with spruce that cloaks the slopes of Pine Mountain. Spring branches cross the trail at many points. Come to a stile at mile 13.4 and enter a field. A rock outcrop atop the field provides the last high country views for the AT in this section. Skirt the meadow's edge for about 200 yards before clearing another stile and intersecting the Pine Mountain Trail. The Pine Mountain Trail leaves left and heads 1.9 miles to Rhododendron Gap. The AT continues forward in rich woods, dropping off the rocky northern slope of Pine Mountain.

At mile 14.1, enter the Lewis Fork Wilderness. Northern red oaks join the forest as the path continues to descend below 4,000 feet. The mountainside flattens out just before reaching the Old Orchard trail shelter at mile 15.2. This shelter—an older, wooden, Adirondack-style structure—is backed by trees and fronted by a field offering good views to the north of Hurricane Mountain across the Fox Creek valley. A spring is located away from the AT. Leave the Old Orchard and descend through a flat to intersect the Old Orchard Trail. It leaves left 0.3 mile to intersect the Lewis Fork Trail and right 1.4 miles to Fairwood Valley and VA 603. Keep dropping toward Fox Creek, intersecting the Old Orchard Trail once again at mile 16.1. Keep going forward and leave the Lewis Fork Wilderness for the final time. Swing around a small knob while descending through rhododendron to cross a feeder stream of Fox Creek. Walk a few yards beyond the stream and emerge onto the Fox Creek Trailhead at mile 17.0. From here, the AT crosses VA 603 and heads north for 8.5 miles to VA 16 and Dickey Gap. Across the road, the Fairwood Valley Trail leads left 1.6 miles to the Flat Top Trail and right 0.2 mile to Fox Creek Horse Camp.

Access

Southern Access: From the Little Red Caboose in Damascus, drive 11.0 miles east on US 58. Here, US 58 curves right; keep going forward, now on VA 603 (Konnarock Road). Stay on 603 for 2.6 miles to VA 600 (Whitetop Road). Turn right on VA 600 and follow it for 5.1 miles to the Elk Garden trailhead, where the AT crosses VA 600.

Northern Access: From exit 45 on I-81 near Marion, drive 6.0 miles south on VA 16, passing the Jennings Visitor Center. Remain on VA 16 for 11.0 more miles to VA 603 (Fairwood Road) in Troutdale. Turn right on VA 603 and follow it for 4.3 miles to the Fox Valley trailhead, which will be on the left.

Appalachian Trail, Fox Creek to Dickey Gap

Type:	Foot only
Length:	8.5 miles
Difficulty:	Moderate
Use:	Moderate to heavy
Condition:	Excellent
Highlights:	Comers Creek Falls, rich woods
Book Map #:	8, 4, 8
USGS Topo:	Whitetop Mountain, Trout Dale
Connections:	Hurricane Mountain Trail, Virginia Highlands Horse Trail, Iron Mountain Trail, Hurricane Creek Trail, Dickey Gap Trail, Comers Creek Falls Trail

This section of the Appalachian Trail leaves the Mount Rogers high country to climb Hurricane Mountain through rich woods. After gaining the crest of Hurricane Mountain, the AT intersects the Iron Mountain Trail and the Virginia Highlands Horse Trail, then drops along the north slope of Hurricane Mountain. Here, it picks up an old road for a bit, before turning east and following a footpath to reach Comers Creek, where there is an attractive fall. From the fall, the trail veers northeast for Dickey Gap and the end of this section. The grades are never overly steep or long, making for a nice woodland walk.

Leave the Fox Creek trailhead in Fairwood Valley, and immediately cross VA 603. Take a few more steps, passing two large stones and intersect the Fairwood Valley Trail. This trail leaves 1.6 miles left to intersect the Flat Top Trail and the Mount Rogers Trail. It leaves right 0.2 mile to intersect the Fox Creek Horse Camp. Keep going forward on the AT and enter deep woods, crossing Fox Creek on a plank footbridge. Begin climbing along a rock wall to enter the valley of a feeder stream of Fox Creek. Keep climbing through oak-maple-magnolia woods to reach the spine of a rib ridge on Hurricane Mountain at 0.7 mile. Continue a steady uptick on a single-track path to reach the right side of a flat and a trail junction at mile 1.5. To the left, the blue-blazed, unsigned Hurricane Mountain Trail leads 0.4 mile to intersect the Iron Mountain Trail. There is also a spring and tiny pond to the west, on the far side of the flat and down a hollow beyond a grove of white pine.

The AT swings away from the flat and makes for the top of Iron Mountain, achieving the rocky crest at mile 2.0. Descend around a spring to meet the Iron Mountain Trail/Virginia Highlands Horse Trail. Here, those two trails coincide, leaving left, west, 1.7 miles to Flat Top. To the right, the IMT leads 3.3 miles to VA 16. The AT continues forward and makes a forest cruise in tall oak woods, gently descending. Soon, pick up an old woods road and keep going northeasterly. Make a pair of wide switchbacks and come along a small, rhododendron-choked stream. Just ahead is the spur trail to the new Hurricane Mountain shelter. It is a cabin-style shelter with a large overhang in the front. At mile 3.0, leave left away from the feeder stream and descend sharply down the north slope of Hurricane Mountain to meet the Hurricane Creek Trail at mile 3.9. The Hurricane Creek Trail continues forward on the roadbed 0.4 mile to reach Hurricane Creek and Forest Road 84. The AT makes a hard switchback to the right, now an eastbound footpath on the north slope of Hurricane Mountain.

Undulate along the richly forested slope to cross little streams in coves where tulip trees grow straight and tall. Pass under a small power line at mile 5.2. Keep heading easterly, mostly in steep-sided woods, to reach the Dickey Gap Trail at mile 6.4. Here, the Dickey Gap Trail leaves left 0.4 mile to reach Hurricane Campground. The AT turns right here on an old railroad grade and heads past a tiny rill and then up the Comers Creek valley. Comers Creek soon becomes audible before reaching a trail junction at mile 7.3. Here, the Comers Creek Falls Trail continues forward and heads 0.2 mile to VA 741, intersecting the Iron Mountain Trail along the way. The AT veers left, downhill, to soon reach Comers Creek Falls. This 15-foot waterfall cascades down a rock face in stairstep fashion before landing in a small pool below. A plank bridge with handrails crosses the stream and doubles as a fall viewing platform.

Climb away from Comers Creek, briefly passing through pine–oak–mountain laurel woods before returning to rich woods broken with occasional rhododendron tunnels. Cross a plank bridge over a gully and pass a tiny stream before making a short, final ascent to reach VA 650 at mile 8.5. From here, the AT turns right, crosses the road, and enters the far side of the woods to make the Jennings Visitor Center in 15.0 miles.

Access

Southern Access: From exit 45 on I-81 near Marion, drive 6.0 miles south on VA 16, passing the Jennings Visitor Center. Stay on VA 16 for 11 more miles to VA 603, Fairwood Road, in Troutdale. Turn right on VA 603 and follow it for 4.3 miles to the Fox Valley trailhead, which will be on the left.

Northern Access: From exit 45 on I-81 near Marion, head south on VA 16 for 6.0 miles to the Jennings Visitor Center. From the Jennings Visitor Center, continue south on VA 16 for 8.7 miles to VA 650 (Comers Creek Road). Turn right on Comers Creek Road and immediately look for the Appalachian Trail, marked by a sign, crossing the road here.

Appalachian Trail, Dickey Gap to Jennings Visitor Center

Type:	Foot only
Length:	15.0 miles
Difficulty:	Moderate
Use:	Heavy to moderate
Condition:	Good
Highlights:	Views, trail shelters
Book Map #:	8, 7, 6
USGS Topo:	Trout Dale, Atkins
Connections:	Hickory Ridge Trail, Virginia Highlands Horse Trail, Bobbys Trail, Slabtown Trail

This section of the Appalachian Trail is less used than other sections that pass through the recreation area. Furthermore, only 5.0 of the nearly 15.0 miles of this section of AT are within the official boundaries of Mount Rogers NRA. But these last 10.0 miles are included in this guidebook because they end at the Mount Rogers Visitor Center (a.k.a. the Jennings Visitor Center). This section of the AT leaves Hurricane Mountain and heads north past a good view from High Point and on to the South Fork Holston River, only to climb Brushy Mountain and head east to end at the Visitor Center. Three trail shelters make backpacking trips here more viable.

Leave Comers Creek Road, pass a trail register, and come to the Hickory Ridge Trail, which leaves left to intersect the AT once again on the far side of a knob. The AT swings around a grassy field below and climbs up the south side of the knob. There are views of Straight Mountain across the valley. Crest out and then drop down to a gap and a trail junction at 0.8 mile. The Hickory Ridge Trail comes in from your left. A few feet farther down in the gap, intersect the Virginia Highlands Horse Trail. It leads left 2.0 miles to Comers Creek Road near Hurricane Campground and right 4.0 miles to Raccoon Branch campground.

Leave the gap and climb the south side of Bobbys Ridge to reach a rock outcrop at mile 1.3. Here are good views of Pine Mountain and the Mount Rogers high country. Continue on the AT and come to Bobbys Trail at 1.5 miles. To your right, it is 3.3 miles to Raccoon Branch Campground. The old Raccoon Branch shelter has been torn down.

Continue north on the AT, climbing into a rock jumble, and make Dickeys Ridge. Veer right on Dickeys Ridge and then come to the side trail for High Point at mile 2.1. Make this 0.2-mile side trip left to view Rye Valley and the ridges beyond. The AT begins an extended downgrade toward South Fork Holston River. At mile 2.4, on a turn, the Mullins Branch Trail leaves right 2.9 miles down to Rye Valley. Swing below High Point with occasional views of a now-closer Rye Valley. At mile 3.7, come to gap and veer left, switching sides of the ridge.

At mile 4.0, come to another gap and a trail junction. To your right, a blue-blazed side trail leads 0.1 mile to the Trimpi trail shelter. This is an attractive three-sided stone shelter with a fireplace inside. A spring is in the hollow down below. Straight ahead is the blue-blazed Slabtown Trail. It travels 2.1 miles to connect to the AT again at VA 670.

Stay left and continue north on the AT, switching back to the right to cross an old road and survey marker at mile 4.5. Soon cross over a stile and enter open pastureland with good views of Brushy Mountain. The AT is marked with posts across the open field. At an open fence line, make a sharp right on an easily missed turn. Drop down, passing old outbuildings, and cross another stile. Follow a farm road a short distance to gravel-surfaced VA 672 (Slab Town Road) at mile 5.1. Cross the road and swing around a knoll, descending to a small stream at mile 5.9. Drop down and intersect the Slabtown Trail, coming in from your right at mile 6.0. Pass an old homesite and immediately cross the South Fork Holston River on a wood bridge, coming to VA 670 (South Fork Road).

Climb away from South Fork Road and come to a wide railroad grade at mile 6.6. The level grade makes for easy walking. Leave the railbed and head uphill to your left along a feeder stream of the South Fork. Step over the small stream and climb, making the crest of Brushy Mountain at mile 8.4. Veer right, easterly, and top a knob at mile 9.2. Drop down and undulate along the ridgeline with occasional views of the recreation area to the east and the small hamlet of Teas below. Stay generally on the south side of the slope.

Come to gravel-surfaced VA 601 at mile 10.8. The AT crosses the road, heads a few feet east, and then veers right as a foot trail. Climb easterly as the ridgeline narrows. Descend sharply to pass under a power line at mile 12.5; then pick up an old roadbed and begin an extended downgrade. Step over the first of three streams at mile 13.5. Rhododendron escorts the trail as it ascends the upper reaches of Georges Branch, which flows on your right. At mile 14.6, make a near "U" turn to the right and then keep climbing, passing a reclamation pond from strip mining on your right.

At mile 14.9, come to the Partnership trail shelter. This is a newer log model, with a porch, picnic table, fire grate, and a hot shower in the warm season. Come to the parking area for the Jennings Visitor Center, where there is a spigot. The Visitor Center is open Monday through Friday during winter and seven days a week during the warmer months. If leaving a car here during winter, park your vehicle outside the gate if you will be retrieving your car on a Saturday or Sunday, or after 4:30 p.m. on weekdays. At mile 15.0, come to VA 16. From here it is 7.0 miles north to Chatfield shelter on the AT.

Access

Southern Access: From exit 45 on I-81 in Marion, head south on VA 16 for 6.0 miles to the Jennings Visitor Center. This is the northern terminus of this section of the AT. Continue south on VA 16 for 8.7 miles beyond the Visitor Center to VA 650 (Comers Creek Road). Turn right on Comers Creek Road and follow it just a short distance to the Appalachian Trail, which crosses Comers Creek Road. To hike this section, head north on the AT.

Northern Access: From exit 45 on I-81 near Marion, head 6.0 miles to the Jennings Visitor Center. The Appalachian Trail passes directly beside the Visitor Center. Before parking inside the gates of the visitor center, check the hours of operation to make sure you can get your vehicle upon returning to it.

Iron Mountain Trail

The Iron Mountain Trail (IMT) is a long trail that also extends beyond the borders of the Mount Rogers National Recreation Area. For most of its distance, it is a multiuse trail shared by hikers, bikers, and equestrians. The pathway continues along the Iron Mountain Range, starting in Tennessee's Cherokee National Forest, and travels north, where it enters Virginia. Here, the Iron Mountain Range is broken by Beaverdam Creek at Damascus. Once again the Iron Mountain Range rises, and the Iron Mountain Trail culminates in its highest point along Grosses Mountain. Many trails spur off this backbone path, allowing for loop possibilities. Impressive oak forests with an understory of mountain laurel cloak much of these mountain lands. Long-distance travelers can use the three trail shelters spaced along the path; these were built as shelters for AT through-hikers since this was once the route of the AT. The IMT continues easterly to reach VA 16, where it temporarily ends. The ridgeline continues through a mix of private and public land. Eventually, the forest service intends to have the IMT continue past VA 16, but for now the trail resumes at Hale Lake, where it continues northeasterly over Comers Rock and beyond for 14.0 more miles. In places, the trail here is rocky and spectacular. In other places, it traverses logged lands and is very hard to follow. However, solitude seekers will love this last slice of the Iron Mountain Range, which ends at the New River. The IMT once continued almost to the New but was abandoned. Plans call for the trail to ultimately extend more easterly.

Iron Mountain Trail, Damascus to Tennessee State Line

Type:	Foot only
Length:	1.4 miles
Difficulty:	Moderate to difficult
Use:	Low

Condition:	Good
Highlights:	Some views
Book Map #:	1
USGS Topo:	Damascus, Laurel Bloomery
Connections:	Iron Mountain Trail in Tennessee's Cherokee National Forest

This part of the Iron Mountain Trail is mostly used by hikers heading south on the IMT to follow Iron Mountain south into Tennessee, where the trail continues in the Volunteer State's Cherokee National Forest. A grand loop of approximately 50.0 miles can be made using the IMT and the Appalachian Trail, starting in Damascus and heading south to near the AT, then taking the AT north back into Virginia and Damascus.

On the Iron Mountain Trail, leave VA 1212 and head south, uphill, passing around a pole gate and a sign indicating the IMT. The path starts out as a wide, gravel-speckled roadbed and rises alongside a small branch lying beneath shady rhododendron and imperiled hemlock. Bridge the small stream and enter a wildlife clearing. Beyond this, the trailbed becomes much smaller as it knifes through a young forest of spindly trees and vines on a rocky slope. At 0.5 mile, abruptly climb left, tracing the yellow blazes steeply uphill. The ascent moderates via switchbacks while passing a rocked-in spring on the right.

There are occasional views of Damascus through the woods. At mile 1.1, tunnel through a gap in a rhododendron thicket and keep climbing. Far below to your right are the headwaters of Sugarcamp Branch. The bulk of Butt Mountain is to your left. At mile 1.4, come to the boundary between Tennessee and Virginia. This border is indicated by a sign stating, "Wildlife Management Area, Tennessee Wildlife Resources Agency." Behind you, a sign welcomes hikers to Mount Rogers NRA. Beyond this point, the Iron Mountain Trail climbs another mile to Butt Mountain and the crest of the Iron Mountains, continuing southwest for 16.0 miles through the Cherokee National Forest and coming very near the AT at Cross Mountain on Cross Mountain Road.

Access

From the Little Red Caboose in Damascus, drive east on US 58 for 1.4 miles to VA 91. Turn right on VA 91 and follow it just a short distance, crossing over Laurel Creek. Just beyond this crossing, turn right on VA 1212. Follow VA 1212 for 0.2 mile to the Iron Mountain trailhead. The trail leaves left, uphill, from VA 1212, and the trailhead parking is on the right of VA 1212.

Iron Mountain Trail, Damascus to Skulls Gap

Type:	Foot, bicycle, horse
Length:	12.8 miles
Difficulty:	Moderate
Use:	Heavy near Damascus, less use farther east
Condition:	Good
Highlights:	Old AT, trail shelters
Book Map #:	1, 3, 2, 4
USGS Topo:	Damascus, Konnarock, Whitetop Mountain
Connections:	Appalachian Trail, Beech Grove Trail, Feathercamp Ridge Trail, Feathercamp Trail, Bushwacker Trail, Rush Trail, Shaw Gap Trail, Beartree Gap Trail, Chestnut Ridge Trail, Lum Trail, Skulls Gap Trail

The Iron Mountain Trail is a mountaintop path that generally heads east to west along a series of ridges collectively known as the Iron Mountains. Numerous side paths spur off the main trail. This section of the Iron Mountain Trail was once the Appalachian Trail, before the AT was rerouted to the south in the early 1970s. This path is enjoyed by all types of recreation area enthusiasts. Mountain bikers like to pedal out of Damascus and make loop rides using the side trails that spur off Iron Mountain. Equestrians also ride this section where it nears other bridle paths. Backpackers can enjoy a one-way hike using the two trail shelters along the route, or they can use side paths to make loops of their own.

Start your hike by leaving Mock Hollow on the east side of Damascus at 2,000 feet, and heading up an old roadbed. Pass a sign indicating the Iron Mountain Trail and begin to climb along an unnamed feeder stream in a forest of rhododendron and beech. Soon, make the first of seven crossings of the small stream in the first 0.7 mile, which can be easily stepped over in times of normal flow.

Climb away from the watercourse into a drier forest of chestnut oaks, white pine, and mountain laurel. Note the particularly large chestnut oak on trail left, at mile 1.3. Swing around the head of the hollow and top out on the ridge. An unmaintained path leads right to "The Cuckoo" (a strangely named peak) and a view of Damascus.

Stay left on the Iron Mountain Trail, which leads left up Feathercamp Ridge. At mile 1.7, a blue-blazed side trail leads right 0.2 mile to the Appalachian Trail. Keep heading forward, following the yellow blazes of the Iron Mountain Trail. Undulate along Feathercamp Ridge, soon dropping down onto an old forest road, which is the northern section of the Beech Grove Trail. The Beech Grove Trail heads left 2.3 miles down to lower Beech Creek. Stay right on the forest road and walk a bit to a gap and a trail junction at mile 2.7. The continuation of the Beech Grove Trail leaves right to connect to the AT and US 58. The Iron Mountain Trail traces the wide forest road for 0.2 mile before splitting off and rising right on a single track, up the narrow ridgeline in a pine-oak woodland.

Continue a steady ascent as the trail becomes rocky. Begin to gain some views of the South Fork Holston River valley off to your left. Feathercamp Ridge levels off in places, but generally climbs, reaching 3,450 feet by mile 4.8, where there is a trail junction. Here, the Feathercamp Ridge Trail leaves left to intersect the Sawmill Trail. The Iron Mountain Trail veers up and to the right. Straight up the ridgeline is an unmaintained manway climbing to the site of a former lookout tower.

Angle up around the right side of Feathercamp Ridge. Top out and descend toward Forest Road 90, coming to another junction at mile 5.6. Here, the Iron Mountain Trail diverges. Horses and bikers continue forward to intersect Forest Road 90 at 0.1 mile and then follow FR 90 through the gap at Sandy Flats and uphill to reconnect with the Iron Mountain hiker trail in 0.5 mile. The hiker-only portion of the IMT makes a sharp right at the junction and drops down to intersect the Feathercamp Trail at mile 5.8. This blue-blazed trail leads right 2.2 miles to the Appalachian Trail. Drop down on the Iron Mountain Trail and cross the headwaters of Feathercamp Branch before climbing up a hollow and bridging another small stream at mile 6.2. Here lies the Sandy Flats trail shelter. This board shelter is in an open flat beside a small stream. There is a privy nearby and a spring within sight of the structure. Just a few feet in front of the shelter is another trail junction, this time with the Bushwacker Trail, which leads left a short distance to Sandy Flats and right 1.1 miles to Forest Road 90.

Stay forward on the Iron Mountain Trail, climbing over a small knob before coming to Forest Road 90 at mile 6.5. Cross the road, climb a hill, and intersect the Rush Trail. The Rush Trail leaves left and drops down to Rush Creek after 1.8 miles. The Iron Mountain Trail leads forward and climbs Grosses Mountain. Stay in an oak forest with an understory of striped maple. Climb to a high point of 3,800 feet and then drop down to Shaw Gap, reaching a trail junction at mile 8.0. To your right are the Beartree Gap Trail and the Shaw Gap Trail. The Shaw Gap Trail leads 1.0 miles down to Beartree Group Camp. The Beartree Gap Trail leads down to Beartree Lake and on to the AT after 3.3 miles. To your left is Chestnut Ridge Trail. It leads 1.8 miles down to Forest Road 615.

Climb away from Shaw Gap on the Iron Mountain Trail and soon top out on the ridge crest, continuing northeasterly along the southeast side of Grosses Mountain. Rollercoaster along the ridgeline, passing old cattle fencing wire and posts on your left. There are large trees in this section of trail. Later, the ridge becomes narrow and rocky before coming to a conspicuous rhododendron thicket at mile 10.1. From here, the evergreen becomes more prevalent. Make an extended drop to reach a gap and a trail junction at mile 11.1. This attractive flat graced with large white pines is the site of the Straight Branch trail shelter, just a few steps to your right. This is a three-sided board shelter with an open front. A side trail leads from the shelter front to a spring. There is a privy behind the shelter. The Lum Trail leads past the shelter 1.0 mile down to Beartree Campground.

Keep descending on the Iron Mountain Trail, crossing a couple of small streams, picking up a road and entering an old farm field. Leave the hilly former pastureland, cross another stream, and enter the woods. Parallel a feeder stream as it flows to the roadbed of old VA 600 and a trail junction at mile 12.0. The Skulls Gap Trail follows old VA 600 left for 0.9 mile down to an overlook on the current VA 600. Turn right on the old roadbed, passing a homesite on the right. Come to and leave Forest Road 84 at mile 12.3, now aiming for VA 600 on a descent, which is reached at 12.8 miles. From here it is 9.7 miles north to VA 16 on the Iron Mountain Trail.

Access

Western Access: From the Little Red Caboose beside US 58 in Damascus, drive east on 58 for 0.6 mile to Fourth Street. Turn left on Fourth Street and follow it up and to the right 0.3 mile into Mock Hollow. The Iron Mountain Trail starts just at the curve over a creek on the road. There is parking here for two cars.

Eastern Access: From the Little Red Caboose in Damascus, drive east on US 58 for 11.0 miles to VA 603 (Fairwood Road). Continue forward on VA 603 (US 58 curves right) and follow it for 2.7 miles to VA 600 (Whitetop Road). Keep going forward on VA 600, and VA 603 leaves right in 0.1 mile. (VA 603 and VA 600 coincide for 0.1 mile.) Continue forward on VA 600 and follow it for 2.6 miles to the IMT trail crossing on the improved VA 600.

Iron Mountain Trail, Skulls Gap to Hurricane Mountain

Type:	Foot, bicycle, horse
Length:	9.2 miles
Difficulty:	Moderate
Use:	Moderate
Condition:	Good
Highlights:	Trail shelter, great views, numerous trail connections
Book Map #:	4, 8
USGS Topo:	Whitetop Mountain, Trout Dale
Connections:	Little Laurel Trail, Flat Top Trail, Hurricane Mountain Trail, Virginia Highlands Horse Trail, Appalachian Trail, Comers Creek Falls Trail

This section of the Iron Mountain Trail climbs east away from VA 600 and then leaves Skulls Gap and climbs to a high gap at Cherry Tree Camp and beyond into a northern hardwood forest and Cherry Tree Shelter, an alluring camping locale. Beyond this, the path continues east with easy traveling over Flat Top and along Hurricane Mountain, where there are great views of the Mount Rogers high country from ridgetop pastureland, eventually dropping to VA 16. Along the way are several side trails, including the Appalachian Trail and the Virginia Highlands Horse Trail.

Leave VA 600 and walk northeast up an open roadbed. Veer right into the woods past a trail sign. Ascend, swinging around a point in the ridge at 0.3 mile. Continue ascending the south-facing slope, which is grown up with pine and mountain laurel. Off to your right is the Little Laurel Creek Valley and Grave Mountain. On the far side of Grave Mountain is Whitetop Mountain. Achieve the crest of the ridge at mile 0.7, and keep climbing on the narrow land. Drop to a gap; then stay fairly level to intersect Forest Road 84 at 1.9 miles. For the next mile, the Iron Mountain Trail traces Forest Road 84. Slightly ascend on the road and come to a wildlife clearing on your right at mile 2.9. This is known as Cherry Tree Camp. The little-used Little Laurel Trail leaves right from the clearing and dead-ends down on Little Laurel Creek. Notice the two huge sugar maple trees on the edge of the clearing.

Just past Cherry Tree Camp, a road leaves right. The Iron Mountain Trail traces this road uphill past a vehicle barrier. Notice how the beech, yellow birch, and cherry trees, components of a northern hardwood forest, have increased with the elevation. You are now at over 4,200 feet. There are views back to Double Top and Round Top, as well as mountains to the north. Ascend the side of Graves Mountain. Springs run down the side of the mountain. Crest the ridge at mile 3.6 and enjoy easy walking to a grassy gap and a trail junction at mile 4.1. This is the site of the Cherry Tree shelter. This rustic lean-to of notched round logs with a wood shingle roof stands at 4,400 feet. A spring is down from the front of the shelter, and a privy is within sight. The Flat Top Trail follows the old roadbed right and downhill to VA 603.

Hiker at Cherry Tree shelter.

The Iron Mountain Trail leaves left as a footpath. Make a gradual descent on Flat Top to intersect Forest Road 828 at mile 4.4. Turn right on 828 and walk a bit, until you see the Iron Mountain Trail leading left into the woods again, along Hurricane Mountain. This is also the intersection with the Virginia Highlands Horse Trail, which has come up from Fairwood Valley on 828. These two paths run together for 1.7 miles.

Keep going east, now on Hurricane Mountain, which forms the border of Smyth and Grayson counties. The grades are moderate as the trail rolls along the crest of Hurricane Mountain in deciduous woodland heavy with oaks. Drop to a prominent gap at mile 5.4. Just as the Iron Mountain Trail begins to climb out of the gap, intersect the Hurricane Mountain Trail on your right. It is blue-blazed, marked with a "No Horses" sign, and leads 0.4 mile to intersect the Appalachian Trail.

Climb out of the gap on the yellow-blazed Iron Mountain Trail and swing around the north side of the ridge to intersect the Appalachian Trail at mile 5.9. To your left, it is 6.2 miles to Dickey Gap and, to your right, 2.3 miles to Fairwood Valley. Continue forward and come to another junction at mile 6.1. The Virginia Highlands Horse Trail diverges from the IMT and leads 2.6 miles to Fox Creek Horse Camp. The IMT drops down to a perennial stream, passing an old road leaving left. Climb out of the creek bed only to drop and pass a second stream at mile 6.7. Rise again and come directly alongside fenced pastureland to your right. The grassy mountaintop offers great views of Pine Mountain in the Mount Rogers high country. Beyond the pasture, begin an extended descent and enter lower pastureland.

At mile 7.5, intersect gated Forest Road 4022. It drops down a quarter mile to VA 741. Bikers and equestrians must use FR 4022 in combination with a left turn on VA 741 (Homestead Road) to access VA 16, as the continuation of this segment of the Iron Mountain Trail is for hikers only. Hikers stay left at the junction and step over a stile to climb a hill. Past the hill, the trail opens into a field, where there are awesome views of Pine Mountain. The trail is marked with yellow blazes on wooden posts.

Leave the cleared area at mile 8.1 and step over another fence stile. Soon, beside a survey marker, the trail makes a sharp right turn and drops down to a stile and a field. Just past this stile, make a very sharp left turn back into the woods and pass over another stile. Comers Creek is audible off to your right as you drop down to this watercourse and a trail junction at mile 8.7. The Comers Creek Falls Trail crosses the Iron Mountain Trail, leaving left 0.3 mile to the AT and 0.1 mile right to VA 741. Stay right, heading upstream along the upper stretch of Comers Creek. Look on your left for a footlog crossing Comers Creek. Span the creek and continue forward along the steep hillside of Comers Creek valley. Crashing Comers Creek is off to your left. Begin to switchback up and away from the stream to pass by VA 741. Parallel VA 741 and pick up an old roadbed, descending to VA 16 at mile 9.2. One hundred yards to your right is potential parking at the top of a gap at the

Smyth-Grayson county line. There is no parking at the exact point where the Iron Mountain Trail meets VA 16.

Access

Western Access: From the Little Red Caboose in Damascus, drive east on US 58 for 11.0 miles to Virginia 603 (Fairwood Road). Keep going forward on VA 603 (US 58 curves right) and follow it for 2.7 miles to VA 600 (Whitetop Road). Continue forward on VA 600, and VA 603 leaves right in 0.1 mile. (VA 603 and VA 600 coincide for 0.1 mile) Keep going forward on VA 600 and follow it for 2.6 miles to the gap where the IMT crosses VA 600.

Eastern Access: From exit 45 on I-81 near Marion, head south on VA 16 for 6.0 miles to the Jennings Visitor Center. From the Jennings Visitor Center, continue south on VA 16 for 9.4 miles to VA 741 (Homestead Road) just beyond the Smyth-Grayson county line. The Iron Mountain Trail meets VA 16 just before the county line.

Iron Mountain Trail, Hale Lake to Jones Knob

Type:	Foot-only first two miles, horse and bike rest of trail
Length:	15.6 miles
Difficulty:	Moderate
Use:	Low
Condition:	Good
Highlights:	Views, Comers Rock, loop possibilities, solitude
Book Map #:	11, 13, 15
USGS Topo:	Speedwell, Cripple Creek
Connections:	Hale Lake Trail, Little Dry Run Trail, Comers Rock Trail, Unaka Trail, Dry Run Gap Trail, Perkins Knob Trail, Divide Trail

This is the least used section of the Iron Mountain Trail. Start at Hale Lake and head east on a foot-only path to Comers Rock Campground. From here, travel Forest Road 57 to Dry Run Gap. Reenter the wilds on a rerouted narrow section of the IMT to wrangle along a rocky divide. Intersect the Perkins Knob and Divide trails before continuing east into a rough, seldom-traveled section of Iron Mountain. Here, the trail borders private land and logged-over areas, which obscure the path. Occasional clearings make for spectacular views, but keep your eye peeled for the correct trail, which becomes difficult to follow at times. Emerge onto gravel-surfaced VA 653. From here the IMT continues east on VA 653, past Jones Knob to intersect a closed forest road. Pick up the forest road, passing a few wildlife clearings and an old homesite. After the last clearing, the IMT drops along the north side of Iron Mountain, passing a couple of more homesites before ending near a cabin south of Bournes Branch. The trail once continued farther east, but the final section has been abandoned. The trail currently ends near the cabin, though plans for an extension are being worked out. There is no current public auto access beyond Jones Knob.

Start this section of the IMT by leaving the Hale Lake parking area and heading up the wooden steps to Hale Lake on the Hale Lake Trail. Head right, around the lake, and soon pass over a wooden bridge. Just past this bridge, begin to look for a trail leading uphill to the right. This is the Iron Mountain Trail. Climb astride a hollow to cross Forest Road 57B at 0.2 mile. Keep heading easterly, following the yellow blazes in a rich oak forest. Swing along the headwaters of Kinser Creek to ascend to a trail junction in an open area of dead and living white pine. An unmaintained trail leaves right a short distance and connects to Forest Road 57. Stay left and climb; there are occasional views to the west. At 0.9 mile, begin to swing around the knob of Comers Rock. Notice the stonework along the trail. Top out on a side ridge at mile 1.4; there is a rock outcrop to the left. The trail moderates and comes to a trail junction at 2.0 mile. To the left, the Little Dry Run Trail heads downhill 4.4 miles to US 21, connecting with the Virginia Highlands Horse Trail along the way. To the right, the Little Dry Run Trail leads 100 feet to Comers Rock Campground. Acutely right, the Comers Rock Trail leads 0.4 mile to Comers Rock. On the far side of Comers Rock Campground, the Unaka Mountain Trail makes a 1.0-mile loop through a section of old-growth forest.

The IMT now follows Forest Road 57 east, away from Comers Rock Recreation Area. The section along FR 57 is not blazed. Pass a couple of small cabins on private land at mile 2.3. Undulate on the spine of Iron Mountain, catching occasional obscured views to the left. At mile 3.6, dip to a prominent gap with closed forest roads leaving both sides of the gap. Ascend out of the gap to make a sharp left turn at mile 4.1, passing a small wildlife clearing on the right. Mostly descend from here to reach Dry Run Gap and US 21 at mile 5.6. From here the IMT heads left. Walk a short distance, looking for a gravel road across the paved highway. Very carefully cross US 21 over to the gravel road, blocked with a metal vehicle barrier. Just ahead is a trail sign indicating the Iron Mountain Trail. Keep going forward and pass a huge mound of rock to reenter the woods at 5.8 miles. Swing around a feeder stream of East Fork over an ancient culvert. The trail is now on the old US 21. At 5.9 miles, intersect the Dry Run Gap Trail. It continues forward on the old US 21 1.0 mile to intersect the Virginia Highlands Horse Trail.

Swing right, uphill, onto a single-track path, part of the trail rerouting that occurred when Dry Run Gap was modified to prevent slides. Wind uphill in pine-oak woods with an understory of mountain laurel. Do not cut the switchbacks here: it causes erosion, and you can't count your full trail mileage. Work around the head of a hollow to reach the crest of Iron Mountain at mile 6.7. A trail sign indicates the left, easterly, turn here. Continue along the rocky ridge crest, undulating up and down the border between Wythe and Grayson counties. At mile 9.2, come to a fairly open gap where there are many sawn logs that make good seats. The unsigned Perkins Knob Trail leaves right, 0.2 mile down to the Perkins Knob Spur Trail and 2.0 miles beyond that to US 21.

Keep heading forward, ascending gently to arrive at a second trail junction, this one signed, at mile 9.4. The Divide Trail leaves steeply left 0.8 mile to Forest Road 14. Continue forward and, at mile 9.6, swing around the right side of a rocky knob. The woods here are heavy with rhododendron and mountain laurel. Look for occasional yellow blazes. At 10.0 miles, emerge onto a grassy ridgeline dotted with locust trees, heading downhill. Look left for a huge pile of rocks surrounded by trees, before dropping to a gap and climbing uphill back into the woods. The land here is posted on both sides. At 10.3 miles, come to a junction. A road drops sharply right. Continue forward uphill, topping out on a knob. Head downhill and leave tall woods to drop very steeply through a sprouting forest broken by dead white pine snags. There are good views here. Drop down to a gap—a road leaves sharply right downhill. Keep heading forward on a grassy roadbed 0.1 mile, until it drops steeply downhill at 10.6 miles. Just before the drop, look left across the broken grass–and–tree hillside for a grove of white pines. Leave the road and cut to the left about 80 yards to pick up the ridgeline in the white pine grove. Continue right on the ridgeline, through the woods, to emerge onto a grassy, canopied, level logging road. Travel this road 200 feet to a moderate right turn and look left for a faint yellow blaze on a chestnut oak. Head left, uphill on the IMT for 0.1 mile, to emerge from the woods onto a wide-open grassy roadbed at 11.1 miles. Keep to the left and parallel the national forest border. Watch for occasional national forest property boundary signs. Logging roads spur away from the main path. Stay on the ridgeline and look for occasional faint yellow blazes.

The path winds among sporadic trees and grass. In late summer, blackberries may crowd the way. This open area allows great views of the Devils Den and Chestnut Knob on Ewing Mountain to the left. Veer right onto a grassy trail, soon passing under a power line in a clearing. The IMT passes through private land here; please respect landowners' rights. A house is uphill to your left. At 12.0 miles, make a sharp right, staying with the yellow blazes. Pass a pole gate and descend. At 12.2 miles, emerge onto a gravel road at a curve. This is VA 653. The left, downhill portion of VA 653 leads to Brush Creek. On the far right, a dirt road leads to private land. The IMT takes the middle, gravel road, which is the part of VA 653 that continues along the spine of Iron Mountain. The trail is not blazed past here. Stay with VA 653, heading uphill in pine-oak woods. At 12.9 miles, pass the gated forest road leading left up to Jones Knob. Descend to reach a closed forest road on the left at 13.1 miles. The IMT continues beyond the gate of this closed forest road. Note that this gate is currently the most easterly road access for the IMT.

Pass around the pole gate and soon reach a wildlife clearing. Undulate along the ridgeline to reach a second wildlife clearing at 13.8 miles. On the far side of the clearing is an old homesite. The chimney is still standing. Cruise easterly around the 3,400-foot level to enter a third wildlife clearing at mile 14.1. The IMT continues directly across the clearing here. Do not take the ORV trail leading uphill to the right.

Descend along the north side of Iron Mountain on a much narrower trail. There are occasional views to the left of Brush Creek valley and Ewing Mountain. Rhododendron and mountain maple become more prevalent as the trail descends. At mile15.0, enter an old homesite growing up with locust trees and brush. Look for old bricks and other artifacts. Just past this homesite is a trail junction. To the left, an unmaintained trail leads down to Bournes Branch. The Iron Mountain Trail makes an acute right turn down to a perennial stream, where it resumes an easterly course. At mile 15.3, look for another homesite in a flat, growing up in white pines, on the left of the trail. Here are piles of rock and woods roads spurring off the flat.

Shortly beyond the third homesite, pass another perennial stream. Climb away from this stream to emerge onto a clearing and a gravel road at mile 15.6. To the left is a wooden cabin with a brick chimney. This is the current end of the IMT. This end of the trail cannot currently be publicly accessed by auto, but changes are planned for the future. The IMT once turned left here, but this section has been abandoned. Any further progress on the old IMT is considered off-trail travel.

Access

Western Access: From exit 70 on I-81 near Wytheville, drive south on US 21 for 17.8 miles to Forest Road 57, passing through Speedwell. Turn right on FR 57 and follow it for 5.1 miles to Hale Lake, which will be on your right.

Eastern Access: From exit 80 on I-81 near Fort Chiswell, head south on US 52 for 1.2 miles to VA 94. Turn right on VA 94 and follow it 14.9 miles to VA 602 (Brush Creek Road). (There is a convenience store at this turn.) Turn right on Brush Creek Road and follow it for 5.4 miles to VA 653 (Arrowood Road). Turn left on Arrowood Road and follow it for 3.9 miles to a gate to the left of 653. This is the farthest-west public auto access for the IMT.

Virginia Highlands Horse Trail

After the designation of Mount Rogers as a national recreation area, local horse enthusiasts clamored for a horse trail extending the length of the preserve. In the early 1970s, horse clubs and the forest service began to actually lay out trail. As always, money became an issue, but now we have an equestrian trail extending from Elk Garden on the western edge of the Mount Rogers high country and traveling easterly over the high country. It then drops down to Fairwood Valley and passes by Fox Creek Horse Camp.

Equestrians tackle the Virginia Highlands Horse Trail.
Photo courtesy of U.S. Forest Service.

Beyond the camp it rises to meet Iron Mountain. The VHHT then shares treadway with the Iron Mountain Trail and Forest Road 84 before entering some of the least visited sections of the recreation area on the east side of VA 16. Later, it emerges from this little-used section to skirt the Little Dry Run Wilderness and enter the Hussy Mountain area, where many other trails avail loop opportunities. Finally, the horse path meanders among more quiet forestlands before dropping down to meet the New River Rail Trail, covering nearly 80.0 miles.

Virginia Highlands Horse Trail, Elk Garden to Fox Creek Horse Camp

Type:	Foot- and horse-only in wilderness areas, bicycle rest of trail
Length:	12.9 miles
Difficulty:	Moderate to difficult
Use:	Moderate
Condition:	Mostly good
Highlights:	Great views in high country, spruce-fir forest, access to Fox Creek Horse Camp
Book Map #:	5, 9, 8
USGS Topo:	Whitetop Mountain, Trout Dale
Connections:	Appalachian Trail, Helton Creek Spur Trail, Helton Creek Trail, Crest Trail, Rhododendron Gap Trail, Virginia Highlands Horse Connector Trail, Wilson Creek Trail, Scales Trail, First Peak Trail, Switchback Trail, Old Orchard Spur Trail, Virginia Highlands Horse Trail, Fox Creek Horse Camp to Raccoon Branch

This is the most heavily used section of the Virginia Highlands Horse Trail. It starts at Elk Garden on the western edge of the high country, which it then traverses, offering numerous and spectacular views, before it descends to Fairwood Valley, where it passes by Fox Creek Horse Camp. The VHHT here isn't overly steep, save for the drop from Scales to Fairwood Valley. However, expect occasional muddy conditions, especially following rains.

Leave the Elk Garden parking area and immediately pass through a gate. The Virginia Highlands Horse Trail leaves right, following the orange diamonds through the open slope of Elk Garden Ridge. There are immediate views southward, to the right. There may be cattle grazing in this meadow during the summer. Buckeye and hawthorn trees dot the field. Mount Rogers lies dead ahead. Downhill to the right at 0.3 mile is a fenced-in spring. Shortly after the spring, intersect the Helton Creek Spur Trail. It leads right 1.3 miles down to the Helton Creek Trail. Continue forward to reach a gate at 0.5 mile. Pass through the gate and enter the Lewis Fork Wilderness and a canopy of red maple, buckeye, beech cherry, and sugar maple. The trail may be muddy in places here.

Intersect the Helton Creek Trail at 1.0 mile. The Helton Creek Trail descends 3.1 miles to reach VA 783. The VHHT keeps ascending on a wide track to reach Deep Gap at mile 1.7. This is a no-camping area. Across the gap, to the left, the Appalachian Trail has come 1.8 miles from Elk Garden.

The VHHT now turns southerly along the rocky lower slope of Mount Rogers. Pass several spring branches flowing off Mount Rogers. Make a little jump just before reaching a gate at mile 2.4. Leave the Lewis Fork Wilderness and enter a meadow. Switchback up a rock path that has been rerouted to prevent erosion. Gain the crest of Brier Ridge, adorned with rock outcrops, and enjoy views of Whitetop, down into the Cabin Creek watershed, and southward to North Carolina. Intersect the abandoned Cabin Ridge Trail, which leaves right 1.2 miles to enter private land. Continue forward through the meadow of Brier Ridge, passing a spring and then coming to another gate at mile 2.7. Clear the gate and reenter northern hardwoods complemented by Fraser fir and spruce trees.

Undulate along the sometimes muddy south slope of Mount Rogers. Spruce and fir become the dominant tree species. The forest canopy breaks open before reaching a gate at mile 3.6. A meadow opens up beyond the gate, allowing wide vistas to the south and of Mount Rogers to the north. Gently ascend to the crest of Cabin Ridge and a trail junction at mile 4.0. Here, the Crest Trail leaves acutely left 3.1 miles to Scales. To the right, the old, now-closed VHHT crosses a field and deadends. The current VHHT continues forward to descend from Cabin Ridge.

There are good views to the left of Wilburn Ridge as the gravel trail drifts in and out of woods. At mile 4.8, the VHHT leaves sharply left, and closed Forest Road 4033 leaves right down to Middle Fork Helton Creek. There are more good views of Wilburn Ridge ahead. Stay along a fence line to clear a gate and cross the headwaters of Cabin Creek at mile 5.3. The landscape becomes increasingly open as the trail parallels Grayson Highlands State Park. There are more good views south before intersecting the Appalachian Trail at mile 5.8. Here, the AT leads left 6.3 miles to Elk Garden and 9.7 miles to Fairwood Valley. Just past this intersection, the VHHT meets the Rhododendron Gap Trail, which leads left 1.2 miles to the Crest Trail. Keep descending to meet the Virginia Highland Horse Connector Trail at mile 5.9. The connector trail leads right beyond the gate, 1.0 mile to the state park Horse Trail.

Beyond these junctions, the trail continues in mostly open country with more views. Make four downhill switchbacks and briefly slip into the state park. After a long, canopied straightway, the trail crosses Big Wilson Creek at mile 7.5. The landscape opens once again beyond this stream. This time, most views— primarily of Stone Mountain and Pine Mountain—are from "the down looking up" instead of "the up looking down." The state park's Fraser fir seed orchard is easily visible. Cross a feeder stream of Big Wilson Creek and cruise along a fence line to intersect the Wilson Creek Trail at mile 8.7. This trail leads right 0.7 mile to meet the Scales Trail and the Seed Orchard Road Trail near lower Big Wilson Creek.

Keep heading northerly for Scales, reaching a gate and then Scales at mile 9.3. Here is a gap centered by a corral. To the right, the Scales Trail leads down to Big Wilson Creek. The Appalachian Trail leads right 12.1 miles to Elk Garden and left 4.9 miles to Fairwood Valley. The First Peak Trail leads right 3.2 miles to the Hightree Rock Trail. The Crest Trail leads left 3.4 miles back to the VHHT. Stay to the left of the corral and follow Forest Road 613, now going downhill. Look left for views into Opossum Creek. Pass over a cattle guard and a spring branch before turning left into the woods. Steeply drop through mixed hardwoods on a narrower, rocky trailbed. There is a profusion of Fraser magnolias among the rocky woods. Intersect the Switchback Trail at mile 10.4. It leads right, uphill, on a much narrower track than the VHHT to cross FR 613 once before reaching 613 a second time after 1.2 miles.

The VHHT keeps descending and soon reaches Forest Road 613. Turn left on 613 and follow the gravel road to a sharp right turn. Make this turn; then look left for the orange diamonds as the VHHT leaves the road at 10.6 miles. Shortly cross Opossum Creek and undulate through woodland on a rerouting of the VHHT. Clear a gate at 11.9 miles and descend to meet the Livery Trail, which leads right 0.2 mile to a horse-rental facility that may or may not be open. The VHHT stays left here, spanning a small stream via culvert. Open into meadows broken by lines of trees. There are views across the valley of Hurricane Mountain. Intersect the Old Orchard Spur Trail at mile 12.8. It leads forward 1.7 miles to meet the Old Orchard Trail. The VHHT turns right and crosses a feeder stream of Fox Creek. Emerge onto VA 603 at mile 12.9. Fox Creek Horse Camp is just to the left. From here, the VHHT continues 16.4 miles to Raccoon Branch near VA 16.

Access

Western Access: From the Little Red Caboose in Damascus, drive 11.0 miles east on US 58. Here, US 58 curves right; keep driving forward, now on VA 603 (Konnarock Road). Stay on 603 for 2.6 miles to VA 600 (Whitetop Road). Turn right on VA 600 and follow it for 5.1 miles to the Elk Garden trailhead, where the AT crosses VA 600.

Eastern Access: From exit 45 on I-81 near Marion, drive 6 miles south on VA 16, passing the Jennings Visitor Center. Stay on VA 16 for 11.0 miles to VA 603 (Fairwood Road) in Trout Dale. From the village of Trout Dale, head west on VA 603 (now called Fairwood Valley Road) for 4.0 miles. Fox Creek Horse Camp will be on your right. The VHHT starts next to the campground.

Virginia Highlands Horse Trail, Fox Creek Horse Camp to Raccoon Branch

Type:	Foot- and horse-only first 2.6 miles and first 2.0 miles beyond VA 650, bicycle rest of trail
Length:	16.4 miles
Difficulty:	Moderate to difficult
Use:	Moderate
Condition:	Very good
Highlights:	Numerous trail junctions, some views from Bobbys Ridge, wildlife clearings
Book Map #:	8, 4, 8, 7
USGS Topo:	Whitetop Mountain, Trout Dale
Connections:	Fairwood Valley Trail, Iron Mountain Trail, Hickory Ridge Trail, Bobbys Trail, Dickey Knob Trail, Appalachian Trail, Virginia Highlands Horse Trail, Raccoon Branch to Middle Creek

This bridle path has several different sections. It first follows gravel road up to Locust Ridge to meet Hurricane Mountain. It then traces Hurricane Mountain to meet and follow two other forest roads. After this, the VHHT becomes a narrow steep path climbing to the crest of Bobbys Ridge, picking up an old roadbed and becoming easier to travel, but is still limited to foot and horse travel only, until it meets the Appalachian Trail. Beyond the junction with the AT, this part of the VHHT is also open to bicycles and thus is a little busier than the previous section of trail. The path then leaves the AT to climb up and over Bobbys Ridge, then descend to Raccoon Branch. Once on Raccoon Branch the trail drops easterly past numerous wildlife clearings to ford Dickeys Creek. Pass directly by Raccoon Branch Campground to end at a trailhead on the far side of VA 16.

Start this section of the Virginia Highlands Horse Trail by tracing VA 741 away from the lower Fox Creek Horse Camp on the left to bridge Fox Creek. Head uphill on VA 741 and continue passing the upper portion of the camp. Ascend the side of Locust Ridge, making a sharp left curve at 0.7 mile. At 1.1 miles, look left for a sign and trail indicating the reentry of the VHHT into the woods. Climb onto a single-track path, soon making a switchback left. Head westerly through hickory-oak woods on Locust Ridge toward a larger knob of Hurricane Mountain. Pass by an unusual, large pile of rocks at mile 2.0. The trail steepens beyond the rocks. Look for an old barbwire fence and large northern red oaks beside the trail. Top out at mile 2.3, and switch to the north side of Hurricane Mountain on a slender path. Intersect the Iron Mountain Trail at mile 2.6. The Virginia Highlands Horse Trail and the Iron Mountain Trail share the same treadway atop Hurricane Mountain for the next 1.7 miles. Turn left on the Iron Mountain/VHHT and soon intersect the Appalachian Trail. Descend to intersect the Hurricane Mountain Trail at 3.2 miles. It is marked by a "No Horses" sign and leaves left to intersect the Appalachian Trail in 0.4 mile. Climb out of a gap and come to Forest Road 828 at 4.3 miles.

The VHHT turns right onto FR 828. Stay on the road as the IMT soon turns left back into the woods. Continue on the rough dirt-and-gravel road, which is laden with soil berms to cut down on erosion. At 5.1 miles, come to Forest Road 84. Turn right on FR 84, which is less rough. Continue descending on the road toward Hurricane Gap. Come to a trail junction at mile 5.6. To the left, the Rowland Creek Trail leaves to intersect the Old 84 Trail; continue 1.5 miles farther to Rowland Creek Falls. Stay forward on the VHHT and pass by Hurricane Gap. Descend into the watershed of Hurricane Creek, passing wildlife clearings at 6.3 and 6.8 miles. Come to another trail junction at mile 7.5. The Barton Gap Trail leaves left 1.6 miles to Barton Gap on FR 643. The Hurricane Creek Trail leaves 0.4 mile right to intersect the Appalachian Trail.

Continue descending on the VHHT, soon passing another wildlife clearing. Briefly come alongside Hurricane Creek and then veer away. Keep dropping to intersect the paved portion of FR 84 near Hurricane Campground at mile 9.6.

Turn right and head uphill along the paved Hurricane Campground Road for 0.3 mile to gravel-surfaced Comers Creek Road. Turn left on Comers Creek Road (VA 650) and follow it 0.1 mile to a curve. The VHHT then leaves the road and heads right, uphill, ascending sharply on a narrow treadway alongside a feeder stream of Comers Creek. It soon turns away from the stream and angles up the steep slope of Bobbys Ridge. To your left are views of Hurricane Knob in the foreground and Hurricane Mountain beyond. Look for squawroot along this trail. It is a white bulb-like parasite feeding on oak roots; it starts popping out of the ground around mid-April. It is an important early spring food for bears, when they emerge from hibernation. Achieve the western crest of Bobbys Ridge at 10.7 miles, after a climb of over 500 feet. Veer right, working easterly along the south slope of the ridge amid tangled vines and downed trees. Soon pick up an old roadbed that is being reclaimed by mountain laurel and young pines. A single-track trail is open on the roadbed. At mile 11.2, split a gap with a small knob to your right. Continue in a moderate ascent and look for occasional views of Hurricane Mountain and Pine Mountain. The trailbed widens and opens overhead as it reaches a gap and a trail junction between Hickory Ridge and Bobbys Ridge at mile 12.0. The Appalachian Trail leads right 0.8 mile to Dickey Gap at VA 650 and left 0.7 mile to meet Bobbys Trail. To your right, just a short distance on the AT, is the junction with the Hickory Ridge Trail, which leaves right and climbs over Hickory Ridge to intersect the AT again near Comers Creek Road. Stay forward on the wide roadbed of the VHHT and swing around the headwaters of Scott Branch, which is downhill to your right. At 12.3 miles, ascend the piney south side of Bobbys Ridge to make a sharp left and cross to the north side of the ridge at mile 13.1. Begin to descend steadily into the valley of Raccoon Branch. The stream becomes audible before intersecting Bobbys Trail at mile 14.0. Bobbys Trail leads left 0.9 mile to intersect the Appalachian Trail.

The VHHT turns sharply right, downhill, thorough a rhododendron-choked valley. Now heading easterly, cross Raccoon Branch; then pass an old road coming in from your left at mile 14.3. Small streams coming off Dickey Ridge to your left flow under the roadbed via culverts. Shortly come to the first of many wildlife clearings along the trail. Pass another clearing on your right that is reached by a very short road. Reach a stand of planted white pines and then come to a large grassy clearing. To your right, the north-facing slope of Bobbys Ridge favors rhododendron and moisture-loving trees, such as sweet birch. To your left, the south-facing side of Dickeys Ridge harbors drier-condition species, such as oak, table mountain pine, and mountain laurel. It is a somewhat confused forest, a mix of species types. However, it does indicate the biodiversity of the Southern Appalachians, which are rich in ecosystems not perfectly delineated from one another; rather, they represent a mixing and melding of forest habitats. The technical term for this is "an overlapping of ecotones."

Keep walking down the valley. More wildlife clearings appear on both sides of Raccoon Branch. At mile 15.5, cross Raccoon Branch; then pass two more clearings. Make two quick crossings of Raccoon Branch in succession. Pass a pole gate at mile 16.2. Keep going forward to enter a grassy area growing up in pines. Soon go around another pole gate. Make a sharp left here and come to Dickey Creek. There is no bridge here, and hikers will have to ford the stream in high water. Ford Dickey Creek and then immediately turn right up a gravel path. Ahead on the paved road is Raccoon Branch Campground. The Dickey Knob Trail can be accessed near campsite #6 here. On the VHHT, follow the gravel path right to cross VA 16 and come to a parking area and trailhead at mile 16.4. From here, it is 14.7 miles east on the VHHT to Middle Creek.

Access

Western Access: From exit 45 on I-81 near Marion, drive 6.0 miles south on VA 16, passing the Jennings Visitor Center. Stay on VA 16 for 11.0 miles to VA 603

(Fairwood Road) in Trout Dale. From the village of Trout Dale, head west on VA 603 (Fairwood Valley Road) for 4.0 miles. Fox Creek Horse Camp will be on your right. The VHHT starts next to the campground.

Eastern Access: From exit 45 on I-81 in Marion, head south on VA 16 for 6.0 miles, passing the Jennings Visitor Center. Continue 5.8 miles beyond the visitor center on VA 16 to the Virginia Highlands Horse Trail parking area, which is on your left 0.1 mile beyond Raccoon Branch campground.

Virginia Highlands Horse Trail, Raccoon Branch to Middle Creek

Type:	Foot, bicycle, horse, except for 1.5 mile section
Length:	14.7 miles
Difficulty:	Moderate
Use:	Low to Moderate
Condition:	Very good
Highlights:	Wildlife clearings, mountain views
Book Map #:	7, 10
USGS Topo:	Trout Dale, Atkins, Cedar Springs
Connections:	Kirk Hollow Trail, Horne Knob Trail

This section of the Virginia Highlands Horse Trail primarily follows old or closed forest roads, making for a wide path and moderate grades while staying generally around 3,000 feet. The exception is the part from VA 601 to Sugar Pond, where the VHHT becomes a narrow rocky path that eventually opens up near the impoundment. This particular section is closed to mountain bikes.

The VHHT leaves VA 16 to make an extended climb between Brushy Butt and Green Ridge and then heads east along Straight Mountain to descend to Cressy Creek. It continues around Little Mountain, passing Sugar Pond and a former mining area. This section of forest was once strip-mined for manganese. The VHHT drops down to Dry Creek and then ascends the north slope of Snake Den Mountain, passing in and out of shallow coves. The east end of Snake Den Mountain offers excellent views. Finally, the path drops down to Middle Creek and Forest Road 16.

Head east away from VA 16 and pass around a pole gate. Begin to climb along Hutton Branch on a closed forest road in a pine-oak forest. The road is sparingly used by forest personnel to maintain wildlife clearings in the area. Pass two small dynamite sheds on your left. Bridge Hutton Branch at 0.3 mile; then climb steeply up the side of Brushy Butt. At mile 1.4, come to a wildlife clearing. Keep ascending to pass a vehicle barrier at mile 2.0 in a grassy gap. Stay left and head east, now descending. At mile 2.3, look right for a wooden post indicating a former forest research experimental area. Keep going east to intersect another road at mile 3.1. Stay right and downhill; you will parallel a small feeder stream, bridging the watercourse several times to pass around a pole gate. Keep going forward to intersect VA 601 at mile 4.1. Turn left and span Cressy Creek on the VA 601 bridge. Turn right just past the bridge and ascend a narrow rocky path, marked with orange diamonds, curving around Little Mountain. This begins the "no bikes" section. There are views from the end of Little Mountain into Sugar Grove. Pick up an old woods road at mile 4.6 and enter a forest of maple, Fraser magnolia, and tulip trees and many vines.

Come to a strip-mined section and then Sugar Pond at mile 5.5. Cross the pond dam and keep going forward. Pass through more mined areas on the north slope of Little Mountain, indicated by sporadically exposed soil, evenly aged trees, and land leveling. At mile 7.1, look for a small pond off to your right. At mile 7.2, come to the Kirk Hollow Trail, entering on your left after a sharp right turn. This wide path leads 0.9 mile down to VA 675 (Vipperman Hollow Road). Just beyond this junction is a sign that says, "Horse, Foot and Wagon Travel Only."

The trail swings into the upper cove of Kirk Hollow before working around an outlying ridge of Little Mountain. A single-track path is overlain on the roadbed as it turns south into the Dry Creek watershed at mile 8.6. Ahead, there are views of Canadays Ridge, part of the Iron Mountain Range. Come to a trail junction at mile 9.4. To your right, the Horne Knob Trail leads 0.4 mile up to Forest Road 16.

Stay forward and come to a crossing of Dry Creek, a perennial stream at this elevation. Continue past the watercourse along the Dry Creek valley, working around Horne Knob to the right. At mile 10.6, the bridle path bridges a rhododendron-choked feeder stream of Bullins Branch. Undulate around the upper hollows of Bullins Branch to achieve a gap at mile 11.8. The bridle path is now on Snake Den Mountain. Make a mild descent toward Granny Branch, winding into rich coves of striped maple and piney rib ridges. Enter a previously burned area at mile 12.6. The trail once acted as a firebreak. To the left, the forest is intact; to the right, the trees were burned.

The low forest opens the canopy overhead to the elements but also allows views of Little Mountain to the north. Just before the trail swings into Middle Creek, there are wide views to the east of Huckleberry Knob, Harvel Knob, and Buzzard Rock. At mile 14.4, a road leads left to a wildlife clearing. Stay to the right and drop into the Middle Creek watershed, now heading west. The Iron Mountains block the sky to the left. Pass around a pole gate, bridge Middle Creek, and come to Forest Road 16 at mile 14.7. Across the road, it is 13.1 miles on the VHHT to US 21.

Access

Western Access: From exit 45 on I-81 in Marion, head south on VA 16 for 6.0 miles, passing the Jennings Visitor Center. Continue 5.8 miles beyond the visitor center on VA 16 to the Virginia Highlands Horse Trail parking area, which is on your left 0.1 mile beyond Raccoon Branch campground. The VHHT leads uphill, away from VA 16.

Eastern Access: From exit 45 on I-81 near Marion, drive south on VA 16 for 6.0 miles to the Jennings Visitor Center. Continue south on VA 16 for 3.7 miles farther to VA 601 (Flat Ridge Road). Turn left on Flat Ridge Road and follow it for 2.6 miles to Forest Road 16 (Dry Creek Road). Turn left on Forest Road 16 and follow it for 5.4 miles to the trailhead on Middle Creek, where the Virginia Highlands Horse Trail leaves right.

Virginia Highlands Horse Trail, Middle Creek to Upper East Fork

Type:	Foot, bicycle, horse
Length:	19.2 miles
Difficulty:	Moderate
Use:	Low to moderate
Condition:	Good
Highlights:	Attractive watersheds, Little Dry Run Wilderness
Book Map #:	10, 11, 13
USGS Topo:	Cedar Springs, Speedwell
Connections:	Little Dry Run Trail, Henley Hollow Trail, Divide Trail, East Fork Trail, Virginia Highlands Horse Trail, Upper East Fork to New River

Lightly used, this section of the Virginia Highlands Horse Trail heads from Forest Road 16 into the quiet side of the recreation area. The VHHT leaves Middle Creek, passing through several attractive watersheds to skirt the Little Dry Runs Wilderness, where the bridle path is actually the wilderness boundary. It then drops into the Dry Run watershed before climbing to Horse Heaven, only to drop again to the upper reaches of East Fork Dry Run and end on Forest Road 14. Gated forest roads, used by the forest service to maintain wildlife clearings, are the primary trailbed for this mid- to low-elevation pathway.

Leave Forest Road 16 and head uphill away from Middle Creek, soon bridging a small feeder branch. Pass a vehicle barrier and work east along the lower valley of Middle Creek in piney woods. At mile 1.5, in a clear area, intersect the unmaintained Leading Ridge Trail. It leads left downhill 0.4 mile to posted private land and uphill to VA 672. Continue forward with the orange diamonds. At mile 2.0, span Crigger Creek on a wide plank bridge. The bridle path then makes a 180-degree curve around a feeder stream of Crigger Creek, undulating around small hollows.

At mile 4.0, the trail swings easterly toward Harvel Creek. There are obscured views to the left of mountains and farmland to the north. Curve very near the forest border by a couple of cabins at mile 5.0. Drop down toward Harvel Creek, coming to gravel VA 798 at mile 5.3. Keep going forward, downhill past the road, and bridge

Harvel Creek. There are three roads here. Dead ahead is a sign that says, "Wythe County." Veer left sharply and pass a green pole gate to bridge a feeder branch. Keep to the right here, uphill on the gated forest road, heading east to a gap. Harvel Knob stands to the right. At mile 6.2, reach the grassy gap and then make an easy descent into the Kinser Creek watershed.

Reach the attractive drainage cloaked in white pine and imperiled hemlock at mile 6.9. Kinser Creek lies to the right of the path. At mile 7.4, span Kinser Creek on a bridge and then bisect a small wildlife clearing. Shortly come to a ford of Kinser Creek. At mile 7.6, the VHHT leaves sharply right to span Kinser Creek on a mossy plank bridge. Ahead, a trail leaves to a wildlife clearing and then peters out near private land. Head up along a feeder stream of Kinser Creek. Make a switchback just before coming to a gap at mile 8.2. Several unmaintained trails spur out from this gap. Continue forward and follow the orange diamonds downhill toward Jones Creek, which is reached at mile 8.6. To the left, a trail leads across Jones Creek to posted land. The VHHT continues to the right, up Jones Creek.

The trail now forms a border of the Little Dry Run Wilderness. Head upstream in a pretty wooded valley. Easily cross Jones Creek at mile 9.0. Soon after, cross a small feeder stream and then Jones Creek again at mile 9.3 and mile 9.6. Come to a split in the trail. A road leaves left a short distance to a wildlife clearing; stay to the right. The valley widens to the right as Jones Creek breaks up into numerous prongs. Make a steeper ascent after passing another wildlife clearing. The bridle path is now far above the stream, and views open of Comers Rock to the south. Wind around a hickory hollow; then briefly descend to a gap and trail junction at mile 10.8. Here, the Little Dry Run Trail leaves right 1.2 miles to Comers Rock Campground and left 3.2 miles through the Little Dry Run Wilderness to US 21.

Keep going forward on the VHHT and soon gain views of the mountains to the north. Pass by a clearing and switch sides of the ridge, now descending. The VHHT forms the southern border of the Little Dry Run Wilderness. Reach the valley of the West Fork at mile 11.4. Pass grassy wildlife clearings. Ford West Fork and then immediately cross it again via bridge. Look for a small waterfall on the West Fork just beyond the bridge. Pass a vehicle barrier at mile 12.6, come to a large clearing, and begin to follow Forest Road 728 downhill. Continue on the gravel road, fording West Fork one last time before coming to US 21 at mile 13.1. Cross US 21 and turn upstream, now along East Fork. Cross East Fork and keep heading upstream on a single-track path to emerge onto Forest Road 14 at mile 13.4. To the right, across a bridge and about 50 yards down the road, the Dry Run Gap Trail leads left 1.0 mile uphill to the Iron Mountain Trail. On the VHHT, turn left onto FR 14 and trace the road for 0.2 mile, turning left again onto another gravel road heading uphill. Pass around a pole gate and ascend. Look for signs of burned woods on trail right. Make a sharp switchback to the left; then crest out on the gap between Porter Mountain and Horse Heaven to intersect the Henley Hollow Trail at mile 14.3. The Henley Hollow Trail leaves left 1.6 miles down to US 21. Keep going forward on the closed forest road. Continue ascending along the western slope of Horse Heaven. The wide road eliminates an overhead canopy. Alongside the bridle path is a pine-oak-hickory woodland. Swing around the north side of the ridge, availing obscured views to the north of Cripple Creek valley and the mountains beyond. At mile 15.4, come to a gap and grassy clearing. Wind along the slender mountaintop, availing views on both sides of the ridge. Resume the climb, passing more wildlife clearings. At mile 16.3, on a sharp right turn, pass a sign that says, "Horse Heaven Trail." The path becomes narrow and rocky here, as it meanders up to level out in Horse Heaven at mile 16.7. At mile 17.2, curve sharply right and begin to drop down the south side of Horse Heaven. There are occasional views of the Iron Mountains. Continue downhill, switchbacking again.

At mile 18.1, a wildlife access road leaves left. Stay forward and drop down along the headwaters of East Fork Dry Run. Pass through wildlife clearings at mile 18.8 and then come to a pole gate. Pass around the gate to briefly climb; then come to Forest Road 14 at mile 19.2. From here it is 12.1 miles forward on the VHHT to VA 94. To the right, 0.1 mile down FR 14, is the beginning of the East Fork Trail. It leads past Hussy Mountain Horse Camp and then down East Fork valley to intersect the VHHT again, making a nice equestrian loop. Ahead, across FR 14, the Divide Trail leads 0.8 mile up to the Iron Mountain Trail.

Access

Western Access: From exit 45 on I-81 near Marion, drive south on VA 16 for 6.0 miles to the Jennings Visitor Center. Continue south on VA 16 for 3.7 miles farther to VA 601 (Flat Ridge Road). Turn left on Flat Ridge Road and follow it for 2.6 miles to Forest Road 16 (Dry Creek Road). Turn left on Forest Road 16 and follow it for 5.4 miles to the section on Middle Creek where the Virginia Highlands Horse Trail leaves right.

Eastern Access: From exit 70 at I-81 near Wytheville, take US 21 south through Wytheville, driving 16.8 miles to Forest Road 14, passing through Speedwell. Turn left on Forest Road 14 and follow it 2.9 miles to a gap on FR 14, where the Virginia Highlands Horse Trail crosses the road. Turn right here and drive up a hill to a parking area. The VHHT comes in from across FR 14.

Virginia Highlands Horse Trail, Upper East Fork to New River

Type:	Foot, bicycle, horse except for 7.8-mile section between VA 602 and VA 94
Length:	16.4 miles
Difficulty:	Moderate to difficult
Use:	Low

Condition:	Good
Highlights:	Mountain views, wildlife clearings, solitude
Book Map #:	13, 12, 14
USGS Topo:	Speedwell, Cripple Creek, Austinville
Connections:	Mikes Gap Trail, Ewing Mountain Trail, New River Rail Trail, Virginia Highlands Horse Trail, Middle Creek to Upper East Fork

This section of the Virginia Highlands Horse Trail traverses the seldom-visited "far east." It leaves the Hussy Mountain area to dip into Francis Mill Creek drainage and then climbs steeply up the Devils Den on a narrow track, running the length of Ewing Mountain, where there are occasional views. Top out on Chestnut Knob, before dropping down to VA 94. Beyond here, the VHHT picks up a forest road and descends to the New River. The grades are mostly moderate, but heading west from the New River up to Chestnut Knob is challenging. Solitude reigns here, but it should be traveled more in late May, when the flame azalea, mountain laurel, and Catawba rhododendron bloom in profusion on Ewing Mountain.

Start the trail by leaving the parking area and heading downhill. The Divide Trail leaves uphill to the right. Pass around a pole gate and follow a roadbed, passing an antenna on trail right. Orange diamonds mark the eastbound trail. At 0.3 mile, pass a small clearing. Tiny rivulets flow off the slope of the Iron Mountains to the north. The lack of canopy overhead allows occasional views. At 0.6 mile, an old road leaves left to a wildlife clearing. Dip into watersheds and then wind around dry ridges. The trail turns north at mile 2.3, following the length of a rib ridge to a small knob at mile 2.7. A trail sign indicates the VHHT leaving right. To the left, a side road leads a short distance to a grassy clearing with views of Hussy Mountain, High Point, Little Horse Heaven, and Iron Mountain. Trace the VHHT downhill on a much narrower path. Switchback right, just before crossing Francis Mill Creek; then come to Forest Road 14 at mile 3.2. The VHHT turns sharply right here, away from the forest road, to recross Francis Mill Creek and head up an old roadbed along a feeder stream of Francis Mill Creek. Gently ascend through rich valley woods, crossing the stream at mile 3.5.

Keep going uphill along a small drainage, as the path becomes single-track. Level out in a gap and drop down to a flat with many white pines. The trail abruptly turns right and climbs to reach VA 602 at mile 4.8, near a sign marking the Grayson-Wythe county line. This section is closed to bikes. Briefly follow VA 602 into Grayson County; then cross 602, turning left onto a gravel road and passing a chain gate. Climb past a cabin on the left; by mile 5.1, the trail has narrowed again as it makes for the Devils Den, topping out at mile 5.7. There are intermittent views of Iron Mountain to the right. The trail is now on the western shoulder of Ewing Mountain. Rise again to the next knob, weaving up two switchbacks. Just past these

Rhododendron blooms along the Virginia Highlands Horse
Trail.

curves, look right for a rock outcrop. From the outcrop, there are good vistas of Jones
Knob and the Brush Creek valley.

Continue east on the now-rocky path and descend through a young forest.
These woods are the comeback effort after Hurricane Hugo in 1989. The storm
swept through Mikes Gap, which is reached at mile 7.1. Here, locust trees are
reclaiming a grassy clearing. Locusts are a pioneer species that invade a disturbed
area. Other trees eventually grow in the shade of the locust, and the forest changes
composition to its predisturbance state. The Mikes Gap Trail leaves left 1.5 miles to
VA 602 and right 1.3 miles to VA 690.

The VHHT continues forward, sloping left away from a knob in pine-oak
woods. Soon, turn sharply right, straddling the crest of Ewing Mountain. Meander
easterly, climbing more often than not. Look left for a sign indicating the intersection of Wythe, Carroll, and Grayson counties, at mile 8.4. Continue easterly, now
paralleling private property on the left. Enter a long grove of planted white pine on
the national forest side of the ridge. In a gap at mile 8.9, an unmaintained trail leads
right, down to VA 667. Just beyond is a sign indicating the Wythe-Carroll county

line. Veer right, up and away from the woods road. Stay uphill on the ridgeline, heavy with oak. At mile 9.2, intersect the Ewing Trail, which leaves left downhill to Collins Cove Horse Camp. Climb to top out on Chestnut Knob in a small grassy clearing at mile 10.1. Make a moderate but steady descent; old roads intersect the main path, which remains obvious. Pass a pole gate at 11.4 miles, and keep going downhill on a gravel road, passing a decrepit cabin on the left. Soon pass a newer house on the right before coming to VA 94 at mile 12.1. Turn right and travel VA 94 a few feet to Forest Road 270. Descend on FR 270 with a view of Iron Mountain ahead. Pass posted private land on both side of the gravel road. Work down the south side of Cold Ridge, passing dry hollows to arrive along Big Branch at mile 13.0. Continue down along the tiny watercourse to a pole gate at mile 13.2. Pass around the pole gate and a sign erroneously indicating 4.0 miles to New River Rail Trail State Park. Continue down the valley of Big Branch, which is not so big. Intermittent rills come in from the left off Cold Ridge. Come to a trail junction at mile 13.7. The now-closed Big Branch Trail leaves right, beyond a "No Horses" sign.

The VHHT heads left, up the south flank of Cold Ridge. The forest canopy is mostly absent. Pass a wildlife clearing at mile 14.0 and keep climbing. Turn easterly and wind in and out of dry hollows of Cold Ridge. Come to a second wildlife clearing at mile 15.0. The VHHT veers left onto a dirt path bordered by sun-loving pioneer species such as locust and sumac. Pass beneath a power line at mile 15.4; then begin to switchback down toward Big Branch, reaching the stream at mile 16.0. Turn left, now heading downstream, and immediately ford Big Branch. Pass around a pole gate, cross Big Branch twice more, and then emerge onto a gravel road. Stay to the left on the gravel road, continuing along the sometimes dry streambed of Big Branch. At mile 16.4, the road continues forward, but the VHHT drops steeply right a few feet to intersect the New River Rail Trail. This is the eastern terminus of the nearly 80-mile-long Virginia Highlands Horse Trail. From here, on the rail trail, it is 0.9 miles upstream to Byllesby Road and 11.9 miles downstream to Foster Falls.

Access

Western Access: From exit 70 at I-81 near Wytheville, take US 21 south through Wytheville. Drive 16.8 miles to Forest Road 14, passing through Speedwell. Turn left on Forest Road 14 and follow it 3.0 miles to a gap on FR 14, where the Virginia Highlands Horse Trail crosses the road. Turn right here and drive up a hill to a parking area. The VHHT heads downhill beyond the gated road.

Eastern Access: From exit 80 on I-81 near Fort Chiswell, head south on US 52 for 1.2 miles to VA 94. Turn right on VA 94 and follow it 13.0 miles to VA 602 (Byllesby Road). Turn left on Byllesby Road and follow it for 3.6 miles down to Buck Dam Road. Turn left on Buck Dam Road and follow it 3.0 miles to the end of the road. From here, take the New River Rail Trail 0.9 mile to intersect the VHHT.

Rail Trails

Virginia Creeper Trail

The Virginia Creeper Trail was nearly a century in the making. Of course, those who originated the idea for a railroad through this slice of southwest Virginia had no vision whatsoever of plastic-clad pedalers, backpack-toting hikers, and equestrians plying their railbed for pleasure and exercise. This would all come later, after entrepreneurs vying for iron and timber resources in the nearby mountains raised funds to build a rail and after many men sweated to construct trestles and blast through hillsides. It came after a period of economic prosperity borne of untold millions of timber feet cut from the Virginia Highlands, followed by a period of slow decline in business for the Virginia-Carolina Railroad, or V-C, until the train whistles stopped in 1977 and the V-C was nothing but fodder for railroad nostalgia buffs. After that, the reality of a rail trail was still uncertain, and a lot of effort by local groups led to the complete rail trail, which now extends from Whitetop Station to Abingdon, a distance of over 34.0 miles.

At some point in its history, the railroad was nicknamed the Virginia Creeper, maybe because of the same-named vine that thrives locally, or maybe because of the slow progress of the train as it climbed through the mountains. Today, the Virginia Creeper is the most popular trail in the Old Dominion, and its popularity is well deserved. From Whitetop Station at 3,525 feet, the Creeper courses down through the mountains, passing vistas near and far, deep woods, small farms, and clear, fast streams. It passes Green Cove, where an original train station still stands. And it crosses numerous trestles that offer treetop views looking down and all around the area to finally open up at Damascus, one of the friendliest towns in a friendly state. The second section of the Creeper, from Damascus to Abingdon, heads through somewhat different terrain— farmlands, meadow, and woods—but it is absolutely worth the time it takes to travel it.

Virginia Creeper Trail, Whitetop Station to Damascus

Type:	Foot, bicycle, horse
Length:	17.4 miles
Difficulty:	Moderate
Use:	Heavy
Condition:	Good
Highlights:	Restored rail trail through mountains and river gorge, views, history
Book Map #:	17
USGS Topo:	Park, Grayson, Konnarock, Damascus
Connections:	Appalachian Trail, Beech Grove Trail, Virginia Creeper Trail, Damascus to Abingdon

Start the Creeper at Whitetop Station, where a replica of the old Whitetop Station stands. Here, soft drinks, water, and information are dispensed in warmer months. The rail trail actually extends 1.0 mile south to the Virginia–North Carolina line, but beyond that the old rail, which once went to Wilkesboro, North Carolina, has reverted back to landowners.

Begin cruising down the obvious old roadbed. The temptation is to travel fast, since the trail is downhill all the way to Damascus, but stop, take your time, and look around. And keep an eye peeled for other trail enthusiasts, whether bikers, hikers, or horseback riders. Views of Whitetop Mountain are immediate. Look also for Christmas tree farms, a growing agricultural industry in these mountains. Drift down the valley of High Trestle Branch. Immediately cross the first of 31 trestles in this section. Enjoy these thrills, but if a horse is on a trestle, always let it pass before proceeding.

At 3.0 miles, come to Green Cove Station. This is the last remaining original station on the Virginia Creeper. This mountain community is just a short distance from the point where Virginia, Tennessee, and North Carolina meet. Reenter the woods. The canopy is closed overhead more often than not. Keep descending, now along Green Cove Creek. Stay mostly on the north side of the stream but span the watercourse on trestles occasionally.

Cross VA 726 at mile 3.6 and keep descending, mostly on national forest land. The forest service purchased the right-of-way and land shortly after the trains stopped, giving the rail trail early momentum when it needed it. It was seen as a potential jewel in the Mount Rogers National Recreation Area trail system. And so it is.

Occasional mile markers from the railroad days can be seen on the side of the trail. The gravel and cinder path makes for easy travel, though occasional storms can rut out the trailbed. At mile 6.2, the Appalachian Trail comes in from the

Hiker crosses trestle on the Virginia Creeper Trail.

right. From here the AT has come 8.7 miles from Elk Garden. The Virginia Creeper and the Appalachian Trail, two historic paths, share the same trail across the long Luther Hassinger Memorial Bridge. Descend to Whitetop Laurel Creek and another trail junction at mile 6.6. Here, a spur trail leads left along Whitetop Laurel Creek 0.4 mile to the Creek Junction parking area.

The rail trail and the AT share the path for another 0.2 mile before the AT splits right, leading 13.8 miles to Damascus. This path is foot-only. The Creeper continues along Whitetop Laurel Creek as a wider, more graveled path. Trestles become more frequent, allowing view upon view of Whitetop Laurel Creek. Pass a few homes along the way. Please respect landowners' rights, and honor the request that opened gates be closed after you pass. The next major intersection comes in Taylors Valley, at mile 10.6. Here is a small community center in an old caboose.

Leave the area of homes and head back into national forest land. The trail once again has a wilderness feel. Whitetop Laurel Creek crashes down the valley, flanked by rhododendron with steep cliffs for a backdrop. At 13.2 miles, come to the Straight Branch parking area. From here, the Beech Grove Trail heads across US 58 and intersects the Appalachian Trail in 0.3 mile and the Iron Mountain Trail in 0.7 mile.

Back on the Creeper Trail, at mile 14.5, pass over a steel bridge—an exception on this trail, as most of the bridges are wooden. Frequent floods washed out these wooden trestles during the logging days and afterward, disrupting service and cutting into the profits of Norfolk and Western Railroad (the company that owned and operated the railroad for most of its existence).

Keep going through the outskirts of Damascus, come alongside US 58, and then cross VA 91. Pass through town, and, at mile 17.4, reach the Little Red Caboose, where you can find information as well as a nearby park and parking area. From here the Virginia Creeper Trail continues for 16 more miles to Abingdon. To the left, the Appalachian Trail leads through the community park 3.5 miles to the Tennessee state line and, to the right, through Damascus and into the recreation area.

Access

Upper Access: From the Little Red Caboose in Damascus, take US 58 east for 18.0 miles to VA 726 (Whitetop Gap Road). Turn right on VA 726 and follow it 3.0 miles to the Whitetop Station. The trail starts behind the replica of the original Whitetop Station. There are shuttle services in Damascus that drive bicyclists and hikers up to Whitetop and Creek Junction for a fee.

Lower Access: This section of trail ends at the Little Red Caboose in Damascus, on US 58.

Virginia Creeper Trail, Damascus to Abingdon

Type:	Foot, bicycle, horse
Length:	16.0 miles
Difficulty:	Moderate
Use:	Heavy
Condition:	Good
Highlights:	Rail trail through farm country, good views
Book Map #:	17
USGS Topo:	Damascus, Abingdon
Connections:	Appalachian Trail, Virginia Creeper Trail, Damascus to Abingdon

The Virginia Creeper Trail is one of the most popular rail trails in the eastern United States. The lower section of the trail is second in popularity to the upper section, which heads from Whitetop to Damascus. As part of the original railroad, the lower section was actually constructed first and was in operation by early 1900. Ironically, this first section to be built as a railroad was the last to be secured as a rail trail. Thanks to the cities of Abingdon and Damascus—and a whole lot of people—the 16-mile trip between the two towns is now a great way to spend a day.

This section has a more pastoral feel than the upper section. From Damascus, the Creeper passes by many homes, where there are gates to cross. It also passes through farms, where there are more gates to open—and close. Please do so out

Bicyclist on the Virginia Creeper Trail by the Little Red Caboose in Damascus.

of respect for the landowners, who are gracious enough to cooperate and make a path for all to enjoy. And there is plenty of scenery to enjoy, as the trail descends alongside Laurel Creek and the South Fork Holston River. A highlight of the trip is the long, high trestle that spans the confluence of the South and Middle forks of the Holston River. This also a low point, literally, as the Creeper leads away from its lowest elevation at nearby Alvarado, 1,750 feet, and then begins to climb toward Abingdon. From here, the trail continues its march toward civilization, finally reaching Abingdon and an old steam engine that once powered up and down the Creeper. Outfitters in Damascus provide shuttle service for trail travelers who want to travel the entire length of this section of the Creeper.

Leave the Little Red Caboose in Damascus and immediately cross US 58; then pass some homes. Laurel Creek lies off to your right as you pass along the Damascus outskirts, which include industry, homes, and campgrounds. The trail becomes single-track, bordered by grass overlain on the roadbed when in front of most homes. Gradually, the homes become more scarce. The trail is canopied more often than you would expect, although the open areas offer good vistas of the surrounding mountains and quaint farm scenes.

By mile 3.0, Laurel Creek has met the South Fork Holston River, which is on the right of the trail. At mile 3.4, pass under US 58 at an area known as Drowning Ford. Ahead, past a gate, is a "bull lot," literally a pasture full of bulls. Close the gate behind you on your way out. Pass through a mix of wooded and pasture lands, clearing many gates.

Come to Alvarado at mile 7.0, once a stopping point for the Creeper. Now there is a small store on the left that was once the Alvarado post office. Keep going westerly for the confluence of the forks of the Holston River, reached at mile 8.2. The trestle over the confluence is 529 feet long. There are great views up the South Fork Holston from here. Keep climbing through many wooded sections and also spots where part of the hillside was blasted out. Cross several more trestles before reaching VA 677 (Watauga Road) at mile 12.2. Even as the trail nears Abingdon, it stays well forested until about a mile from the end, where the town has crept outward. You know the end is near when the trail passes under I-81 at mile 15.2.

From here, begin to look for the "Y" on the right. This is the site of a railroad engine turnaround. The grade splitting right from the main track is easily visible at this area, which is now a little park. Pass some restrooms just before one last trestle and the end of the line at 16.0 miles. Across the street is a parking area, and just beside the end of the trail is an old steam engine that made the grade just as you did.

Access

Damascus Access: This section of the Virginia Creeper trail starts at the Little Red Caboose in Damascus, on US 58.

Abingdon Access: From exit 17 on I-81, take Cummings Road west for 0.2 mile. Turn right on Main Street and follow it 0.4 mile to the Creeper Trail. You will see the large black locomotive on the right. Parking is across the street. The parking area on the left.

New River Rail Trail

New River Rail Trail State Park is Virginia's longest park, extending over 57.0 miles along a former railroad bed. The rail trail is the primary attraction, as it courses along a cinder bed and over trestles that span Chestnut Creek and the New River. Bikers are the primary users, though equestrians and hikers will travel portions of the path. The trail demonstrates how, in our modern era, we can preserve scenic natural areas in the midst of human habitation.

New River Rail Trail, Galax to Foster Falls

Type:	Foot, bicycle, horse
Length:	27.7 miles
Difficulty:	Moderate to difficult
Use:	High
Condition:	Excellent
Highlights:	Diverse landscapes, tunnels, views of New River, Shot Tower
Book Map #:	16

USGS Topo: Galax, Austinville, Sylvatus, Foster Falls
Connections: New River Rail Trail, Fries to Fries Junction; Virginia High
lands Horse Trail, Upper East Fork to New River; New River
Rail Trail, Foster Falls to Pulaski

This is a scenic section of the rail trail that follows the old railroad bed of the Norfolk and Western Railroad. It starts out along intimate Chestnut Creek, passing through attractive woodlands, pasturelands, and a few houses. It then crosses the thousand-foot Fries Junction trestle and enters the much larger New River Valley. Occasional rapids and riverside bluffs satiate the visual palate. It closes out at Foster Falls, the site of a campground and other facilities.

Shot Tower, along the rail trail near Foster Falls, is an old stone structure once used to make shot, or "bullets," for the rifles of yesteryear. Stop by for a glimpse of this interesting aspect of frontier life. You will pass through a dark, 200-foot tunnel that adds spice to a great trail. The trailside is generally forested, though it does bisect humanized areas. Occasional picnic areas make nice stopping points. Don't pass up a chance to see this jewel of the Old Dominion.

The trail has a very slight decline, as it follows the water north through the mountains of southwest Virginia. Mile per mile, the trail is easy, but the sheer length of this section, nearly 28.0 miles, may make it hard for those in less than reasonable shape to get from Galax to Foster Falls. Arrive at the trailhead early and allow yourself plenty of time to take breaks, even if you are bicycling as most trail enthusiasts do. One outfitter rents bikes at Galax, and another outfitter offers bike rentals and shuttle service at Foster Falls.

Cyclist pauses at Chestnut Creek Falls on the New River Rail Trail.

Start the New River Rail Trail at the city of Galax. Surprisingly quickly, you will leave the civilized world behind. Pretty Chestnut Creek lies to the right. Woods are all around. Look for the painted white posts that are mile markers from the old railroad days. Come to Cliffview at mile 1.8. There is a ranger station here and also a little store for drinks and snacks. The wilderness feel resumes beyond Cliffview as the trail passes Cliffview Campground. Note that campers here must register in advance.

Come to a trestle and Chestnut Creek Falls at mile 5.4. The wide falls drop over a rock base. There is a little covered shelter here. The American chestnut tree was the once-dominant giant of the Southern Appalachians. This tree formerly ranged from Maine to Mississippi, and in southwest Virginia it grew to massive proportions. The fruit of this tree was very important. Chestnut acorns were the staple food for everything from bears to birds. Of course, humans ate them, too. Remember the words from "The Christmas Song": "chestnuts roasting on an open fire." In addition to its edible nuts, the tree provided some of the best wood for everyday use by pioneers. It was also coveted by the timber companies that harvested the Smokies. Just as the era of settlers at Mount Rogers are gone, the era of the mighty chestnut is gone, too. In the early 1900s, Asian chestnut trees were imported to the United States, bringing a fungus with them. The Asian trees had developed immunity to the fungus, but the American chestnut was helpless. Before long, chestnuts were dying in the Northeast, and the blight worked its way to the South in the 1920s. Two decades later, the day of the chestnut was over. But there is hope. To this day, chestnut trees sprout from the roots of the ancients, growing up but always succumbing to the blight. We can hope that these chestnuts are building a resistance to the blight and will one day tower over the mountains again, long after we are gone. Scientists are expediting this process, and experiments are underway to graft American chestnut trees with the Asian chestnuts in an effort to develop a blight-resistant American chestnut.

Pass Chestnut Yard at mile 6.2. Cross a road and travel between areas where the rock walls were blasted to clear the way for the railroad. The path curves in places and crosses a trestle. Enjoy the clear waters of Chestnut Creek. Ahead, at mile 11.4, is a 200-foot tunnel. Bikers should stay in the middle of the tunnel as the edges are somewhat rough. Not far after this is the Fries Junction trestle. Stop for a minute on the trestle and enjoy the river and ridge views. Beyond the trestle is Fries Junction, reached at mile 12.0. There is a covered picnic area here. To the left, the Fries arm of the trail leads 5.5 miles to Fries.

Keep downstream along the New River, passing an island. Notice the waters backing up. Clear the Brush Creek trestle before reaching Byllesby Dam and Byllesby Road at mile 14.4. To your left is an old power station, and the old dam is on the right. These structures were built in 1913, and they look it! Swing around a flat and cross the gravel-surfaced Buck Dam Road, which accesses the New River Campground. A short distance ahead, look for the side trail that leads left from the rail trail up to the camping area.

Pass Buck Dam. Cross a small trestle over Big Branch and intersect the Virginia Highlands Horse Trail at mile 17.9. The VHHT leads left 16.4 miles to Upper East Fork and beyond to Elk Garden and the Mount Rogers high country. Cross into Wythe County before coming to the Ivanhoe area. Look left for J & T Sales on VA 94. This business offers sandwiches and cold beverages. Come to the state park's Ivanhoe access at mile 20.1. At mile 21.4, cross the New River on a high trestle. Next, pass through an old industrial area. Signs advise one to stay on the trail. Cross the road to Austinville and come to a tunnel shorter than—and not so dark as—the one you encountered earlier on the trail. In this tunnel, you can still see light at both ends when you're in the middle of it.

The trail resumes a pastoral feel until it goes beneath I-77. This signals a return to civilization. Just past this point, at mile 26.5, reach the side trail to Shot Tower. Take time to check out this relic built in 1807. Beyond Shot Tower, the trail stays on a bluff beside the New River before returning to Foster Falls at mile 27.7. Here is an outfitter, a campground, and access to the New River at some picturesque rapids, Foster Falls. From here it is 22.0 miles to Pulaski on the rest of the New River Rail Trail.

Access

Galax Access: From exit 14 on I-77, head west on US 58. Follow US 58 for 10.0 miles to the city of Galax. Just after crossing Chestnut Creek on a bridge, look on the right-hand side of the road for the brown New River State Park sign and a parking area. The New River Rail Trail starts here.

Foster Falls Access: From exit 24 on I-77 south of Wytheville, take VA 69 (Lead Mine Road) for 0.2 mile east to US 52. Turn left on US 52 (Fort Chiswell Road) and head north for 1.5 miles to VA 608 (Foster Falls Road). Turn right on 608 and follow it for 1.8 miles to VA 623 (Orphanage Drive). Turn left on Orphanage Drive and shortly enter Foster Falls State Park, part of the New River Rail Trail State Park. The New River Rail trail cuts right through the park.

New River Rail Trail, Fries to Fries Junction

Type:	Foot, bicycle, horse
Length:	5.5 miles
Difficulty:	Easy
Use:	High
Condition:	Excellent
Highlights:	Views of New River
Book Map:	16
USGS Topo:	Galax, Austinville
Connections:	New River Rail Trail, Galax to Foster Falls

Heading south to north, the upper New River Rail Trail splits into two sections at Fries Junction. The primary arm of the New River Rail Trail follows Chestnut Creek to Galax. The other arm of the trail follows the New River up to Fries. This description covers this second arm. On this second arm, the rail trail leaves the town of Fries at the city park and begins a northerly journey down the New River Valley. It travels alongside VA 721 for a distance before 721 crosses the river. Here, the New River Rail Trail continues down the valley, passing over several trestles to meet the main arm of the rail trail coming from Galax just after the main arm has crossed the New River on a 1,000-foot trestle. The paths now join for the remainder of the journey to Foster Falls and on toward Pulaski.

Leave the Fries City Park and begin a northward journey away from town, passing a couple of yellow vehicle barriers that will be seen often along the trail. The river lies on the right. Occasional fields, houses, and crop areas lie between the trail and the river, which is often back by a bluff. Soon come alongside VA 721, which is crossed at mile 2.0. The Riverside Market is just on the right for refreshments.

This section continues through quiet farm and pastureland. Pass over several trestles along the way before reaching Fries Junction at 5.5 miles. Here is a covered picnic shelter. The 1,000-foot Fries Junction trestle is just to the right. Beyond the trestle, it is 12.0 miles to Galax. To the left, it is 15.8 miles to Foster Falls.

Access

Fries Access: From exit 80 on I-81 near Fort Chiswell, head south on US 52 for 1.2 miles to VA 94. Turn right on VA 94 and follow it 19.2 miles to VA 1001 and the hamlet of Fries. Turn left on VA 1001 and trace it just a short distance to a side road, passing the Fries Volunteer Fire Department. Take this side road and look for a red caboose. The Fries parking area is near the caboose.

Fries Junction Access: This end of the trail can be reached by traveling 12.0 miles from Galax or 15.8 miles from Foster Falls.

New River Rail Trail, Pulaski to Foster Falls

Type:	Foot, bicycle, horse
Length:	22.0 miles
Difficulty:	Easy to moderate
Use:	High
Condition:	Excellent
Highlights:	Views of New River, long trestles, remoteness
Book Map #:	16
USGS Topo:	Foster Falls, Hiwassee, Dublin, Pulaski
Connections:	New River Rail Trail, Galax to Foster Falls

This section of the New River Trail has a variety of scenery and situations. From Pulaski it climbs a bit and then heads downhill to Claytor Lake, an impoundment

Cyclist on the New River Rail Trail near Pulaski.

of the New River. There are some homes in the vicinity of the lake. It then keeps up the New River valley where the watercourse runs free. In this free-flowing section beyond Claytor Lake, the trail takes on a wilder character, where towering bluffs loom over the path. As opposed to the upper section, there is no distinct advantage to going downstream along the New here, as there are ups and downs in either direction. Many trail users will take advantage of the shuttle service at Foster Falls, which drops trail users in Pulaski and lets them head back to Foster Falls. Biking is the most popular way to enjoy this section of trail, though hikers will be found near access points, and equestrians will ride some sections as well, especially on summer weekends, when the Foster Falls horse livery is operating.

This section of the New River Trail starts at mile marker #2, because the last 2.0 miles into Pulaski are currently in dispute. However, this trail description starts at mile 0. Leave the parking area and immediately pass between soil and rock berms, which form walls on both sides of the trail where the grade was blasted through a hill. This practice was common in constructing the railroad bed to keep the grade as level as possible. Trail travelers will notice a slight uptick in the path over the first few miles. Soon pass the Peak Creek trestle. Just beyond the trestle, look for an old railroad signal on the left. Pass under I-81 at mile 1.6. Keep south thorough rolling pastureland to reach a picnic shelter at McAdam Bench, at mile 2.8.

The climbing ends just beyond McAdam Bench. Now enjoy the extended downgrade past Draper, at 4.2 miles. Here is an access point and a little store with snacks and drinks. Continue the downgrade alongside pastoral and mountain views broken by closed wooded sections where the rock berms close in on the rail trail. Pass two trestles in succession, with the second one encountered along the shore of Claytor Lake, an impoundment of the New River. Even though there are homes in the area, the trail stays beneath canopied woodland.

At 7.0 miles, cross Claytor Lake on the Delton trestle. This one is framed by iron supports and offers good views. Come to the more civilized side of Claytor Lake and keep heading southwest on a long riverside bench. Cross the Hiwassee River Bridge at mile 8.2 before reaching Allisonia. Here, the trail passes directly through the small former railroad community, where travelers can purchase supplies at a little store.

The trail reenters woodland beyond Allisonia, only to emerge into open country on the Big Reed Island trestle at mile 11.2. While crossing the trestle, look left for an interesting rock formation up the valley to the left. The trail becomes wilder after this trestle. Sheer walls lie just beside the trail, with the river on the right. Overhead are tall woods. This wild character is broken only by an occasional grassy flat between the trail and the river. Pass a covered picnic shelter at mile 13.6, seemingly in the middle of nowhere. This is a remote section of trail.

Keep heading southwest in wild country, which is broken while passing under the high bridge of VA 100 at mile 15.6. After this, come to the lonesome community of Lone Ash and a gravel road, VA 622. There are just a few houses here. Come to equally quiet Bertha and another gravel road at mile 18.3. There is more heavily wooded country, but abandoned and occupied houses become more frequent. Enter the Foster Falls Village to pass by the Foster Falls entrance station. End the trail just past here, at 22.0 miles, at the Foster Falls covered shelter. Enjoy the view from this bluff. Just below is the state park livery.

Access

Foster Falls Access: From exit 24 on I-77 south of Wytheville, take VA 69 (Lead Mine Road) for 0.2 mile east to US 52. Turn left on US 52 (Fort Chiswell Road) and head north for 1.5 miles to VA 608 (Foster Falls Road). Turn right on 608 and follow it for 1.8 miles to VA 623 (Orphanage Drive). Turn left on Orphanage Drive and shortly enter Foster Falls State Park, part of the New River Rail Trail State Park. The New River Rail Trail cuts right through the park, near the river.

Pulaski Access: From exit 94 on I-81, turn north on VA 99 (Mount Olive Road) and follow it for 2.0 miles to Xaloy Way. Turn right on Xaloy Way and follow it just a short distance to the parking area, which is on the right.

Ridges and Rivers Route

The Ridges and Rivers Route is a great way to see the a large piece of the recreation area on one epic trip. This route is an agglomeration of five different trails that collectively connect the town of Abingdon to the town of Pulaski, 132.0 miles distant. The Ridges and Rivers Route derives its name from using rail trails that head along the Holston and New rivers and paths along the high ridges between them. The route encompasses a variety of scenery and trail types.

The Ridges and Rivers Route starts in Abingdon. It is not marked or blazed in any unique way other than with the blazes or markings of the trails it is using. Begin on the Virginia Creeper Trail and continue along the old railbed beyond Damascus for 20.0 miles to the Beech Grove Trail. Turn left on the Beech Grove Trail, crossing US 58, and head up a mile to meet the Iron Mountain Trail. Turn right and continue easterly on the IMT for nearly 15.0 miles to meet the Virginia Highlands Horse Trail at Forest Road 828. Follow the VHHT as it parallels FR 828 to reenter the forest near Hurricane Campground. (Hikers can bypass this road section by staying on the Iron Mountain Trail and then taking the Appalachian Trail to the Dickey Gap Trail to Hurricane Campground.)

Stay east on the VHHT as it comes to VA 16. By this point, the Ridges and Rivers Route has covered over 40.0 miles. Cross VA 16 on the VHHT and stay with it for the next 50.0 miles, covering some of the least visited sections of the recreation area. Descend to reach the New River and the New River Rail Trail. Turn right on the New River Rail Trail and follow it upstream through an attractive valley in the linear state park. Contact the state park about campsite reservations along the way. The old railbed makes for fairly easy travel, as the Ridges and Rivers Route ends in Pulaski at 132.0 miles.

West Side Trails

....
Beartree Gap Trail

Type: Foot, bicycle
Length: 3.3 miles
Difficulty: Moderate
Use: Moderate
Condition: Good
Highlights: Accesses Beartree Recreation Area and connects with many
                side trails
Book Map #:   3, 2
USGS Topo: Konnarock
Connections: Chestnut Ridge, Iron Mountain Trail, Shaw Gap Trail, Bear-
                tree Lake Trail, Appalachian Trail
....

The Beartree Gap Trail extends from the Iron Mountain Trail to the Appalachian Trail. Along the way, it connects with numerous other paths and crosses a couple of roads, making traversing portions of the trail feasible. It is popular with mountain bikers looping through the Iron Mountains and backpackers making a loop using the Iron Mountain and Appalachian trails. The path starts at Shaw Gap on Grosses Mountain. It descends westerly downslope toward a feeder stream of Straight Branch to pass by Beartree Lake. It then crosses US 58 at Beartree Gap and heads south a short distance to intersect the AT.

Leave Shaw Gap on the Beartree Gap Trail and head just a few feet before intersecting the Shaw Gap Trail, which leads left down to Beartree Group Camp. Veer right past this junction and pick up an uphill single-track marked with yellow diamonds and purple blazes and running over a roadbed. Head west on the south slope of Grosses Mountain in a dry forest dominated by chestnut oaks and mountain laurel. At 0.3 mile, level out and begin descending. There are winter views of

Whitetop Mountain to your left. Make a brief climb at mile 1.1 and resume the downgrade on a steep rocky side ridge of Grosses Mountain.

Come to a gap and a trail junction at mile 1.7. The Yancy Trail leaves left 0.3 mile down to Forest Road 837. Continue forward on the Beartree Gap Trail, still descending, now on a path crowded by rhododendron. Pass a dammed pond at mile 1.9. Beyond the pond, cross a small stream and continue down the valley of this watercourse, eventually crossing the stream again on a wooden bridge at mile 2.6. Just past this crossing, come to Forest Road 837. Past the forest road, Beartree Gap Trail is for hikers only.

Hikers continue on the path by crossing FR 837 and taking wooden steps down to a conventional trail, which shortly climbs to the Beartree Lake fisherman's parking area. Veer left across the parking area and pick up a paved path down to Beartree Lake and the Beartree Lake Trail. Turn right and cross the lake dam at mile 2.9. The paved Beartree Lake Trail leaves left to skirt the lake. The Beartree Gap Trail, however, leaves right, away from the water, and climbs on a natural footbed in woods to reach Beartree Gap and US 58 at mile 3.0. Cross the highway and stay with the trail as it opens into a brushy clearing with great views of Laurel Mountain. More travel reveals better views of Laurel Mountain, as well as views of Lost Mountain, Beech Mountain, and Whitetop Mountain. At mile 3.3, in a grassy gap growing up with young pines, intersect the Appalachian Trail. From here, on the AT, it is 2.3 miles left to Creek Junction and 11.7 miles right to Damascus.

Access

Northern Access: The Beartree Gap Trail starts at Shaw Gap, which can be reached by the Shaw Gap Trail, the Iron Mountain Trail, or Chestnut Ridge Trail. The Beartree Gap Trail can be accessed in its middle portions on US 58 near Beartree Recreation Area, or near Beartree Lake.

Southern Access: The south end can be accessed by walking south on the Appalachian Trail, 2.3 miles from Creek Junction.

Beartree Lake Trail

Type:	Foot only
Length:	1.0 mile
Difficulty:	Easy
Use:	Heavy
Condition:	Excellent
Highlights:	Lake views, fishing access
Book Map #:	2
USGS Topo:	Konnarock
Connections:	Beartree Gap Trail

This is a wide, purple-blazed path that encircles the mountain impoundment of Beartree Lake. Anglers use it to access their favorite fishing spots. This is a family hike that stays around 3,000 feet in elevation.

Drop down from the anglers' parking area on a paved path and soon come to a split in the trail. Take the left route around the lake. Pick up a gravel footpath cut into the mountainside. There is a steep drop-off to the lake to your right. Short fisherman's paths descend to the lake.

Step over a small creek at 0.4 mile and come to a brushy area. Cross a small bridge and on your right is a fishing dock. Below another bridge is a canoe launch. The trail becomes paved just past the launch. Stay right and walk beside a swim beach—this is the more developed side of the lake. Stay along the shoreline, where there are a few repose benches. At 0.7 mile, come to a second fishing dock. Swing right over the lake dam at the junction for the Beartree Gap Trail, which leaves left 0.4 miles to intersect the Appalachian Trail. Walk beside the outflow and intersect the paved path to the parking area, retracing your steps a short distance to complete the loop at 1.0 mile.

Access

From the Little Red Caboose in Damascus, head east on US 58 for 8.2 miles to paved Forest Road 837. Turn left and drive for 0.2 mile to the Beartree Lake anglers' parking area on the right. The Beartree Lake Trail starts on the north side of the parking area as a paved footpath. Do not confuse this with the Beartree Gap Trail, which starts on the south side of the parking area as a dirt path.

Beaver Flats Trail

Type:	Foot only
Length:	0.6 mile
Difficulty:	Easy
Use:	Moderate
Condition:	Good
Highlights:	Loops around beaver pond wetland
Book Map #:	2
USGS Topo:	Konnarock
Connections:	None

The Beaver Flats Trail is a nature trail that primarily serves campers at Beartree Campground. It makes a loop through a flat of Straight Branch, where beavers have backed up the stream's waters and made dams. This high country wetland is worth a visit, and so is the campground. This narrative starts where the Beaver Flats Trail leaves Forest Road 837.

Leave FR 837 and walk beneath white pine to a split in the trail. Take the right fork. Soon cross Straight Branch on a bridge to pass a side trail leading directly to the Beaver Flats loop of Beartree Campground. Walk up some steps and cruise along the edge of Grosses Mountain. There are views of Straight Mountain across the valley. Descend to cross a bog on a boardwalk and then Straight Branch again. The area is open overhead. Cross more wet areas on boardwalks and bridges. Come to an area overlooking a beaver dam and pond. Beaver dams create shallow ponds such as this, which attract other wildlife, especially waterfowl, and are in general a boon to any ecosystem. Their dams slow watercourses, settling sediment and filtering waters to make them cleaner. In the 1800s, beaver hats became very popular. Large trading companies shipped beaver pelts around the world. By the late 1800s, the high demand for beaver pelts led to the extirpation of beavers over much of their natural range in the Old Dominion, as well as much of North America. The Virginia Game Commission began a reintroduction program for beavers between 1932 and 1938, when 35 beavers were purchased from states that still had native beaver populations and released them into nine counties within Virginia. These beavers bred, and their offspring were subsequently restocked to other parts of Virginia. By the early 1950s, beavers had reoccupied many parts of their former range in Virginia. Beavers are believed to inhabit every county in the Old Dominion.

Continue through a forest of many yellow birches to return to the white pine grove. Stay right and retrace your steps a short distance to FR 837.

Access

From the Little Red Caboose in Damascus, head east on US 58 for 8.2 miles to paved Forest Road 837. Turn left on FR 837 and drive for 3.3 miles to the Beaver Flats Trail, which is on the left.

Beech Grove Trail

Type:	Foot, bicycle, horse
Length:	3.3 miles
Difficulty:	Moderate
Use:	Low to moderate
Condition:	Good
Highlights:	Good connector, solitude and views on lower end
Book Map #:	3, 1
USGS Topo:	Konnarock, Damascus
Connections:	Virginia Creeper Trail, Appalachian Trail, Iron Mountain Trail, Clark Mountain Trail

This is a tale of one trail with two very different sections. First, the Beech Grove Trail heads away from Whitetop Laurel Creek and the Virginia Creeper Trail along a feeder branch to pass the Appalachian Trail. The moderately narrow path then climbs more sharply up to Feathercamp Ridge and the Iron Mountain Trail. From a gap on Feathercamp Ridge, it leaves left and picks up a very wide roadbed to wind down to the lower end of Beech Creek. The trail receives moderate usage from Whitetop Laurel Creek to Feathercamp Ridge, and once it follows the old road, it is hardly used at all. The system of old roads and trails near lower Beech Creek is not signed and can be very confusing.

Leave US 58 and begin up a shady dirt path broken by numerous rock and wood water bars. A feeder branch flows off to the left. At 0.3 mile intersect the Appalachian Trail. From here it is 4.9 miles left to Damascus and 0.7 mile right to the Feathercamp Trail. Keep climbing on the Beech Grove Trail, marked with yellow diamonds, and pass more erosion bars to cross the feeder stream. Steeply ascend from here via switchbacks to reach a gap on Feathercamp Ridge and the Iron Mountain Trail at 0.7 mile.

The Iron Mountain Trail leaves right 3.5 miles to Sandy Flats shelter. Turn left on the Beech Grove Trail, which shares the wide grassy roadbed with the IMT for a short distance. The IMT then leads left, uphill, to reach Damascus in 2.5 miles. The Beech Grove Trail stays on the wide roadbed and begins a long descent down the northern end of Feathercamp Ridge. The trail canopy is often absent overhead. At mile 1.4, there are views to the right of Beech Creek and Clark Mountain. At mile 1.7, a road comes in from the right; stay forward and continue descending among blackberries, black locust, sumac, and other invasive sun-loving plants. Later, impressive views of farms and mountains to the north open up. At mile 3.0, the Clark Mountain Trail leaves left and skirts the national forest border. Keep going downhill, now sharing the treadway with the Clark Mountain Trail, and pass a road leaving sharply left; stay forward. A grassy field lies to the left through the trees. Come to a second road split at mile 3.2. A grassy road leaves left to cross Beech Creek and end on private property overlooking an old two-story log cabin. This is the end of the Beech Grove Trail. To the right, the Clark Mountain Trail continues up Beech Creek to cross the stream on old bridge supports and climbs up Clark Mountain along the national forest border to drop down, cross Henry Widener Branch, and continue to meet the Wright Hollow Trail.

Access

From the Little Red Caboose in Damascus, drive east on US 58 for 4.5 miles to the Straight Branch Virginia Creeper Trail parking area, off US 58 to the right. After parking, return to US 58 and walk a few steps east on 58, past two picnic tables; the Beech Grove Trail starts on the far side of the road.

Bushwacker Trail

Type:	Foot, bicycle
Length:	1.2 miles
Difficulty:	Moderate
Use:	Moderate
Condition:	Good
Highlights:	Part of good mountain biking loop
Book Map #:	3
USGS Topo:	Konnarock
Connections:	Iron Mountain Trail, Feathercamp Branch Trail, Sawmill Trail

The Bushwacker Trail is a popular mountain biking path. It is used in combination with one or more of the following trails to make a loop: Iron Mountain Trail, Sawmill Trail, Rush Trail, and Beartree Gap Trail. Hikers also use it sometimes, as the Sandy Flats trail shelter is found along the way. The Bushwacker Trail leaves Forest Road 90 on a wide roadbed and swings around the southwest side of Sandy Flats Knob, passing the trail shelter, and then drops down to Sandy Flats, which is an important junction for area trail travelers.

Leave FR 90 and then clear a pole gate and stone vehicle barrier. Head uphill in an open area on a wide-open roadbed. There is very little shade. The sandy path ascends in fits and starts, leveling off in a little hollow at 0.5 mile. Take a sharp right here, leaving the roadbed at a location marked with piled rocks. The trail here is narrow. Mountain bikers will have to carry their bikes up this section. Soon pick up a small roadbed and veer right, passing a few intermittent rills.

Top a hill in pine-oak woods; then drop to a gap and a trail junction at 1.0 mile. To your left, it is but a few feet to the Sandy Flats shelter, a three-sided board affair with a spring and privy nearby. Beyond this to the left, the Iron Mountain Trail (for hikers only here) heads 0.4 mile to connect with the Feathercamp Trail. To your right, the Iron Mountain Trail heads 0.3 mile to FR 90. Continue forward on the Bushwacker Trail and descend along a spring branch to end at Sandy Flats at mile 1.2. The Feathercamp Trail leaves left down the lower gated road. On the upper gated road, it is 0.1 mile to the bicycle and horse portion of the Iron Mountain Trail and 0.2 mile to the Sawmill Trail.

Access

From the Little Red Caboose in Damascus, drive east on US 58 for 7.3 miles to Forest Road 90. Turn left on FR 90 and follow it 0.5 mile to the trailhead, which will be on your left. Park off the road and don't block the pole gate in front of the trail.

Buzzard Den Trail

Type:	Foot, bicycle, horse
Length:	1.6 miles
Difficulty:	Difficult
Use:	Low
Condition:	Good but narrow
Highlights:	Solitude
Book Map #:	2
USGS Topo:	Damascus
Connections:	Wright Hollow Trail, Sawmill Trail

This is a steep and narrow path that ascends the spine of Buzzard Den Ridge to intersect the Sawmill Trail. The path stays spindly throughout from the north end, where it spurs off the Wright Hollow Trail to the south end on Feathercamp Ridge. Be apprised: there is one short ultra-steep section and no water along the way.

Leave the Wright Hollow Trail 0.1 mile uphill from the gate at Forest Road 287. Look for the yellow metal triangle nailed to a tree and a path leading steeply left up the nose of Buzzard Den Ridge. Pick up an old trail coming in from your left at 0.1 mile; the climb moderates. Stay in pine-oak woods and reach the ridgeline at 0.2 mile, where the path then switches over to the left side of the ridge.

The trail soon ascends radically for about 200 feet into a white pine woods and keeps leading uphill. It is a steep drop to Creasy Hollow on your left. At 0.6 mile, level off and then resume the climb to pass a rock outcrop on your left. There are some large oaks along the narrow ridgeline here. Keep climbing, only to reach another gap at 1.3 mile. Descend from here on a path lined with mountain laurel and intersect the Sawmill Trail at 1.6 miles. From here it is 0.3 mile right to the Feathercamp Ridge Trail and 1.4 miles left to the Rush Trail.

Access

From the Little Red Caboose in Damascus, drive east on US 58 for 0.5 mile to VA 91. Turn left on VA 91 and drive for 1.3 miles to VA 605 (Widener Valley Road). Turn right on VA 605 and follow it 5.8 miles to the gravel-surfaced Forest Road 287. FR 287 is just beyond Birdsong Road. Turn right on FR 287 and follow it 0.9 mile to a gap and a parking area. After arriving at the trailhead on FR 287, trail users will have to walk up the closed portion of the forest road 0.1 mile past the pole gate on the Wright Hollow Trail to the yellow diamond–marked path leading steeply left up Buzzard Den Ridge. The southern end of the Buzzard Den Trail can be accessed by heading 1.4 miles from Sandy Flats on the Sawmill Trail.

Chestnut Ridge Trail

Type:	Foot, bicycle, horse
Length:	1.8 miles
Difficulty:	Difficult
Use:	Low
Condition:	Good
Highlights:	Solitude, views
Book Map #:	2
USGS Topo:	Konnarock
Connections:	Beartree Gap Trail, Iron Mountain Trail, Shaw Gap Trail

Hikers, bikers, and equestrians all enjoy this single-track path. But all the users still add up to a low number. The path is attractive but steep, as it winds up the north slope of Grosses Mountain. It starts in the upper Mill Creek valley to climb up a slender ridge to the headwaters of Rush Creek. It then picks up an old railroad grade for the final climb to end at Shaw Gap. This gap is an important trail junction in the NRA's west side.

This path is not signed at either end, possibly accounting for low usage. Follow the directions carefully to get started. Leave FR 615 near the white pine blazed with two yellow horizontal stripes. Follow an old woods road a short distance along upper Mill Creek in a young forest of slender trees. At 0.2 mile, veer left and cross Mill Creek. Keep going uphill, where the trailbed and creekbed merge. Come to a switchback left and leave the valley, now climbing a rib ridge cloaked in maple–pine–oak–mountain laurel woodland. The trail weaves up the nose of the ridge, slightly moderating the sharp ascent. Briefly level out in a flat covered in blueberry bushes at 0.7 mile. Resume the climb and look left for intermittent views of the South Fork Holston Valley and mountains beyond.

Reach the ridgeline at 1.2 miles. An unmaintained trail leaves sharply right toward Rush Creek. Stay forward on a slim spine, soon dropping off toward upper Rush Creek, reaching the waters to pick up a railroad grade. At the stream, an unmaintained manway leads left up and over a gap to drop down Buzzard Den Branch. The Chestnut Branch Trail traces the railroad grade right to reach Shaw Gap at mile 1.8. From Shaw Gap it is 2.6 miles forward on the Beartree Gap Trail to Forest Road 837. It is 1.0 mile forward on the Shaw Gap Trail to Beartree Group Camp. It is 2.1 miles left on the Iron Mountain Trail to Straight Branch shelter. It is 1.8 miles right on the IMT to the Sandy Flats shelter.

Access

From the Little Red Caboose in Damascus, drive east on US 58 for 0.5 mile to VA 91. Turn left on VA 91 and drive for 1.3 miles to VA 605 (Widener Valley

Road). Turn right on VA 605 and follow it 8.9 miles to VA 604 (Mill Creek Road). Turn right on VA 604 and follow it 1.9 miles to VA 730 (Blevins Road). Turn right on gravel-surfaced VA 730 and follow it 2.0 miles. Then look for a white pine with two yellow bands painted around it on the left side of the road. Just past this is a dirt parking area on the right-hand side of the road. The forest has been thinned around this parking area.

Clark Mountain Trail

Type:	Foot, bicycle, horse
Length:	3.7 miles
Difficulty:	Very difficult
Use:	Very low
Condition:	Very poor
Highlights:	Solitude, navigational challenge
Book Map #:	1, 2, 3
USGS Topo:	Damascus, Konnarock
Connections:	Beech Grove Trail

This is a very rough trail that seems to have been abandoned. Its western end, near Damascus, either is not as portrayed on topographic maps or is completely overgrown. It does meet the Beech Grove Trail and parallels it for a short distance before striking easterly on its own and climbing Clark Mountain, nearing a clear-cut on the forest boundary to reach a gap in Clark Mountain. From here it drops very steeply and faintly down to Henry Widener Branch. The trail sees more use here and heads east up to a gap between Short Mountain and Feathercamp Ridge to intersect a closed logging road. The trail then traces the closed logging road to intersect the Wright Hollow Trail, which follows the logging road east past Buzzard Den Branch. Only hearty and intrepid hikers with map and compass skills should attempt this path.

This description starts at the western end of the Clark Mountain Trail, at a dirt road on private land 0.2 mile from Beech Grove Trail. Leave easterly from the old dirt road beside a decaying outbuilding and head east along an old woods road. Skirt the red-blazed forest border to intersect the wide Beech Grove Trail, coming in from the right. Keep going forward, sharing the sunny blackberry-lined roadbed with the Beech Grove Trail. A road leaves left to a field; stay forward. Soon, come to a second road split. The Beech Grove Trail leaves left and descends a short distance to cross Beech Creek and end at a gate looking out on a two-story log cabin. The Clark Mountain Trail leaves right and enters rich woods to reach the supports of an old bridge over Beech Creek at 0.7 mile.

Climb away from Beech Creek to begin the ascent of Clark Mountain. Old roads and smaller trails split off the main path, which is generally kept open by occasional hunters and hikers. The main trail then ascends very steeply up a rock-lined path to top out on a ridgeline beside a clear-cut at 1.7 miles. There are good views of Widener Valley to the left. Parallel the clear-cut and look for another rock-lined, single-track path leaving right, back into the woods uphill. Follow this single-track path and swing around a knob to the left in pine–mountain laurel woods. There will be numerous blowdowns on the trail. Keep climbing to reach Clark Mountain in a gap at mile 2.2. Drop back down, making a few switchbacks. Then head straight down a very rocky, very rough hollow that narrows to a rhododendron-choked streambed. Open back up at mile 2.5 in a tall forest that runs along Henry Widener Branch. To the left, the unmaintained trail leads 0.2 mile to dead-end at private property. To the right, the Clark Mountain Trail continues, crossing Henry Widener Branch just below its confluence with an unnamed stream. Follow an old woods road up the hollow of the unnamed branch, crossing that stream at 2.8 miles. Leave the woods road and follow a more faint path through thick woods up the now-dry hollow to a gap near Short Mountain, which is on the left. Reach the gap at mile 3.1. Drop straight down just a bit and look out on a huge pile of wood left over from past timbering. Take the seeded logging road right, heading south, moderately uphill. The forest here has been thinned. Top out near a rocky area; then descend to Buzzard Den Branch at mile 3.5. Cross the stream and continue on the road just a short distance farther to a single-track side trail leading to the Wright Hollow Trail. This side trail leaves right, into the woods. Continue forward 0.2 mile on the logging road to intersect the Wright Hollow Trail as it comes in from the right. This is the end of the Clark Mountain Trail. From here the Wright Hollow Trail continues 1.5 miles on closed FR 287 to the Buzzard Den Trail and 1.6 miles to the lower Wright Hollow trailhead.

Access

This trail is accessed by traveling the Beech Grove Trail 3.3 miles from US 58, or by heading 1.1 miles down the Wright Hollow Trail to closed Forest Road 287.

Feathercamp Ridge Trail

Type:	Foot, bicycle
Length:	0.7 mile
Difficulty:	Moderate
Use:	Moderate
Condition:	Good
Highlights:	Mountain bike loop connector trail
Book Map #:	3, 2
USGS Topo:	Konnarock
Connections:	Iron Mountain Trail, Wright Hollow Trail, Sawmill Trail

This interior trail serves as a connector for loop hikes and rides in the Sandy Flats Area. It begins in a high saddle on Feathercamp Ridge and then drops off the ridgeline to Buzzard Den Branch and the upper reaches of Wright Hollow, where it connects to the Wright Hollow Trail and the Sawmill Trail.

Triangular yellow blazes mark the narrow path, which leaves the intersection with the Iron Mountain Trail and swings downhill below the highest point of Feathercamp Ridge. Wind among moist coves and rib ridges to level out and pass through a gap at 0.4 mile. Descend very steeply from the gap to the wide and shallow Buzzard Den Branch. Cross this small stream to pass another intermittent rill, just before intersecting the Wright Hollow Trail. From here, it is 3.0 miles left to Forest Road 287 on the Wright Hollow Trail. The Feathercamp Ridge Trail, however, continues right, 100 feet up a small hill, to intersect the Sawmill Trail at 0.7 mile. From here on the Sawmill Trail, it is 1.1 miles right to Sandy Gap and 0.3 mile left to the Buzzard Den Trail.

Access

The Feathercamp Ridge Trail is an interior trail. It can be reached either by heading west on the Iron Mountain Trail for 1.0 mile from Sandy Flats (on the biker and horse-trail portion of the Iron Mountain Trail), or by heading north for 1.1 miles on the Sawmill Trail from Sandy Flats.

Feathercamp Trail

Type:	Foot only
Length:	2.2 miles
Difficulty:	Moderate
Use:	Moderate
Condition:	Good but rocky
Highlights:	Intimate stream valley
Book Map #:	3
USGS Topo:	Konnarock
Connections:	Sawmill Trail, Bushwacker Trail, Iron Mountain Trail, Appalachian Trail

This foot-only trail leaves Sandy Flats and heads down the exceptionally pretty valley of Feathercamp Branch, a heavily forested rocky hollow. The path stays near the stream and crosses its lower end numerous times to end at the Appalachian Trail. It can be used as a connector path for loop hikes using the Iron Mountain and Appalachian trails. The Feathercamp Trail's beginning is also a terminus for the Sawmill and Bushwacker trails. Start the Feathercamp Trail by leaving the Sandy Flats parking area and circumventing the lower of three pole gates. The upper reaches of Feathercamp Branch lie to your left. Walk down the wide roadbed to intersect

Feathercamp Trail in the spring.

the Iron Mountain Trail at 0.1 mile. Sandy Flats shelter is a short distance left on the IMT.

Hike down the wet roadbed and stay left at a road split, continuing downhill. Open into a wildlife clearing at 0.3 mile. Continue forward through the clearing, staying closely along Feathercamp Branch to pick up a slender, shady footpath blazed in blue. The rate of descent increases as it passes over small rills flowing off the slopes of Feathercamp Ridge to the right. The valley walls rise on both sides. Witch hazel, striped maple, and doghobble line the very stony trail. Doghobble is a low arching shrub that grows only in the Southern Appalachians. In late spring and early summer, it grows clusters of tiny bell-shaped flowers that droop from its branches. The waist-high thickets prove quite an impediment for most creatures, including humans and dogs. In pioneer days, hunted bears would take off through such thickets with their powerful bodies, losing the dogs in pursuit of them and giving the plant its name, doghobble.

Watch for small falls and cascades on the stream. Switchback left along a side stream to soon cross Feathercamp Branch at mile 1.6. This marks the first of eight crossings that can be negotiated dry-footed in times of normal flow. After the eighth crossing, intersect the Appalachian Trail at mile 2.2. From here it is 0.1 mile forward to US 58 and 5.6 miles right to Damascus.

Access

From the Little Red Caboose in Damascus, drive east on US 58 for 7.3 miles to Forest Road 90. Turn left on FR 90 and follow it 1.8 miles to Sandy Flats, where there are two gated roads and Forest Road 615 turns sharply right downhill. Park here and take the lower gated road.

Lum Trail

Type:	Foot, bicycle
Length:	1.0 mile
Difficulty:	Moderate
Use:	Moderate
Condition:	Excellent
Book Map #:	2
USGS Topo:	Konnarock
Connections:	Straight Branch Trail, Iron Mountain Trail

The Lum Trail traces the upper reaches of Straight Branch through a very pretty valley, first of hardwoods, then fading hemlocks, to reach a gap between Grosses Mountain and Straight Mountain. On the lower end is the Beartree Campground, and on the upper end is the Straight Branch trail shelter. Also at the top is the junction with the Iron Mountain Trail. From here, forest travelers can make loop trips in either direction.

Leave Chipmunk Circle Loop of Beartree Campground near the bathhouse and trace an old woods road past a few streamlets. Beech, sweet birch, and yellow birch tower over the rhododendron that covers the forest floor. This trail is a good place to discern between the two types of birch trees. Yellow birches are easy to spot. They have a yellowish-gold bark with horizontal stripes. This ragged bark peels on the tree. However, the larger yellow birches will not have bark peeling on their lower trunks but will still have peeling bark on their upper branches. Sweet birch, also known as black birch, is common and has horizontal stripes on its bark, which is more brownish-gray. The bark does not peel. The tight bark resembles that of a cherry tree. Scratch a twig of black birch, and it smells like wintergreen.

At 0.4 mile, the trail begins to rise. Cross more intermittent streamlets coursing off Grosses Mountain to your left into Straight Branch on your right. At 0.5 mile, imperiled hemlocks become more prevalent as the valley and trail veer left. Keep climbing to arrive at the saddle dividing Grosses and Straight mountains at 1.0 mile. Here, the Straight Branch trail shelter lies beneath tall white pines. To your right, a side trail leaves right to a spring. Dead ahead is the junction with the Iron Mountain Trail. To your left on the IMT, it is 2.1 miles to Shaw Gap, and to your right, it is 1.7 miles to VA 600.

Access

From the Little Red Caboose in Damascus, take US 58 east for 8.2 miles to the paved Forest Road 837. Turn left up 837 and follow it for 0.7 mile to the campground guardhouse. Continue past the entrance for 3.0 miles to the Chipmunk Loop. The trail starts near the first bathhouse on the loop.

Rush Trail

Type:	Foot, bicycle, horse
Length:	1.8 miles
Difficulty:	Difficult
Use:	Low
Condition:	Good
Highlights:	Solitude
Book Map #:	3, 2
USGS Topo:	Konnarock
Connections:	Sawmill Trail, Iron Mountain Trail

The Rush Trail connects the Rush Creek area to the Iron Mountain Trail. It travels along Rush Creek for a distance and then angles up the side of Grosses Mountain to top out on the ridgeline of Grosses Mountain. It is often used as part of many loop possibilities in the Sandy Flats area. Start the Rush Trail by leaving Forest Road 615 and traveling uphill just a few feet, coming to a wooden vehicle barrier. Rush Creek gurgles and crashes off to your right. Begin ascending an old roadbed in rhododendron with a deciduous overstory. Yellow diamonds mark the path.

At 0.3 mile, briefly descend and then continue up a wet, rocky path. At 0.5 mile, the trail makes a sharp right. An unmaintained path continues left, up Rush Creek. Cross Rush Creek and soon pass a small side stream, while ascending the north slope of Grosses Mountain and winding in and out of small coves. Old roads spur off the main path, but the primary route is obvious, having a single track in the middle of the trailbed.

At mile 1.4, there is a great view of the Holston River Valley off to the right. Keep climbing and intersect the Iron Mountain Trail at mile 1.8. To your right, it is 200 feet down to Forest Road 90 on the Iron Mountain Trail. To the left, it is 1.5 miles to Shaw Gap on the Iron Mountain Trail.

Access

Lower Access: From the Little Red Caboose in Damascus, drive east on US 58 for 7.3 miles to Forest Road 90. Turn left on FR 90 and follow it 1.8 miles to Sandy Flats, where there are three gated forest roads, with Forest Road 615 turning sharply right downhill. At Sandy Flats, turn right down Forest Road 615 and follow it for

1.1 miles to a fenced wildlife clearing by Rush Creek. Veer right at the wildlife clearing and drive just a short distance, bridging Rush Creek on a culvert. The Rush Trail begins just beyond the culvert on the far side of Rush Creek. There is no trail sign here. Pull off to the side of FR 615, and do not to block the gate here. FR 615 continues as a rough road beyond the gate.

Upper Access: From the Little Red Caboose in Damascus, drive east on US 58 for 7.3 miles to Forest Road 90. Turn left on FR 90 and follow it 1.3 miles to the Iron Mountain Trail, which crosses FR 90. To the right, just a bit up the IMT, the Rush Trail leaves left.

Saunders Trail

Type:	Foot, bicycle
Length:	2.1 miles
Difficulty:	Moderate
Use:	Low
Condition:	Good
Highlights:	Connects with Appalachian Trail near Saunders trail shelter
Book Map #:	3
USGS Topo:	Konnarock
Connections:	Appalachian Trail

This trail follows closed Forest Road 832 past many wildlife clearings and side trails to other wildlife clearings to come near and then intersect the Appalachian Trail. It then continues to the Saunders shelter, which is on a spur trail from the AT. Begin the Saunders Trail by passing around the gated FR 832, where a sign states, "Disabled Hunter Access, Permit Required." Soon pass through the first of many wildlife clearings. The roadbed is wide, grassy, and mostly uncanopied, as it climbs the north slope of Straight Mountain in rich deciduous woods draped in vines. Open up to a second wildlife clearing. At 0.6 mile, on a right turn, look left for a sign that states, "Hiker Trail," leading left uphill to shortly intersect the Appalachian Trail. Maintain a moderate ascent on the roadbed; then stay left as the road splits, continuing uphill. Intersect the AT in a gap at mile 1.4. From here on the AT, it is 10.1 miles south to Damascus and 3.9 miles north to Creek Junction. The Saunders Trail stays right, continuing on the old roadbed, and shows signs of less use beyond here. Swing around the north side of a knob on Straight Mountain and intersect the water-access trail for the Saunders shelter at mile 2.0. Veer left, uphill, and pass through a clearing and beside a white pine grove to reach the Saunders shelter at mile 2.1. From here, it is a quarter mile up to the AT on a blue-blazed spur trail.

Access

From the Little Red Caboose in Damascus, drive east on US 58 for 7.9 miles to Forest Road 832. Turn right into a gravel parking area; the Saunders Trail starts beyond the gate on FR 832.

Sawmill Trail

Type:	Foot, bicycle, horse
Length:	2.8 miles
Difficulty:	Moderate
Use:	Low
Condition:	Good
Highlights:	Important connector path in west end
Book Map #:	3, 2
USGS Topo:	Konnarock
Connections:	Iron Mountain Trail, Feathercamp Trail, Feathercamp Ridge Trail, Wright Hollow Trail, Buzzard Den Trail, Rush Trail

The Sawmill Trail is an important connector path in the west end of the recreation area. It leaves Sandy Flats and ascends the side of Feathercamp Ridge, only to descend and intersect numerous trails along the way, eventually ending up along Rush Creek. Trail enthusiasts of every stripe use this path, as there are so many loops possible from it.

The Sawmill Trail actually starts 0.2 mile beyond gated Forest Road 90 at Sandy Flats, but for the purposes of this guidebook, the trail description will start at Sandy Flats. Leave Sandy Flats and take the upper gated road of the two gated roads that are side by side. At 0.1 mile, the Iron Mountain Trail leaves left and heads toward Damascus. Keep climbing up gated FR 90 and come to a second gate. Start the official trail beyond the gate and continue up the grassy road. There are views off to your right of Grosses Mountain. At 0.7 mile, come to a gap and a wildlife clearing on your right. Stay forward and drop back down to another gap to turn sharply left into a shady hollow. Spring seeps keep the trailbed wet here.

Come to a trail junction at mile 1.1. The Feathercamp Ridge Trail leaves left here to drop and then climb to the Iron Mountain Trail in 0.7 mile. Just a few feet down Feathercamp Ridge Trail is the Wright Hollow Trail, which leads right 3.0 miles to Forest Road 287. Keep descending on a drier, narrower trailbed on the Sawmill Trail. Dip down to a saddle and intersect the Buzzard Den Trail. It leaves left and reaches Forest Road 287 in 1.8 miles. From here the Sawmill Trail descends very steeply and then moderates, undulating along the north side of a hill. Gain good views of the Holston River Valley off to your left. At mile 2.3, bridge a few small streams and keep descending to pass a wildlife clearing that is now growing in young pines. Beyond the clearing, trace a feeder stream as it falls steeply to Rush Creek. Pass a trail sign, a pole gate, and a pond to your right, ending the trail near a wildlife clearing at Forest Road 615 at mile 2.8. Ahead, across Rush Creek and to the right, is the beginning of the Rush Creek Trail. It leads 1.8 miles up to Iron Mountain Trail.

Access

Upper Access: From the Little Red Caboose in Damascus, drive east on US 58 for 7.3 miles to Forest Road 90. Turn left on FR 90 and follow it 1.8 miles to Sandy Flats, where there are three gated forest roads with Forest Road 615 turning sharply right downhill. Park here and take the upper gated road 0.2 mile uphill to a second gate. The Sawmill Trail starts here.

Lower Access: To reach the lower terminus of Sawmill Trail, continue past Sandy Flats and turn right down Forest Road 615 and follow it for 1.1 miles to a fenced wildlife clearing by Rush Creek. The lower Sawmill terminus is to the left of the clearing by a small pond.

Shaw Gap Trail

Type:	Foot, bicycle
Length:	1.0 mile
Difficulty:	Moderate
Use:	Moderate
Condition:	Good
Highlights:	Good loop trail for Beartree Recreation Area
Book Map #:	2
USGS Topo:	Konnarock
Connections:	Beartree Gap Trail, Iron Mountain Trail, Chestnut Ridge Trail

The Shaw Gap Trail is a vital leg for making loops out of the Beartree area. It leads moderately from the Beartree Group Camp up the south side of Grosses Mountain to Shaw Gap and a five-way trail intersection. From here, trail travelers can diverge in numerous directions.

Start the trail by leaving the group camp and walking a paved path just a short distance into the woods. Look left for an old woods road leading uphill past a square yellow blaze nailed to a yellow birch tree. Follow a single-track trail overlain on the woods road lined with rhododendron. At 0.1 mile pass a pair of cleared areas on the left. The path here is often wet. A deciduous forest of maple, hickory, and oak stands overhead. At 0.5 mile, cross a feeder stream of Straight Branch and keep ascending. The final climb angles north toward Shaw Gap, intersecting the Beartree Gap Trail at mile 1.0. The Beartree Gap Trail leads left 2.6 miles to Forest Road 837 and 3.3 miles to the Appalachian Trail. Veer right past the Beartree Gap Trail and travel just a few feet to reach Shaw Gap. From here, the Chestnut Ridge Trail leads forward 1.8 miles to Forest Road 615. The Iron Mountain Trail leads left 1.8 miles to Sandy Flats shelter and 2.1 miles right to Straight Branch shelter.

Access

From the Little Red Caboose in Damascus, head east on US 58 for 8.2 miles to paved Forest Road 837. Turn left and drive for 1.2 miles to the Beartree Group Camp. Turn left and then quickly left again, toward the RV Group Camp. The Shaw Gap Trail starts near the bathrooms on the right.

Skulls Gap Trail

Type:	Foot, bicycle, horse
Length:	1.0 mile
Difficulty:	Moderate
Use:	Low
Condition:	Good
Highlights:	Views
Book Map #:	4
USGS Topo:	Konnarock
Connections:	Iron Mountain Trail

This trail follows the roadbed of old VA 600 from an overlook on the north side of Straight Mountain up to intersect the Iron Mountain Trail near Skulls Gap and the old and now-closed Skulls Gap Picnic Area. The views from the overlook are among the best in the recreation area. After that, it's uphill, with more occasional views of Widener Valley and Walker Mountain in the distance.

Leave the overlook and pass around a wooden fence near VA 600. Start heading up the roadbed, which was abandoned in 1998. Wind up the north side of Straight Mountain. The road has been seeded, but there are still pieces of crumbling asphalt and gravel strewn about. There are good views of the lands to the north. At 0.5 mile look right, down the steep embankment, for an old jalopy that met a terrible fate long ago.

Keep the steady ascent. The headwaters of Grosses Branch tumble steeply off to your right. At 0.9 mile, the roadbed and creek come together. Just ahead is the junction with the yellow-blazed Iron Mountain Trail. To your right, the Iron Mountain Trail leads away from old VA 600 to climb to a trail junction and the Straight Branch trail shelter in 0.9 mile. To your left, the Iron Mountain Trail picks up old VA 600 and comes to a short side trail leading to the old Skulls Gap Picnic Area in 0.3 mile and to VA 600 in 0.5 mile.

Access

From the Little Red Caboose in Damascus, drive east on US 58 for 11.0 miles to Virginia 603 (Fairwood Road). Keep driving forward on VA 603 (US 58 curves right) and follow it for 2.7 miles to VA 600 (Whitetop Road). Continue forward on VA 600 and VA 603 leaves right in 0.1 mile. (VA 603 and VA 600 coincide for 0.1 mile.) Keep following VA 600 for 2.6 miles to the IMT trail crossing at the gap on VA 600.

Straight Branch Trail

Type:	Foot, bicycle
Length:	1.7 miles
Difficulty:	Moderate
Use:	Moderate
Condition:	Excellent
Highlights:	Good mountain biking trail, clearing in a gap
Book Map #:	2
USGS Topo:	Konnarock
Connections:	Lum Trail

The Straight Branch Trail follows a closed and seeded forest road up the valley of a side stream of Little Laurel Creek to a gap on Straight Mountain. Once over the gap, the trail drops down the headwaters of Straight Branch to end at the Chipmunk Circle of Beartree Campground. Mountain bikers use this trail along with the Lum Trail, Iron Mountain Trail, and VA 600 to make a loop. Campground visitors also use this path to stretch their legs.

Leave the gravel parking area around a wooden gate and climb up a mixed forest dominated by sweet birch and white pine. A rhododendron-filled hollow lies off to your left. Intermittent streams flow over the wide roadbed off the slopes of Straight Mountain to your right. Make a moderate climb and come to a sharp switchback to your right and then to the left, to top out in a gap at 0.7 mile. In the gap a sign tells of forest damage here by Hurricane Hugo in 1989.

Keep heading forward in the grassy clearing and begin a drop into the Straight Branch watershed. The wide path makes for easy travel. Pass a smaller grassy clearing at 1.0 mile and a stone wall beyond that. Piles of discarded picnic tables and other forest service junk are stored within sight of the trail. One hopes this debris will be removed one day. Pass through a wooden gate and come to the paved campground road that leads right into Chipmunk Circle at mile 1.7. To your left it, is 2.5 miles to down Forest Road 837 to the Shaw Gap Trail. To your right, it is 0.1 mile to the Lum Trail, which leaves right to intersect the Iron Mountain Trail atop Straight Mountain.

Access

Eastern Access: From the Little Red Caboose in Damascus, drive east on US 58 for 11.0 miles to Virginia 603 (Fairwood Road). Continue forward on VA 603 (US 58 curves right) and follow it for 2.7 miles to VA 600 (Whitetop Road). Keep going forward on VA 600, and VA 603 leaves right in 0.1 mile. (VA 603 and VA 600 coincide for 0.1 mile.) Keep heading forward on VA 600 and follow it for 1.4 miles to a gravel road leading uphill on your left. Climb this gravel road just a few feet to the parking area for the Straight Branch Trail, which starts behind the pole gate at the back of the parking area.

Western Access: From the Little Red Caboose in Damascus, take US 58 east for 8.2 miles to paved Forest Road 837. Turn left up 837 and follow it for 0.7 mile to the campground guardhouse. Continue past the entrance for 3.0 miles to the campground.

Taylors Valley Trail

Type:	Foot, bicycle, horse
Length:	2.6 miles
Difficulty:	Moderate
Use:	Low
Condition:	Good
Highlights:	Creek fords, old homesite, potential loop with Virginia Creeper Trail
Book Map #:	3
USGS Topo:	Grayson, Konnarock
Connections:	Virginia Creeper Trail, Appalachian Trail

This trail is one half of an excellent loop in conjunction with the Virginia Creeper Trail. The path begins by immediately fording Whitetop Laurel Creek and soon afterward fording Green Cove Creek. It then climbs a bit to an old homestead to join a roadbed that meanders the mountainside of Laurel Mountain, running parallel to Whitetop Laurel Creek. Finally, the trail drops down a hollow to meet a gravel road, which in turn leads a short distance to the Virginia Creeper Trail.

From the Creek Junction parking area turnaround, look for the blue blaze on a tree beside Whitetop Laurel Creek. Immediately ford Laurel Creek, a year-round wet ford. Dead ahead through the woods is the Appalachian Trail, which has just come over the span to the right. Follow the blue blazes downstream to head beneath the large trestle of the Virginia Creeper Trail/Appalachian Trail. Pass under the trestle and immediately turn left, paralleling the trestle, walking away from the stream. Soon make a sharp right away from the trestle and come to Green Cove Creek. Make another wet ford, this time of Green Cove Creek, and then ascend an old woods road through a rich forest of tulip trees, striped maple, black birch, and buckeye.

At 0.7 mile, open to a glade shaded by occasional maple trees. Look left for the remains of an outbuilding. This was once a mountainside farmstead. Turn sharply left here, passing through the clearing. The bulk of the clearing is uphill to the left. Past this, the trail opens up and passes alongside an area that was selectively logged. Continue westward along the slope of Laurel Mountain, traveling through smaller clearings that avail views of Straight Mountain across the Whitetop Laurel Valley. Bridge Steep Branch at mile 1.7 via road culvert. Rise away from the stream and come to a clearing. Bisect another wildlife clearing at mile 2.2. Reach a pole gate at mile 2.6. Travel just a few feet farther to come to a gravel road. This is the end of the Taylors Valley Trail. However, to continue to the Virginia Creeper Trail, turn left on the gravel road, (Forest Road 49100). Follow FR 49100 mostly downhill for 0.7 mile to intersect the Virginia Creeper Trail. From here it is 4.0 miles to the right, heading upstream, to Creek Junction.

Access

Eastern Access: From the Little Red Caboose in Damascus, head east on US 58 for 11.6 miles to VA 728 (Creek Junction Road). Turn acutely right and follow VA 728 for 1.0 mile to dead-end at the Virginia Creeper Trail. At the parking area turnaround, look for the blue blaze on a tree beside Whitetop Laurel Creek. The Taylors Valley Trail starts here, immediately fording Whitetop Laurel Creek.

Western Access: From Little Red Caboose in Damascus, drive east on US 58 for 1.5 miles to VA 91. (This is the second turnoff for VA 91.) Continue on VA 91 for 2.2 miles into the state of Tennessee to Dollarsville Road. Turn left on Dollarsville Road, which is also marked Taylors Valley Road, and follow it 1.1 miles to the state line where it turns into VA 725 (Taylors Valley Road). Continue 2.2 miles from the state line to the road's end near some cabins and the Virginia Creeper Trail. Finally, take the gravel road leading uphill into the forest, Forest Road 49100. Follow FR 49100 for 0.7 mile to a dead end. The Taylors Valley Trail leaves right, around a pole gate.

Tennessee Trail

Type:	Foot, horse, bicycle
Length:	1.1 miles
Difficulty:	Difficult
Use:	Low
Condition:	Good
Highlights:	Connects national recreation area to Appalachian Trail in Tennessee
Book Map #:	1
USGS Topo:	Damascus
Connections:	Appalachian Trail

This trail traces a former jeep track up Pond Ridge onto Holston Mountain, where it enters the state of Tennessee and continues on to meet the Appalachian Trail. This trail is maintained but infrequently used, though it passes through an attractive woodland with sporadic views of the ridges around it.

Leave the parking area on Forest Road 32 and cross the gravel road uphill. Pass around a pole gate that states, "Foot Travel Welcome." Work your way around the gate and start uphill among a fast-growing forest of pine, oak, and striped maple with an overstory of chestnut oaks. A single-track path overlays the roadbed. The Tennessee Trail soon steepens. Many drainage cuts in the path minimize erosion but make the trailbed somewhat uneven.

At 0.5 mile, the trail angles up over to the left side of the ridge and briefly moderates its ascent. Occasional views of Holston Mountain open to the left. At 1.0 mile, the path levels out at the state line. The trail is now part of the Cherokee National Forest of Tennessee and has left the Mount Rogers National Recreation Area. Pass by a pond on the right at mile 1.1. Keep heading south and descend to the headwaters of Ramsey Branch. Beyond the streamlet, the Tennessee Trail continues sharply uphill to intersect the Appalachian Trail in a half mile. This last part of the path is faint and rugged. Continue left up the ridge and the AT can be intersected. To the left, it is 5.5 miles south to Damascus on the AT.

Access

From the Little Red Caboose in Damascus, drive west on US 58 for 0.7 mile to VA 757 (Government Road). Turn left on VA 757 and follow it for 1.2 miles, where it turns into Forest Road 32; continue following it for 2.2 miles farther for a total of 3.4 miles from US 58. Look for metal pole gates on both sides of FR 32. The Tennessee Trail leads left, uphill, from the parking area by the two gates on FR 32.

Wright Hollow Trail

Type:	Foot, bicycle, horse
Length:	3.0 miles
Difficulty:	Difficult
Use:	Very low
Condition:	Fair to good
Highlights:	Solitude on upper reaches
Book Map #:	2
USGS Topo:	Damascus
Connections:	Feathercamp Ridge Trail, Clark Mountain Trail, Buzzard Den Trail, Sawmill Trail

This is a little-used path that runs down Wright Hollow from Feathercamp Ridge to turn northeast and run along the lower part of Buzzard Den Ridge. It then connects to Forest Road 287. The first mile of the trail drops steeply along Buzzard Den Branch as a rocky narrow treadway that often merges with the stream itself. The trail then picks up an old roadbed to meet the closed west end of FR 287. The last section of trail traces the closed forest road, passing the Buzzard Den Trail just before exiting at a gap and auto-accessible trailhead. The south end of the trail is accessed via the Sawmill Trail and a short piece of the Feathercamp Ridge Trail from Sandy Gap on Feathercamp Ridge. The path is much easier to follow from Feathercamp Ridge down than from the forest road up. This upper portion of trail will be difficult for bikers and equestrians to negotiate, due to the closed forest canopy and rocky, wet treadway.

The Wright Hollow Trail leaves north from the Feathercamp Ridge Trail, steeply descending alongside Buzzard Den Branch in a rhododendron-choked valley. At 0.2 mile, cross Buzzard Den Branch for the first of four times. The trailbed and creek bed intermingle as the path drops down a rocky bed. At 0.9 mile, the trail picks up a road coming in from the left across the stream. (If heading upstream, look for the square yellow blaze, staying on the north side of the creek.)

Continue on the roadbed, which veers away from Buzzard Den Branch. The trailbed furls where large, soil water drains have been dug into the path. At mile 1.2, come to an unmarked junction. Forward, downhill, an unmaintained trail leads to closed Forest Road 287 to intersect the Clark Mountain Trail. The Wright Hollow Trail, however, makes a sharp right at the junction onto another roadbed to meander east along the north slope of Buzzard Den Ridge. Stay right and pass the remains of an old vehicle barrier. Stay on the roadbed until it drops down to intersect closed FR 287 at 1.4 miles. From here, the Clark Mountain Trail leaves left 3.5 very rough miles to Beech Grove Trail. Turn right here on the gravel forest road, continuing northeast on the Wright Hollow Trail. The woods here were thinned in the late 1990s. Meander along the north slope of Buzzard Den Ridge, gaining occasional views of Widener Valley below and Walker Mountain in the distance to your left.

At mile 2.9, as you work around a point in the ridge, the yellow triangle marked Buzzard Den Trail leaves right, steeply, up Buzzard Den Ridge to intersect the Sawmill Trail after 1.6 miles. Ahead, the Wright Hollow Trail continues, dropping steeply downhill to pass a pole gate and veer left to end, after 3.0 miles, at the publicly accessible portion of Forest Road 297.

Access

Upper Access: Head 1.1 miles on the Sawmill Trail (from Sandy Flats); then make a short walk downhill on the Feathercamp Ridge.

Lower Access: From the Little Red Caboose in Damascus, drive east on US 58 for 0.5 mile to VA 91. Turn left on VA 91 and drive for 1.3 miles, to VA 605 (Widener Valley Road). Turn right on VA 605 and follow it 5.8 miles to gravel-surfaced Forest Road 287. FR 287 is just past Birdsong Road. Turn right on FR 287 and follow it 0.9 mile to a gap and a parking area.

Yancy Trail

Type:	Foot, bicycle
Length:	0.3 mile
Difficulty:	Moderate
Use:	Moderate
Condition:	Good
Highlights:	Connects Beartree Recreation Area to Beartree Gap Trail
Book Map #:	3
USGS Topo:	Konnarock
Connections:	Beartree Gap Trail

The Yancy Trail is a short connector route primarily used to make a biking or hiking loop using the Shaw Gap Trail, the Beartree Gap Trail, and Forest Road 837. It climbs out of the upper Straight Fork valley to a gap on a side ridge of Grosses Mountain. Start this trail by leaving FR 837 near the recreation area gatehouse and heading up an old roadbed alongside a feeder stream of Straight Fork. The trailbed is surfaced with large gravel. The wide path makes for easy travel as it passes a cleared area on the right at 0.1 mile. Continue following the square yellow blazes back into the woods to top out at 0.3 mile at the Beartree Gap Trail. From here it is 1.7 miles right to Shaw Gap and 1.6 miles left to the Appalachian Trail.

Access

From the Little Red Caboose in Damascus, take US 58 east for 8.2 miles to paved Forest Road 837. Turn left up 837 and follow it for 0.7 mile. The Yancy Trail begins just past the gatehouse of Beartree Recreation Area. The trail's northern end can be reached via the Beartree Gap Trail.

Central Area Trails

Barton Gap Trail

Type:	Foot, bicycle, horse
Length:	1.6 miles
Difficulty:	Moderate
Use:	Low
Condition:	Good
Highlights:	Views of Hurricane Mountain, solitude, large oak tree
Book Map #:	4
USGS Topo:	Whitetop Mountain
Connections:	Hurricane Creek Trail

This little-used, mid-elevation path leaves Forest Road 84 to cross Hurricane Creek and ascend to a gap between Seng Mountain and Bear Ridge. It then descends to Barton Gap across from Plummer Ridge. Along the way it passes a very large oak tree. From the parking area, cross Forest Road 84 and drop down just a short distance to Hurricane Creek. The stream is 8 feet wide here and is easily crossed in times of normal flow. Begin climbing on a single-track dirt path overlain on an old woods road up the south slope of Seng Mountain. Gain partial views of Hurricane Mountain across the stream valley. At 0.3 mile, turn north on a point of the mountain to pass the head of a dry hollow. Keep climbing to reach the gap between Seng Mountain and Bear Ridge to your right. Old trails spur off this gap but are not maintained or recommended for travel.

Pass through the gap onto the north side of Bear Ridge. Keep heading easterly to a point on the ridge at 0.9 mile where the trail makes a sharp left and begins to descend, eventually passing through a rhododendron tunnel. Just past the rhododendron, look for a large oak on trail right. Keep descending past the headwaters of Barton Branch and come to an earthen vehicle barrier and then Forest Road 643 at 1.6 miles. Dead ahead is Plummer Ridge.

Access

From exit 45 on I-81 near Marion, drive south on VA 16 for 6.0 miles to the Jennings Visitor Center. From the visitor center, continue south on VA 16 for 8.7 miles to VA 650 (Comers Creek Road). Turn right on VA 650 and follow it for 1.4 miles to Forest Road 84 (Hurricane Campground Road). Turn left on Hurricane Campground Road and follow it 2.2 miles to a gravel parking area, which will be on your left, just past a grassy clearing on the left side of the road. The Barton Gap Trail starts on the far side of the road and is marked by a motorcycle sign.

Bobbys Trail

Type:	Foot only
Length:	0.9 mile
Difficulty:	Moderate
Use:	Low
Condition:	Good
Highlights:	Connector trail
Book Map #:	7
USGS Topo:	Trout Dale
Connections:	Virginia Highlands Horse Trail, Appalachian Trail

This is a short connector trail that leads along the upper reaches of Raccoon Branch to the Appalachian Trail. Most trail users start on the Virginia Highlands Horse Trail, heading up 2.4 miles from Raccoon Branch campground and then using Bobbys Trail to access the AT.

Leave the Virginia Highlands Horse Trail at a sharp left turn coming from Raccoon Branch Campground and keep going forward on an old jeep road, passing a "Hiker Trail" sign. The roadbed here is fast growing up with young trees. Raccoon Branch flows off to your right. Rhododendron soon crowds the path.

At 0.2 mile, the trail leaves the wide roadbed and continues up a much narrower treadway. The path steepens and Raccoon Branch lies far below. The head of the hollow becomes very rocky. Step over the headwaters of Raccoon Branch and come to the old Raccoon Branch trail shelter site at 0.7 mile. Just past the site on the left is a stone-encased spring. Keep climbing through rocky terrain and make a short, steep climb to intersect the Appalachian Trail at 0.9 mile. To your left, it is 1.5 miles to Dickey Gap at VA 16; to your right, it is 2.5 miles to the Trimpi trail shelter.

Access

This is an interior trail. It can be reached by heading north on the AT for 1.5 miles from VA 650 at Dickeys Gap, or by heading 2.4 miles up the Virginia Highlands Horse Trail from Raccoon Creek Campground.

Comers Creek Falls Trail

Type:	Foot
Length:	0.4 mile
Difficulty:	Easy
Use:	Low
Condition:	Good
Highlights:	Large fall and numerous cascades
Book Map #:	8
USGS Topo:	Trout Dale
Connections:	Iron Mountain Trail, Appalachian Trail

This path leaves the Smyth-Grayson county line and drops down into the steep valley of Comers Creek past the Iron Mountain Trail to intersect the Appalachian Trail. To access the actual falls, hikers must continue on the AT for 0.2 mile.

Leave VA 741 and walk downstream along Comers Creek. Bridge a wet area on elevated planks. There is a field off to your left. At 0.1 mile, come to the Iron Mountain Trail, heading east across Comers Creek. Just a few feet ahead, the Iron Mountain Trail leaves west toward Hurricane Mountain. Keep going forward on the blue-blazed Comers Creek Trail, passing a campsite on your right. The stream drops steeply below the path in several small cascades and falls into a rhododendron-choked gorge.

The trail drops at a rapid pace along with the stream, curving northerly to intersect the Appalachian Trail at 0.4 mile. To access the actual Comers Creek Falls, turn right on the AT and continue another 0.1 mile to view the falls. This waterfall drops about 15 feet in a stairstep fashion to a nice pool that allows hikers to cool off in the summer.

Access

From exit 45 on I-81 near Marion, head south on VA 16 for 6.0 miles to the Jennings Visitor Center. From the Jennings Visitor Center, continue south on VA 16 for 9.4 miles to VA 741 (Homestead Road) just beyond the Smyth-Grayson county line. Turn right on Homestead Road and follow it for 0.4 mile to the Comers Creek Falls trailhead, which will be on your right just past the bridge over Comers Creek.

Comers Creek Trail

Type:	Foot, bicycle
Length:	0.7 mile
Difficulty:	Easy
Use:	Moderate

The Comers Creek Trail traces Comers Creek as it flows downstream from Hurricane Campground. The path stays directly alongside the creek for much of the way. Anglers can use this trail to fish for trout. Campers will use the path for a leg stretcher or a bicycle loop, using Comers Creek Road to complete the loop. If you are not staying in the campground, be sure to park in the gravel parking area near the campground entrance and then walk 0.3 mile down the paved campground road to access the Comers Creek Trail, which starts near campsite #20.

Start the trail by leaving the campground road, passing a hiker sign, and making your way around some stone vehicle barriers. Begin walking alongside Comers Creek to your right. Yellow birch, tulip trees, and hemlock shade the trailway. Soon cross a side stream coursing off Hurricane Knob. At 0.2 mile, pass a rock wall beside Comers Creek. Sidle up directly alongside the stream. At this point, the trailbed and creek bed merge together for the next 0.1 mile.

The path becomes arrow-straight until it is pinched in by a rocky hillside on the left. Comers Creek Road is visible across the stream. Keep descending in the north-facing hollow and come to a pole gate and the end of the trail at 0.7 mile. Just beyond the gate is Forest Road 643. Bikers can ford Comers Creek and return to the campground uphill on FR 643.

Access

From exit 45 on I-81 near Marion, drive south on VA 16 for 6.0 miles to the Jennings Visitor Center. From the visitor center, continue south on VA 16 for 8.7 miles to VA 650 (Comers Creek Road). Turn right on VA 650 and follow it for 1.4 miles to Forest Road 84 (Hurricane Campground Road). Turn left on Hurricane Campground Road and follow it a short distance to the campground entrance; then veer left, staying on FR 84 to park in the gravel lot near the campground entrance. The Comers Creek Trail starts 0.3 mile down the Hurricane Campground Road, by campsite #20. Do not park in the campground unless you are camping there.

Dickey Gap Trail

Type:	Foot only
Length:	0.4 mile
Difficulty:	Easy
Use:	Moderate

Condition:	Good
Highlights:	Connects Appalachian Trail with Hurricane Campground
Book Map #:	8
USGS Topo:	Trout Dale
Connections:	Appalachian Trail

This trail connects Hurricane Campground with Appalachian Trail. Campers use this trail in conjunction with the AT to reach Comers Creek Falls. To find the Dickey Gap trailhead from the gravel parking area on Forest Road 84, walk toward the Hurricane campground to the pavement and a stop sign. Just past this stop sign is a trail leading right, up an old woods road. Just a few feet up this trail is a sign indicating the Dickey Gap Trail.

Keep going up the old woods road, flanked with imperiled hemlocks and, in a flat, pass another trail sign giving distances to the AT. Just past the second sign, head right, uphill and still on a woods road, to step over a small rocky prong of Comers Creek. At 0.2 mile, turn sharply up the north slope of Hurricane Mountain. The ascent steepens just before intersecting the Appalachian Trail at 0.4 mile. To your right, it is 6.4 miles to Fairwood Valley and VA 603; to your left it is 1.0 mile to Comers Creek Falls.

Access

From exit 45 on I-81 near Marion, drive south on VA 16 for 6.0 miles to the Jennings Visitor Center. From the visitor center, continue south on VA 16 for 8.7 miles to VA 650 (Comers Creek Road). Turn right on VA 650 and follow it for 1.4 miles to Forest Road 84 (Hurricane Campground Road). Turn left on Hurricane Campground Road and follow it a short distance to the campground entrance; then veer left, staying on FR 84 to park in the gravel lot near the campground entrance. The Dickey Gap Trail starts near the stop sign by the campground entrance.

Dickey Knob Trail

Type:	Foot, bicycle
Length:	2.3 miles
Difficulty:	Difficult
Use:	Moderate
Condition:	Good
Highlights:	Great views from atop Dickey Knob
Book Map #:	8
USGS Topo:	Trout Dale
Connections:	Raccoon Branch Trail, Virginia Highlands Horse Trail, Raccoon Branch Nature Trail

This trail climbs 850 feet from Raccoon Branch campground to Dickey Knob. The trail grade has been moderated for the most part, but the elevation gain is nearly continuous. Though the trail is open to mountain bikers, they will have a tough time making this haul. It is recommended for hikers only and is a popular walk for campers at Raccoon Branch campground.

The trail technically starts at the Raccoon Branch campground, but parking there is for campers only. If you are not camping there, use the Virginia Highlands Horse Trail trailhead on VA 16 and follow the VHHT a short distance across VA 16 to the campground; then walk the campground loop until arriving at the gravel trail between campsite numbers 4 and 6, near a water spigot.

Leave the campground and take the gravel path upstream just a short distance to span Dickey Creek on a plank bridge that is mossy and potentially slick. Walk the planks and then shortly come to a trail junction. Turn right here and follow a portion of the Raccoon Branch Nature Trail past the mouth of Raccoon Branch. Cross Raccoon Branch on a wide bridge. At 0.2 mile, come to a second junction. The Dickey Knob Trail veers right, uphill. Swing into the hollow of a small prong of Raccoon Branch. At 0.4 mile, cross the prong on a little wooden bridge. At 0.7 mile, make a sharp switchback to the right and keep ascending to a piney flat. Veer sharply left here and ascend to a second flat. Turn left again, passing through a cool rhododendron tunnel to cross a second stream at mile 1.4. Keep climbing and gain partial views of Straight Mountain to your right. Up here are nearly pure stands of gnarly Table Mountain pines. Make a sharp switchback to the left and ascend to a grassy gap. Here, an old road comes up from Rye Valley. It connected the valley with an old fire tower that once stood atop Dickey Knob. Cross this old road and ascend the north side of Dickey Ridge. At mile 2.2, come to the eastern edge of Dickey Knob and a cleared overlook. The drop-off here is precipitous. To your left, the village of Sugar Grove is below with Brushy Mountain beyond. Ahead are Brushy Butt, Green Ridge, and Straight Mountain. The Dickey Knob Trail keeps winding around the mountaintop to intersect the fire tower access road again at mile 2.3. Just a few feet to your right, the road leads to the former tower site at 3,649 feet. The tower foundations are still in place, and there is a survey marker embedded in one of the concrete tower supports.

Access

From exit 45 on I-81 near Marion, drive south on VA 16 for 6.0 miles to Jennings Visitor Center. From here, continue south on VA 16 for 5.8 miles to the Dickey Knob and Virginia Highlands Horse Trail trailhead, on the left of VA 16, 0.1 mile beyond the Raccoon Branch Campground.

Fairwood Valley Trail

Type: Foot, horse
Length: 1.8 miles
Difficulty: Easy
Use: Moderate
Condition: Good
Highlights: Views, connects Iron Mountain trails to high country trails
Book Map #:   8, 4
USGS Topo: Trout Dale, Whitetop Mountain
Connections: Mount Rogers Trail, Flat Top Trail, Lewis Fork Trail, Old Orchard Trail, Appalachian Trail, Virginia Highlands Horse Trail

This trail is an important connector trail for the entire Fairwood Valley area. It is a bridge between the trails of the Iron Mountains and the high country. The trail leaves a gap at the west end of Fox Creek and heads east down the Fairwood Valley, passing numerous other trails and a field where there are great views of Pine Mountain. Continue through the woods to end at the far side of Fox Creek Horse Camp and the Virginia Highlands Horse Trail.

Leave the parking area and head downhill, passing a vehicle-barrier post. The path is graveled. Undulate along the hillside of Hurricane Mountain to the left. Swing near a small stream and continue descending to cross Fox Creek at 0.7 mile. Pass through a gate and enter a field. From the field there are excellent views of Pine Mountain across VA 603. Bisect a maple grove and reenter the woods, going through a second gate to intersect the Lewis Fork Trail at 1.0 mile. It leaves right 5.5 miles to reach the crest of Pine Mountain. Continue through rich woods and ford Lewis Fork. Intersect the Old Orchard Trail at 1.3 miles. It leaves right 1.7 miles to intersect the Lewis Fork Trail. Pass alongside VA 603; then intersect the Appalachian Trail at 1.6 miles. It leaves right to cross VA 603 and reach Scales in 4.9 miles and left to reach Dickey Gap in 8.5 miles.

Keep going forward on the Fairwood Valley Trail and soon come to Fox Creek Horse Camp. Head through the center of the camp and come to gravel-surfaced VA 741 at mile 1.8. The Fairwood Valley Trail ends here. VA 741 here is also the Virginia Highlands Horse Trail. It leaves right to cross Fairwood Road and head 12.9 miles to reach Elk Garden. It leaves left and follows VA 741 for 1.0 mile and reenters the woods to intersect the Iron Mountain Trail at 2.5 miles.

Access

Eastern Access: From exit 45 on I-81 near Marion, drive 6.0 miles south on VA 16, passing the Jennings Visitor Center. Continue on VA 16 for 11.0 miles to VA 603 (Fairwood Road) in Troutdale. Turn right on VA 603 and follow it for 4.0 miles to the Fox Creek Campground, which will be on your right. The Fairwood Valley Trail starts on the far end of the campground from the campground entrance.

Western Access: Follow the above directions, except continue 1.6 miles past Fox Creek Horse Camp to the trailhead, which is on the right just before the Grayson-Smyth county line. The Fairwood Valley Trail leaves right from the parking area.

Flat Top Trail

Type:	Foot, horse, bicycle
Length:	1.7 miles
Difficulty:	Moderate
Use:	Low
Condition:	Good
Highlights:	Trail shelter, connects Iron Mountain Trail to high country trails
Book Map #:	4
USGS Topo:	Trout Dale, Whitetop Mountain
Connections:	Iron Mountain Trail, Fairwood Valley Trail, Mount Rogers Trail

This path connects Fairwood Valley and the Mount Rogers high country to the Iron Mountain Trail. Trail enthusiasts use the Flat Top Trail in conjunction with the Iron Mountain Trail and the Fairwood Valley Trail to make a rewarding loop. The Flat Top Trail leaves Flat Top, near the 4,400 foot Cherry Tree trail shelter, and descends along a rib ridge down to the Fairwood Valley, crossing Forest Road 828 a couple of times on the way down.

Leave the grassy area by the Cherry Tree shelter and the Iron Mountain Trail; then follow the blue blazes down a closed forest service road. Reach a pole gate and FR 828 at 0.3 mile. Follow FR 828 past a roadside flat with campsites. Ascend on the road away from the campsites to leave the road right, uphill, back into the woods, at 0.5 mile, passing a metal vehicle-barrier post. Come alongside a wildlife clearing and resume the descent, intersecting FR 828 again at 0.8 mile. Follow the road a short distance and look left for the trail leaving left into the woods, departing FR 828 for good. There is much more rhododendron in this part of the woods. Swing around the head of a hollow and keep descending. Near a fence, look right to a clearing downhill. Make your way through a mucky section of trail before coming to the Fairwood Valley Trail at mile 1.7. Just beyond here is the end of the Flat Top Trail and the lower trailhead. From this trailhead, the Fairwood Valley Trail leaves left for 1.8 miles to Fox Creek Horse Camp and many trail junctions. The Mount Rogers Trail leaves across the road and heads 4.0 miles onto the slope of Mount Rogers.

Access

Upper Access: The upper access can be reached by walking 0.3 mile of the Iron Mountain Trail from Forest Road 828. From exit 45 on I-81 near Marion, drive 6.0 miles south on VA 16, passing the Jennings Visitor Center. Continue on VA 16 for 11.0 miles to VA 603 (Fairwood Valley Road) in Troutdale. Turn right on VA 603 and follow it for 6.4 miles to Forest Road 828. Turn right on FR 828 and follow it 1.8 miles to the junction with the Iron Mountain Trail on the left-hand side of the road, 0.1 mile beyond the right-hand junction with the IMT. Follow the IMT west into the woods for 0.3 mile to reach Cherry Tree shelter. The Flat Top Trail starts in the grassy area near the shelter.

Lower Access: From exit 45 on I-81 near Marion, drive 6.0 miles south on VA 16, passing the Jennings Visitor Center. Stay on VA 16 for 11.0 more miles to VA 603 (Fairwood Road) in Troutdale. Turn right on VA 603 and follow it for 5.6 miles to the trailhead, on the right just before the Grayson-Smyth county line. The Flat Top Trail leaves uphill from the parking area.

Hickory Ridge Trail

Type:	Foot, bicycle
Length:	0.7 mile
Difficulty:	Difficult
Use:	Low
Condition:	Fair
Highlights:	Potential loop trail with AT
Book Map #:	8
USGS Topo:	Trout Dale
Connections:	Appalachian Trail, Virginia Highlands Horse Trail

This path is connected to the Appalachian Trail on both ends. It leaves the AT very near Comers Creek Road to climb straight up and over Hickory Ridge, reuniting with the AT in a gap between Hickory Ridge and Bobbys Ridge. Just below this junction, the AT intersects the Virginia Highlands Horse Trail. The Hickory Ridge Trail can be used in combination with the AT for a short loop hike.

Leave Comers Creek Road on the AT and make a slight ascent, coming to a trail register. To your left, the Hickory Ridge Trail leads uphill and passes a trail sign to climb up the nose of Hickory Ridge in a hickory-oak-pine forest. Rise nearly 300 feet in 0.3 mile, where the trail levels off and then skirts the left side of a high point. Keep going north and drop steeply to intersect the Appalachian Trail at 0.7 mile. From here it is 0.8 mile back to the origin of the Hickory Ridge Trail. Just a few feet farther down in the gap, come to the Virginia Highlands Horse Trail. From here on the VHHT, it is 4.4 miles right to VA 16 and Raccoon Branch campground. To your left, it is 2.0 miles to Comers Creek Road on the VHHT.

Access

From exit 45 on I-81 in Marion, drive south on VA 16 for 6.0 miles to the Jennings Visitor Center. Continue south on VA 16 for 8.7 miles beyond the Visitor Center to VA 650 (Comers Creek Road). Turn right on Comers Creek Road and follow it just a short distance to the Appalachian Trail, on the right. Follow the AT north 100 feet to intersect the Hickory Ridge Trail, leaving left.

Hurricane Creek Trail

Type:	Foot only
Length:	0.4 mile
Difficulty:	Easy
Use:	Light
Condition:	Good
Highlights:	Connects Hurricane Creek and Barton Gap Trail with the Appalachian Trail
Book Map #:	4
USGS Topo:	Whitetop Mountain
Connections:	Appalachian Trail, Barton Gap Trail

This is a short connector path that links Forest Road 84 and the Barton Gap Trail with the AT. It is not signed on either end. The path traces a closed forest road up the north slope of Hurricane Mountain. The closest it gets to Hurricane Creek is at its beginning, which is on the far side of the forest road from the trailhead. On the far side of Hurricane Creek is the Barton Gap Trail.

Leave Forest Road 84 and make your way around the vehicle-blocking boulders. Ascend southeasterly up the side of Hurricane Mountain in a deciduous forest. There are winter views of Seng Mountain and Bear Ridge. At 0.2 mile, the trail steepens as it ascends a more sloped section of mountainside. After an overall gain of 240 feet, intersect the Appalachian Trail, at 3,440 feet, on a sharp curve. To your left, north, it is 4.6 miles to Dickey Gap. To your right, south, it is 3.9 miles to Fairwood Valley.

Access

From the Jennings Visitor Center, head south on VA 16 for 8.7 miles to VA 650 (Comers Creek Road). Turn right on VA 650 and follow it for 1.4 miles to Forest Road 84 (Hurricane Campground Road). Turn left on FR 84 and follow it 2.2 miles to the Hurricane Creek Trail, which will be on your left just beyond a grassy clearing on the left side of the road. The trail is marked with a hiker sign beside a stone vehicle barrier.

Hurricane Knob Trail

Type:	Foot only
Length:	1.1 miles
Difficulty:	Moderate
Use:	Moderate
Condition:	Good
Highlights:	Intimate views of Hurricane Creek, some views of Hurricane Mountain
Book Map #:	8
USGS Topo:	Trout Dale, Whitetop Mountain
Connections:	None

This trail makes a nice loop from Hurricane Campground. It heads up Hurricane Creek to leave the stream and climb up to Hurricane Knob. From the knob, the trail drops back down through an attractive pine flat to emerge near where it started. The primary users of this trail are campers.

Leave the campground near the bathhouse and begin heading upstream in the valley of Hurricane Creek, passing a sign indicating this as the Hurricane Knob Trail. There is a steep hillside to your right. Shortly come alongside the attractive, cascading stream to a bridge. Span Hurricane Creek and continue upstream. Sheer bluffs lie across the watercourse. Small rivulets flowing off Hurricane Mountain bisect the trail.

Turn away from the creek and pick up an old roadbed, continuing upstream. At 0.4 mile, leave the old roadbed and dive right, spanning Hurricane Creek on a foot-bridge. Begin to walk uphill toward Hurricane Knob, switchbacking to gain altitude on the steep mountainside. There are obscured views of Hurricane Mountain across the valley. Level off at 0.7 mile and pass through a small gap to start descending via a pair of switchbacks. Enter a shady white pine grove and make one more switchback before returning to the campground at 1.1 miles. The origin for the Hurricane Knob Trail is 150 feet to your right across the grassy clearing. Note that the sign for the trail terminus states, "Hurricane Knob Nature Trail."

Access

From exit 45 on I-81 near Marion, drive south on VA 16 for 6.0 miles to the Jennings Visitor Center. From the visitor center, continue south on VA 16 for 8.7 miles to VA 650 (Comers Creek Road). Turn right on VA 650 and follow it for 1.4 miles to Forest Road 84 (Hurricane Campground Road). Turn left on Hurricane Campground Road and follow it a short distance to the campground entrance; then veer left, staying on FR 84 to park in the gravel lot near the campground entrance. The Hurricane Knob Trail starts near the bathhouse by campsite #3 inside

Hurricane Campground, but hikers should park outside the campground if they are not camping there.

Hurricane Mountain Trail

Type:	Foot
Length:	0.4 mile
Difficulty:	Easy
Use:	Low
Condition:	Good
Highlights:	Connects Appalachian Trail and Iron Mountain Trail
Book Map #:	4
USGS Topo:	Whitetop Mountain
Connections:	Iron Mountain Trail, Appalachian Trail

This is a short connector trail that links the Iron Mountain Trail with the Appalachian Trail. From the Iron Mountain Trail, leave a gap in Hurricane Mountain and descend along an old road. Level off and climb a bit, coming to a wide flat area at 0.2 mile. From here, descend toward a saddle with a knob dead ahead. The trail levels off in the saddle, where there is a campsite. Stay to the left in the saddle and intersect the AT at 0.4 mile. To the right of the saddle, there is a spring downhill beyond a grove of pines. On the AT, it is 1.5 miles right to Fairwood Valley and 7.0 miles left to Dickey Gap.

Access

This is an interior trail that connects the Appalachian Trail to the Iron Mountain Trail. It can be reached by hiking the Iron Mountain Trail east from Forest Road 828 for 1.0 mile to the Hurricane Mountain Trail. It is marked with blue blazes and a "No Horses" sign. It is not signed but marked with blue blazes at its junction with the AT.

Jerry's Creek Trail

Type:	Foot, horse, bicycle
Length:	4.1 miles
Difficulty:	Moderate
Use:	Low to moderate
Condition:	Good
Highlights:	Good loop with Rowland Creek and Old 84 Trail
Book Map #:	4
USGS Topo:	Whitetop Mountain
Connections:	Rowland Creek Trail, Old 84 Trail

This trail is steep and narrow at first; it then picks up an old forest road and cruises the lowlands. It is one part of a good loop, in conjunction with the Rowland Creek and Old 84 trails. The Jerry's Creek Trail drops off a ridgeline near Round Top to the narrow valley of Jerry's Creek. It then crosses Jerry's Creek and heads east along the lower northern reaches of Chestnut Ridge to swing around Bald Knob and make a final drop into the Rowland Creek Valley.

Start the upper end of the Jerry's Creek Trail by leaving Forest Road 84 on the Old 84 Trail and walking a few feet past a wildlife clearing to the Jerry's Creek Trail. A sign erroneously states the distance to Forest Road 643 to be 5.5 miles. It is actually 4.1 miles. Walk away from the wildlife clearing on an old woods road. Descend into a pine-oak woodland. The path quickly narrows to pass a rocky rill at 0.3 mile. Jerry's Creek is audible to the right. Drop down alongside Jerry's Creek at 1.0 mile and briefly pick up an old railroad grade. Stay a fair distance above the creek on a rocky path. The valley is full of straight tulip trees. Cross Jerry's Creek at mile 1.4. An unmaintained path leads downstream three quarters of a mile to dead-end at private property.

Pick up an old road leading easterly. A young spindly forest lies down the slope. Pass a large wildlife clearing at mile 1.6 and soon bridge Cold Branch. Stay along the lower end of Chestnut Ridge to bridge Long Branch at mile 2.3. Ascend away from Long Branch to loop around now-forested Bald Knob. Top out on a high point at mile 2.9 and begin to wind down toward Rowland Creek. Swing alongside a feeder stream of Rowland Creek at mile 3.6. Pass a sign indicating Jerry's Creek Trail at mile 4.1; then swing around a pole gate to end the Jerry's Creek Trail. To complete the loop with the Rowland Creek Trail, continue 0.1 mile farther to Forest Road 643 and, once on FR 643, turn right and head 0.1 mile to intersect the Rowland Creek Trail.

Access

Upper Access: From the Little Red Caboose in Damascus, drive east on US 58 for 11.0 miles to Virginia 603 (Fairwood Road). Keep driving forward on VA 603 (US 58 curves right) and follow it for 2.7 miles to VA 600 (Whitetop Road). Continue forward on VA 600; VA 603 leaves right in 0.1 mile. (VA 603 and VA 600 coincide for 0.1 mile.) Keep following VA 600 for 2.6 miles to Forest Road 84. Turn right on FR 84 and follow it 1.1 miles to a gravel road on your left leading downhill. This is the Old 84 Trail. Walk just a few feet on the Old 84 Trail to intersect the Jerry's Creek Trail, leaving left.

Lower Access: From exit 45 on I-81 near Marion, head south on VA 16 for 6.0 miles, passing the Jennings Visitor Center. From the Jennings Visitor Center, head south on VA 16 for 3.5 miles to Sugar Grove and VA 601 (Teas Road). Turn right on Teas Road and follow it for 3.4 miles to Teas. Here, stay left as the main road turns into VA 670 and then VA 650. Stay on 650 for 1.7 miles beyond the left turn to Comers Creek Road; then turn left onto VA 656 (Stoney Battery Road). Follow

VA 656 for 1.7 miles to VA 668 (Rowland Creek Lane). Turn left on VA 668 and continue on it for 0.7 mile to pass an "End State Maintenance" sign; enter national forest property, now on Forest Road 643. Look for the first gravel road in national forest land and drive 0.1 mile up the gravel road to a pole gate and the Jerry's Creek Trail.

Little Laurel Trail

Type:	Foot only
Length:	1.0 mile
Difficulty:	Easy
Use:	Very low
Condition:	Good to fair
Highlights:	Solitude, spring wildflowers, angler's path
Book Map #:	4
USGS Topo:	Whitetop Mountain
Connections:	Iron Mountain Trail

This is an old trail that follows an older railroad grade from Cherry Tree Camp, high in the Iron Mountains, down the headwaters of Little Laurel Creek. It then peters out, offering solitude and high-country brook trout fishing. A very attractive northern hardwood forest of yellow birch, beech, sugar maple, and cherry, complemented with groves of imperiled hemlock, offer year-round beauty, while masses of wildflowers make the Little Laurel Trail a spring attraction from mid-April to mid-May. You may see one of North America's strangest wildflowers, Indian ghost pipe. This white plant, with a flower-like end, has no chlorophyll and resembles the white clay pipes used by Indians for smoking tobacco. It can be seen in summer in the Mount Rogers Area. Ghost pipe obtains its nutrients from other plants in a complex relationship with fungi that is not completely understood. Do not pick the ghost pipe—not that you would want it for a bouquet—because its flesh soon blackens when cut or even bruised and oozes a clear, gelatinous substance. Its natural white color and tendency to "melt" on picking also gives it the moniker "ice plant."

Leave Forest Road 84, along which the Iron Mountain Trail travels, and walk into the grassy clearing at Cherry Tree Camp; look right, west, for an old railbed leading downhill. Walk just a few feet before passing an old sign that says, "Little Laurel Creek 0.3 mile." Descend into a northern hardwood forest and come to a wildlife clearing on your right at 0.2 mile. A spring in the clearing marks the headwaters of Little Laurel Creek. At 0.3 mile drop to the right off the railroad grade down to another railroad grade. Keep heading downhill, stepping over seeps flowing off Graves Mountain to your left. Notice the irregular dips in the trail where the rail ties once were.

Little Laurel Creek falls steeply to your right. Small trees dot the old railbed. Irregular maintenance of this trail makes a few blown-down trees inevitable. Finally, at 1.0 mile, the old railbed peters out. Off to your right, Little Laurel Creek lies far down the hollow. Adventurous hikers might want to walk to the stream and return upstream along the watercourse, looking for wildflowers and small cascades.

Access

From the Little Red Caboose in Damascus, drive east on US 58 for 11.0 miles to Virginia 603 (Fairwood Road). Keep going forward on VA 603 (US 58 curves right) and follow it for 2.7 miles to VA 600 (Whitetop Road). Continue forward on VA 600, and VA 603 leaves right in 0.1 mile. (VA 603 and VA 600 coincide for 0.1 mile.) Keep going forward on VA 600 and follow it for 2.6 miles to Forest Road 84. Turn right on FR 84 and follow it 3.0 miles to a gap and a wildlife clearing on the right. The Little Laurel Trail starts on the right-hand side of the clearing as you face it from the road.

Mullins Branch Trail

Type:	Foot only
Length:	2.9 miles
Difficulty:	Difficult
Use:	Very low
Condition:	Fair to poor
Highlights:	Solitude, old homesite
Book Map #:	7
USGS Topo:	Trout Dale, Atkins
Connections:	Appalachian Trail

This trail was once in much better shape and is ultimately slated for rehabilitation. Until then, however, it will be challenging, with numerous blown-down trees and rhododendron and mountain laurel pinching in the pathway. The path leaves Rye Valley, passes through an old farmstead, and then enters the woods, only to pass another farmstead. It later leaves Mullins Branch valley to ascend the north slope of Dickey Ridge via switchbacks to intersect the Appalachian Trail.

Start the Mullins Branch Trail by leaving gravel-surfaced VA 673 and work your way around a gate to enter pastureland on a farm road. Pass a cinder-block barn on your left and drop down to cross Mullins Branch at 0.1 mile. You may have to step over a wire fence here. Continue up the old woods road. In times of high flow, this part of the roadbed may also be a creekbed. Keep heading upstream to cross Mullins Branch again at 0.2 mile. The trail is flanked with rhododendron. At 0.4 mile, come to an obvious split in the trail. To your left, a pathway soon fords Mullins

Branch and leads to the old Henry Rich homesite. The Mullins Branch Trail, however, continues forward through a forest of maple, birch, and northern red oak.

Stay alongside the stream to step over it at 0.8 mile. Span the stream again at 1.0 and 1.2 miles. Beyond this last crossing, the valley opens up and the trail briefly evades Mullins Branch. Make one more stream crossing as the valley narrows at mile 1.4. You are now on the right-hand side of Mullins Branch. Begin to look for a decrepit footbridge leading left across Mullins Branch. Turn left here and trace a roadbed through thick rhododendron. The old roadbed continues forward up Mullins Branch to peter out below High Point.

The foot trail now leaves the creek and begins a wide easterly climb up Dickeys Ridge. Make a sharp switchback to the right at 1.9 miles. Keep rising through moist coves and thickets of rhododendron and mountain laurel to arrive at the Appalachian Trail at 2.9 miles as the AT makes a sharp curve. This is the end of the Mullins Branch Trail. To your left, the AT leads uphill 0.9 mile to Bobbys Trail. To your right, it is 1.7 miles to Trimpi shelter on the AT.

Access

From exit 45 on I-81 in Marion, head south on VA 16 and follow it for 6.0 miles to Jennings Visitor Center. Stay on VA 16 past the visitor center for 3.3 miles to VA 601 (Teas Road) in Sugar Grove. Turn right on VA 601 and follow it for 2.4 miles to VA 672 (Slab Town Road). Turn left on Slab Town Road and follow it for 1.0 mile to VA 673. (Just beyond the turn to 673, Slab Town Road turns to gravel. If you reach gravel, you have gone too far.) Turn left on VA 673 and follow it for 0.5 mile to a dead end. The Mullins Branch Trail starts at the gate at the end of VA 673.

Old 84 Trail

Type:	Foot, horse, bicycle
Length:	4.6 miles
Difficulty:	Easy to moderate
Use:	Low to moderate
Condition:	Good
Highlights:	Good loop with Rowland Creek and Jerry's Creek trails, occasional views
Book Map #:	4
USGS Topo:	Whitetop Mountain
Connections:	Rowland Creek Trail, Jerry's Creek Trail

This trail traces an old forest road on the northern side of Double Top and Round Top through a rich deciduous forest. It has little elevation variance from the 3,900-foot level as it swings into hollows and occasionally passes wildlife clearings on its way to meet Jerry's Creek Trail, which, along with the Rowland Creek Trail, makes for a good loop.

Leave the Rowland Creek Trail and head westerly, away from Hurricane Gap on the Old 84 Trail. A single-track path is overlain on the old road. Open into a grassy area at 0.1 mile. At 0.5 mile, pass a rocky stream. Beyond here are obscured views to the north. Pass over an earthen vehicle barrier at 0.8 mile; then look left for a wildlife clearing. Up here, around 4,000 feet, are both black cherry and pin cherry trees.

At mile 1.4, bridge the highest feeder stream of Rowland Creek. The trail then turns northeasterly. At mile 1.7, on the crest of a side ridge, an unmaintained trail leads left, uphill a half mile, to Cherry Log Camp, a gap between Double Top and Grave Mountain. A very rough unmaintained trail leads right, down to Rowland Creek. Continue forward on the roadbed. Weave around Doubletop to pass a very large wildlife clearing and then generally descend, reaching a gap between Round Top and Chestnut Ridge at mile 2.9.

Make a moderate climb out of the gap and begin to swing around the numerous headwaters of Jerry's Creek, which are bridged via culverts. Look for old logging trails leading very steeply uphill. None of these will be confused with the Old 84 Trail. Ascend up to a clearing and a trail junction at mile 4.6. To the right, the Jerry's Creek Trail leads 4.1 miles to Forest Road 643. The Old 84 Trail continues a few feet beyond the clearing to pass around a pole gate and intersect the current Forest Road 84.

Access

Western Access: From the Little Red Caboose in Damascus, drive east on US 58 for 11.0 miles to Virginia 603 (Fairwood Road). Keep driving forward on VA 603 (US 58 curves right) and follow it for 2.7 miles to VA 600 (Whitetop Road). Continue forward on VA 600, and VA 603 leaves right in 0.1 mile. (VA 603 and VA 600 coincide for 0.1 mile.) Keep going forward on VA 600 and follow it for 2.6 miles to Forest Road 84. Turn right on FR 84 and follow it 1.1 miles to a gravel road on your left leading downhill. This is the Old 84 Trail.

Eastern Access: From exit 45 on I-81 near Marion, drive south on VA 16 for 6.0 miles to the Jennings Visitor Center. From the visitor center, keep heading south on VA 16 for 8.7 miles to VA 650 (Comers Creek Road). Turn right on VA 650 and follow it for 1.4 miles to Forest Road 84 (Hurricane Campground Road). Turn left on Hurricane Campground Road and follow it a short distance to the campground entrance and then veer left, staying on FR 84 for 4.1 miles. The east end of the trail starts 0.1 mile down the upper Rowland Creek trail off FR 84.

Raccoon Branch Nature Trail

Type:	Foot, bicycle
Length:	0.2 mile
Difficulty:	Easy

Use:	Moderate
Condition:	Very good
Highlights:	Creek valley, tree identification signs
Book Map #:	7
USGS Topo:	Trout Dale
Connections:	Dickey Knob Trail

This short path traverses the valley where Dickey Creek and Raccoon Branch meet. Despite its short length, it is worth the time and is walked by almost all who stay at Raccoon Branch Campground. Leave the campground and bridge Dickey Creek on a wooden-plank span; then come to a trail junction. Take the left fork and walk beneath a tall forest of white pine with a smaller understory trees of maple and birch. Ascend a small hill and near the Virginia Highlands Horse Trail, off to the left. The official trailhead of the VHHT is across the road from Raccoon Branch Campground. The Raccoon Branch Trail, however, drops down to cross Raccoon Branch on a short bridge. Begin returning downstream. The Dickey Knob Trail leaves left to ascend to a view on Dickey Knob. Cross Raccoon Branch once more on a plank bridge. Look for a side path leading to the confluence of Dickey Creek and Raccoon Branch. Complete the loop and retrace the trail back to the campground.

Access

From exit 45 on I-81 in Marion, head south on VA 16 for 6.0 miles, passing the Jennings Visitor Center. Raccoon Branch Campground is 5.7 miles beyond the visitor center on VA 16 on the right. The Raccoon Branch Nature Trail starts between campsites 5 and 6.

Rowland Creek Trail

Type:	Foot, horse, bicycle
Length:	3.2 miles
Difficulty:	Moderate
Use:	Low to moderate
Condition:	Good
Highlights:	Waterfall, good loop with Old 84 and Jerry's Creek trails
Book Map #:	4
USGS Topo:	Whitetop Mountain
Connections:	Old 84 Trail, Jerry's Creek Trail

This is one of the prettiest trails in the recreation area. The trail starts out in the wide lower valley of Rowland Creek, which becomes pinched in by rocky Chestnut

Rowland Creek Falls.

Ridge. It then steepens and comes to Rowland Creek Falls, a 150-foot stairstep cascade. The trail climbs the side of Seng Mountain before topping out near Hurricane Gap. There are numerous good camping spots along the way.

Start the trail by following the orange blazes away from Forest Road 643. Walk just a few feet before veering left onto an old woods road, upstream. Rowland Creek is off to the right. Continue heading up the wide flat and cross Rowland Creek at 0.3 mile. By 0.7 mile the hollow has narrowed. The large, mossy outcrops of Chestnut Ridge add a scenic touch to the valley. At mile 1.1, cross Rowland Creek again; then make two sharp switchbacks, again heading upstream, now on a single-track trail. Swing around a side hollow and return to the Rowland Creek valley, now on a precipitous ledge. Look for a side trail leading right, down to Rowland Creek Falls at mile 1.5. Rowland Creek Falls will be seen and heard from the main trail. Numerous rock ledges lend a stairstep effect to the falls. Be careful, as this side trail ends at the upper end of the tall falls.

The Rowland Creek Trail continues climbing, crossing the stream at 1.8, 2.0, and 2.1 miles. Pass an attractive grassy clearing on the right and bridge Rowland Creek via culvert. Beyond this clearing, the trail widens and steepens. Make a sharp switchback at mile 2.4 in a maple-oak woodland with mountain laurel understory. At mile 3.0, pass a trail sign indicating the Rowland Creek Trail. Pass around a pole gate and a wide muddy area near Hurricane Gap. Stay right, tracing the orange blazes, in this confusing area of old roads. At mile 3.1, intersect the Old 84 Trail, which leaves right around a dirt vehicle barrier. The Rowland Creek Trail continues forward and makes a sharp left to pass a second pole gate and intersect the current Forest Road 84 at mile 3.2.

Access

Lower access: From exit 45 on I-81 near Marion, head south on VA 16 for 6.0 miles, passing the Jennings Visitor Center. From the Jennings Visitor Center head south on VA 16 for 3.5 miles to Sugar Grove and VA 601 (Teas Road). Turn right on Teas Road and follow it for 3.4 miles to Teas. Here, stay left as the main road turns into VA 670, then VA 650. Remain on VA 650 for 1.7 miles beyond the left turn to Comers Creek Road; then turn left onto VA 656 (Stoney Battery Road). Follow VA 656 for 1.7 miles to VA 668 (Rowland Creek Lane). Turn left on VA 668 and continue on it for 0.7 mile to pass an "End State Maintenance" sign and enter national forest property, now on Forest Road 643. Continue forward for 0.1 mile farther and look for the orange blazes leading into the woods to the right.

Upper Access: From exit 45 on I-81 near Marion, drive south on VA 16 for 6.0 miles to the Jennings Visitor Center. From the visitor center, continue south on VA 16 for 8.7 miles to VA 650 (Comers Creek Road). Turn right on VA 650 and follow it for 1.4 miles to Forest Road 84 (Hurricane Campground Road). Turn left on Hurricane Campground Road and follow it a short distance to the campground entrance; then veer left, staying on FR 84 for 4.1 miles. The signed Rowland Creek Trail starts on the right-hand side of the road.

Slabtown Trail

Type:	Foot only
Length:	2.1 miles
Difficulty:	Moderate
Use:	Low
Condition:	Good
Highlights:	Potential loop hike with AT
Book Map #:	7
USGS Topo:	Atkins, Trout Dale
Connections:	Appalachian Trail

This trail tracks the old route of the Appalachian Trail from the South Fork Holston River to the Trimpi trail shelter. It leads past an old homesite on the Holston and then climbs to a gap. From there it drops down to Slabtown Valley, only to climb again on a series of old woods roads and through former strip-mining lands to once again intersect the AT near the Trimpi shelter. This former route of the AT, in com-bination with the new route of the AT, makes for a rewarding 4.1-mile loop hike.

To reach the Slabtown Trail, bridge the long wooden span over South Fork Holston River on the Appalachian Trail. Continue past the homesite foundation on your left and come to a grove of white pines. The Slabtown Trail leads left through the pine grove and into an area of scattered trees. Reenter thick woods on a narrow footpath and soon make a switchback to the right, heading up the valley of a spring branch of the Holston. The blue-blazed path clambers steeply through beech, birch, and Fraser magnolia. The trail grade moderates and then picks up a woods road leading left at 0.5 mile. This roadbed soon gives way to another woods road leading right. Stay on this rhododendron-flanked path to level out on a ridgeline at 0.8 mile, where an unmaintained trail leads right. Stay left on the Slabtown Trail and gently gravitate to the Slabtown valley, which is reached at 1.1 miles.

Now cross gravel-surfaced VA 672 (Slab Town Road) and pass through a fence-type stile to enter an open pasture. Head directly away from the road toward a metal stake painted blue on top. Veer right at this stake, walking uphill toward another stake and then reentering the woods. Keep heading uphill to pass by a homesite on your left and come to another pasture. At mile 1.4, walk over a fence stile and trace the blue blazes on a series of woods roads that ultimately lead uphill to make a sharp switchback to the right. Come along a fence line and tunnel through piney woods, which are post-strip-mining plantations. Dip down into a hollow; then swing around a knob to a trail junction at 2.1 miles. To your left, it is 0.1 mile downhill to the Trimpi shelter and a spring. Dead ahead, it is 2.5 miles on the AT to Bobbys Trail. To your right on the AT, it is 2.0 miles back to the beginning of the Slabtown Trail and the Holston River bridge.

Access

From exit 45 on I-81 near Marion, head east on VA 16 for 9.5 miles to VA 601 (Teas Road) in Sugar Grove. Turn right on 601 and follow it 3.4 miles to Teas. Stay left as the main road turns into VA 670 (South Fork Road). Stay on South Fork Road for 1.6 additional miles to the marked crossing of the Appalachian Trail. The Slabtown Trail starts just across the bridge and beyond the old homesite on the far side of the South Fork Holston River.

Two Ponds Nature Trail

Type:	Foot only
Length:	0.5 mile
Difficulty:	Easy
Use:	Heavy
Condition:	Good
Highlights:	Interpretive forest-recovery information
Book Map #:	6
USGS Topo:	Atkins
Connections:	None

This is a short nature trail that drops down from the Jennings Visitor Center to circle by a few small ponds that were part of a reclamation effort following the manganese mining that went on during World War II. Along the way are numbered posts, which, with the accompanying handout from the visitor center, will enlighten walkers about natural aspects of the area. There are actually three ponds along the way, not two, but what's in a name?

Drop away from the visitor center on a gravel path and come to a junction. Stay right, now on a loop, and swing around the head of a hollow. Drop down and pick up an old road that leads down to the largest pond. Cross the dam of the pond and stay left. Descend past two more ponds before climbing back toward the parking area via a series of switchbacks. Come to the original trail junction and turn right, retracing your steps a few feet to the visitor center.

Access

From exit 45 on I-81 at Marion, drive east on VA 16 for 6.0 miles to the Jennings Visitor Center. The Two Ponds Nature Trail starts in the back of the building at the visitor parking area.

Far East Trails

Comers Rock Trail

Type:	Foot only
Length:	0.4 mile
Difficulty:	Moderate
Use:	Moderate
Condition:	Good
Highlights:	Great views from atop Comers Rock
Book Map #:	11
USGS Topo:	Speedwell
Connections:	Iron Mountain Trail, Little Dry Run Trail

This path leads from near Comers Rock Campground up to its namesake, Comers Rock. It starts at a trail junction very near the campground to ascend a knob and then picks up the access road to Comers Rock. It soon leaves the road and ascends a series of well-placed stone steps that reach an outcrop, where there is a viewing platform.

From Comers Rock campground, look for the sign near the campground restroom that states, "Iron Mountain Trail." Walk this path just a short distance to a trail junction. At the junction, look acutely left for the Comers Rock Trail, which leads uphill. Take this footpath up through a deciduous woodland dominated by red oak. Parallel the Iron Mountain Trail, which lies downhill to the right; then head up the east side of the knob upon which Comers Rock sits.

At 0.2 mile, emerge onto the access road for Comers Rock. Keep heading uphill on the road and come to an auto loop. Look for stone steps at the top of the loop and begin to walk up the base of Comers Rock. These heavy, elaborate stones make climbing the rock easier but not less steep. Make two switchbacks before cresting out on Comers Rock at 0.4 mile. A viewing platform has been built here. The best views are to the south toward Point Lookout into Grayson County.

Comers Rock offers first-rate views.

Access

From exit 70 on I-81 near Wytheville, drive south on US 21 for 17.8 miles to Forest Road 57, passing through Speedwell. Turn right on FR 57 and follow it for 3.6 miles to Comers Rock Recreation Area. Look for a sign indicating the Iron Mountain Trail near the campground restroom. Head up this path a short distance to a trail junction. The Comers Rock Trail leads sharply left, uphill, from this junction.

Divide Trail

Type:	Foot, horse, bicycle
Length:	0.7 mile
Difficulty:	Difficult
Use:	Moderate
Condition:	Fair
Highlights:	Quick access to Iron Mountain Trail
Book Map #:	13
USGS Topo:	Speedwell
Connections:	Virginia Highlands Horse Trail, Iron Mountain Trail

This trail provides quick access from the Upper East Fork to the Iron Mountain Trail. But the access has a price, as trail travelers must gain 700 feet in a mere 0.7 mile. That averages out to 1,000 feet per mile! Furthermore, the Divide Trail is in rough shape. In places it is much eroded; in others it is rocky or muddy. This all adds up to a short but rugged climb.

Leave the parking area and begin to ascend the north slope of Iron Mountain. The erosion is quickly evident. Keep heading up a rib ridge of Iron Mountain, climbing very sharply. At 0.5 mile, pass large boulders on your right; then veer left off the side of the ridge. The trail becomes even steeper just before passing over a large outcrop on the left. Make a final right turn and achieve the crest of Iron Mountain at 0.7 mile. To your right, the Iron Mountain Trail heads 0.2 mile to the Perkins Knob Trail and 3.6 miles farther to Dry Run Gap and US 21. To the left, it is 2.8 rough miles on the IMT to VA 653.

Access

From exit 70 at I-81 near Wytheville, take US 21 south through Wytheville. Drive 16.8 miles to Forest Road 14, passing through Speedwell. Turn left on Forest Road 14 and follow it 3.0 miles to a gap on FR 14, where the Virginia Highlands Horse Trail crosses the road. Turn right here and drive up a hill to a parking area. The signed Divide Trail heads uphill to the right.

Dry Run Gap Trail

Type:	Foot, bicycle, horse
Length:	1.0 mile
Difficulty:	Moderate
Use:	Moderate
Condition:	Good
Highlights:	Connector for Virginia Highlands Horse Trail and Iron Mountain Trail
Book Map #:	11
USGS Topo:	Speedwell
Connections:	Virginia Highlands Horse Trail, Iron Mountain Trail

This connector trail leaves the East Fork Valley and the Virginia Highlands Horse Trail to join old US 21. It then climbs up along a feeder stream of East Fork through thick woods to meet the Iron Mountain Trail. Highway noise from US 21 detracts from the scenery, but the trail's usefulness as a connector more than makes up for this.

Leave Forest Road 14 in an open area and pass a sign indicating the Dry Run Gap Trail. The path immediately enters woodland and then ascends steeply for 0.1 mile before moderating. The narrow track intersects the roadbed on old US 21 at

0.3 mile. Look downhill for an antique road bridge. Keep heading uphill on the roadbed, bordered by rhododendron. Rock exposed by blasting for the road lies to the left; the unnamed feeder stream is to the right. Intersect the Iron Mountain Trail at 1.0 mile. To the right, the IMT leads 0.3 mile to Dry Run Gap. To the left, the IMT leads 3.8 miles to the Divide Trail.

Access

From exit 70 at I-81 near Wytheville, take US 21 south through Wytheville. Drive 16.8 miles to Forest Road 14, passing through Speedwell. Turn left on Forest Road 14 and follow it 0.2 mile to the signed Dry Run Gap Trail, which is on the right.

East Fork Trail

Type:	Foot, horse, bicycle
Length:	2.7 miles
Difficulty:	Easy
Use:	Moderate
Condition:	Fair
Highlights:	Big trees in East Fork Valley, loop potential
Book Map #:	11, 13
USGS Topo:	Speedwell
Connections:	Virginia Highlands Horse Trail, Divide Trail, Dry Run Gap Trail

This path meanders down the extremely attractive valley of East Fork Dry Run. Along the way, it heads through Hussy Mountain Horse Camp and passes many large white pines and other trees. The trail, however, is often muddy, as it crosses East Fork and feeder streams. The path nets only a 275-foot change in elevation, making it an easy trek. Bikers will want to stay away from it and instead use Forest Road 14 for loops. The presence of this trail avails two excellent loop possibilities, with the Virginia Highlands Horse Trail through Horse Heaven and with the Iron Mountain Trail via the Divide and Dry Run Gap trails.

This narrative begins at the trail's east end. Leave Forest Road 14 and drop down toward East Fork, heading downstream on a narrow path. Overhead, tall white pines, imperiled hemlocks, and maples crowd the sky. Cross small East Fork at 0.3 mile. The path becomes rocky. Cross a small feeder stream and then shortly span a second feeder stream on a wooden bridge to emerge into Hussy Mountain Horse Camp at 0.8 mile. Continue downhill on the campground road and span East Fork again on a bridge before climbing a small hill to cross Forest Road 14 and reenter the woods.

Soon, switchback left and keep going downstream in a hickory-oak-pine forest. Parallel FR 14; then descend to it at 1.5 miles. Continue along the gravel road and soon look left for the orange blaze and the sign indicating return to the woods. Soaring white pines make for a magnificent forest. Pass through a roadside camp; then cross East Fork at 2.0 and 2.2 miles. Keep heading downstream to cross a tiny feeder stream coming in from the right and pass directly through another roadside camp. Continue following the orange blazes to emerge onto another roadside camp. Look for a trail sign indicating the East Fork Trail and two square concrete slabs. The trail sign erroneously states that Hussy Mountain Horse Camp is 3.0 miles away; the distance is in fact only 1.9 miles. Forest Road 14 runs directly by the camp. Down FR 14 just a short distance is the Virginia Highlands Horse Trail. A half mile distant on FR 14 is the Dry Run Gap Trail.

Access

Western Access: From exit 70 at I-81 near Wytheville, take US 21 south through Wytheville. Drive 16.8 miles to Forest Road 14, passing through Speedwell. Turn left on Forest Road 14 and follow it 0.6 mile to the signed East Fork Trail on the right.

Eastern Access: From exit 70 at I-81 near Wytheville, take US 21 south through Wytheville. Drive 16.8 miles to Forest Road 14, passing through Speedwell. Turn left on Forest Road 14 and follow it 2.9 miles to the signed East Fork Trail. To park, continue 0.1 mile farther on FR 14, where the Virginia Highlands Horse Trail crosses the road. Turn right here and drive up a hill to a parking area.

Ewing Mountain Trail

Type:	Foot, horse
Length:	2.0 miles
Difficulty:	Difficult
Use:	Moderate
Condition:	Good
Highlights:	Connector trail from Collins Cove Horse Camp
Book Map #:	12
USGS Topo:	Cripple Creek
Connections:	Virginia Highlands Horse Trail, Raven Cliff Trail

This path leads through some interesting terrain on its way to the crest of Ewing Mountain and the Virginia Highlands Horse Trail. It leaves Collins Cove Horse Camp and passes through a clearing in the process of returning to forest. It then climbs a ridgeline, only to drop down to a hollow. Then the real climbing begins, straight up on a rocky path. The trail shows a little mercy just before it intersects the VHHT.

Leave the horse camp and make a short passage through trees to enter a large clearing. Locust, pine, and tulip trees are reclaiming the open area. Briars grow in profusion. Veer left up a wide, shallow hollow on an old woods road. The trailside becomes fully forested by 0.3 mile. The trail soon makes an obvious right and continues uphill. At 0.4 mile come to an unmarked trail junction near a large white pine. Take the right path, which keeps going forward and crosses a normally dry streambed. Ascend steeply on a narrow ridgeline between two ravines. The path becomes rocky. Descend at mile 1.2 to cross another dry hollow. Veer right and climb very steeply, straight up the ridgeline on a very rocky path. Angle left below a knob on Ewing Mountain to reach a saddle and the Virginia Highlands Horse Trail at mile 2.0. From here it is 2.9 miles left to VA 94 on the VHHT and 4.4 miles right to VA 602.

Access

Northern Access: From exit 70 on I-81 in Wytheville, drive 13.6 miles south on US 21 to Speedwell. In Speedwell, turn left on VA 619 (Saint Peters Road). Stay with VA 619 for 7.8 miles and turn right on VA 642 (Pope Road). Stay on Pope Road for 0.9 mile, passing Eagle Cliff Furnace, and come to VA 643 (Cove Branch Road). Turn right on Cove Branch Road and follow it for 0.4 mile. Turn left into the Collins Cove Horse Camp. Wooden fences line the road to the camp. Drive to the head of the camp and look for the Ewing Mountain Trail in the far-right-hand corner of the camp.

Southern Access: The south end of the trail can be reached by traveling 2.9 miles west on the Virginia Highlands Horse Trail from VA 94.

Hale Lake Trail

Type:	Foot only
Length:	0.7 mile
Difficulty:	Easy
Use:	Heavy
Condition:	Good
Highlights:	Mountain lake, fishing
Book Map #:	11
USGS Topo:	Cedar Springs, Speedwell
Connections:	Iron Mountain Trail

This is a narrow foot trail that winds around Hale Lake, which lies at 3,400 feet. Anglers come here to fish the five-acre pond. Whether or not you take home a trout, you will certainly remember what a pretty little place it is.

Leave the parking area and climb a set of wooden steps up to the water. The lake is dead ahead. Veer right onto a footpath leading into an imperiled hemlock woodland and rhododendron, with scattered mountain laurel and deciduous trees such as black birch. Rhododendron, with bigger leathery evergreen leaves, prefers shaded ravines and being near streams, but it will also grow along moist slopes and on high-elevation, well-watered ridges. Mountain laurel, with smaller evergreen leaves, prefers dry, south-facing ridges; it often grows amid pine-oaks forests. That being said, the two overlap habitats as is the case here. Adding to the confusion are the historical names. Many mountain pioneers used the word "ivy" to refer to mountain laurel. Rhododendron they called "laurel," and hemlock trees were often called "spruce." Botanists of the last century, while cataloging the vast array of plants in the Southern Appalachians, must have been confounded by all the names the locals had given their flora.

At 0.1 mile span a footbridge over a tiny rivulet. A short distance ahead, the Iron Mountain Trail leaves right, uphill, and heads 2.0 miles to Comers Rock Campground. On Hale Lake, short angler paths periodically dip down to the water. White pines drop their needles along the trail. Pass a second feeder stream before swinging around a third and final feeder stream at 0.4 mile. The path climbs above the lake and then dips down to the lake dam. Grab one last view before returning to the wooden steps and completing the loop at 0.7 mile.

Access

From exit 70 on I-81 near Wytheville, drive south on US 21 for 17.8 miles to Forest Road 57, passing through Speedwell. Turn right on FR 57 and follow it for 5.1 miles to Hale Lake. The lake will be on your right; the parking area will be on your left. The trail starts up the wooden steps toward the lake.

Henley Hollow Trail

Type:	Foot, bicycle, horse
Length:	1.6 miles
Difficulty:	Moderate
Use:	Low to moderate
Condition:	Good
Highlights:	Narrow valley, small waterfalls
Book Map #:	11
USGS Topo:	Speedwell
Connections:	Little Dry Run Trail, Virginia Highlands Horse Trail

This well-maintained, single-track path makes its way up a narrow, attractive valley to open up near Porter Mountain, passing two small waterfalls before intersecting the Virginia Highlands Horse Trail. Beyond US 21 the path soon enters a shady woodland, crisscrossing the stream of Henley Hollow. It then winds around the stream's headwaters, passing just above a cascade before ending on a rocky slope and the wide, road-like VHHT.

Technically, the Henley Hollow Trail starts directly along US 21, across from the lower terminus of the Little Dry Run Trail. Pass the trailhead parking area and kiosk. Head up the vegetation-choked hollow. Waste no time in crossing the stream of Henley Hollow at 0.1 mile. Overhead are tulip trees, black birch, and red maple. Make a brief but sharp upgrade away from the creek to meet the stream again; here the path and watercourse run side by side. Cross the stream twice in succession at 0.6 mile. Look for evidence of footbridges that have now washed away.

Keep climbing up the valley in a series of switchbacks to meet the stream once again at 0.9 mile. Pass directly above a small waterfall, where the watercourse and trail are pinched in by a rock outcrop. Ascend the side of the ridge, entering smaller hollows. On the right, pass another tiny waterfall, which may be nearly dry in late summer and fall. Cross the streamlet of the falls at mile 1.2, before further switch-backing to enter a rocky flat. Just ahead, at mile 1.6, is the junction with the Virginia Highlands Horse Trail. From here it is 0.9 mile downhill to Forest Road 14 and 4.9 miles uphill to Forest Road 14 and the upper East Fork via Horse Heaven.

Access

From exit 70 on I-81 near Wytheville, drive south on US 21 for 13.6 miles to Speedwell. Continue south on US 21 for 2.1 miles to the Henley Hollow trailhead, which will be on the left.

Horne Knob Trail

Type:	Foot, bicycle, horse
Length:	0.4 mile
Difficulty:	Easy
Use:	Low
Condition:	Good
Highlights:	Connects to Virginia Highlands Horse Trail
Book Map #:	10
USGS Topo:	Cedar Springs
Connections:	Virginia Highlands Horse Trail

This trail is a short connector leading from Forest Road 16 to the Virginia Highlands Horse Trail. It makes a brief jaunt through the Dry Creek watershed to connect to the VHHT near the crossing of Dry Creek. Leave Forest Road 16 and descend to a feeder stream of Dry Creek. Cross the stream and then head uphill a short distance where you will circumvent a pole gate. Resume a drop in a deciduous forest under-lain with rhododendron. Intersect the Virginia Highlands Horse Trail at 0.4 mile. To your left, it is 9.4 miles to VA 16. To your right, it is 5.3 miles to Forest Road 16.

Access

From exit 45 on I-81 near Marion, drive south on VA 16 for 6.0 miles to the Jennings Visitor Center. Continue south on VA 16 for 3.7 more miles to VA 601

(Flat Ridge Road). Turn left on Flat Ridge Road and follow it for 2.6 miles to Forest Road 16 (Dry Creek Road). Turn left on FR 16 and follow it for 3.4 miles to a gravel parking area on the left. The trail starts at the end of the gravel parking area near a small stream.

Kirk Hollow Trail

Type:	Foot, bicycle, horse
Length:	0.8 mile
Difficulty:	Moderate
Use:	Low
Condition:	Good
Highlights:	Wildlife clearings, homesite
Book Map #:	10
USGS Topo:	Cedar Springs
Connections:	Virginia Highlands Horse Trail

This trail connects the upper Dry Creek Valley near Sugar Grove to the Virginia Highlands Horse Trail. It leads through or near several wildlife clearings up Kirk Hollow, gently climbing past the remains of an old homesite to end at the VHHT on the north slope of Little Mountain. It is used by few visitors, primarily equestrians.

Leave the circular parking area and pass around a metal gate. Keep going forward in an area rife with tulip trees, passing a wildlife clearing on trail left. The streambed of Kirk Hollow is normally dry and lies to the right. Enter a wildlife clearing and continue forward. The next clearing is near the homesite at 0.3 mile. Pass some piled rocks and then veer right over the streambed. Rhododendron crowds the now-steeper path. Make a sharp switchback to the right just before intersecting the Virginia Highlands Horse Trail at 0.8 mile. To your right, it is 7.2 miles to VA 16. To your left, it is 7.5 miles to Forest Road 16.

Access

From exit 45 on I-81 near Marion, head south on VA 16 for 6.0 miles to Jennings Visitor Center. Stay on VA 16 for 2.1 miles past the visitor center to VA 695 (Slemp Creek Road). Turn left on VA 695 and follow it for 0.6 mile to VA 675 (Horne Hollow Road). Veer left on Horne Hollow Road and follow it for 2.8 miles, where it turns to gravel and its name changes to Vipperman Hollow Road. Follow the gravel-surfaced VA 675 0.1 mile farther and look on the right for a pole gate and a circular parking area with a tree in the center of the circle. The Kirk Hollow Trail starts beyond the pole gate.

Little Dry Run Trail

Type:	Foot, horse
Length:	4.4 miles
Difficulty:	Difficult ·
Use:	Moderate
Condition:	Fair to poor
Highlights:	Little Dry Run Wilderness, views
Book Map #:	11
USGS Topo:	Speedwell
Connections:	Comers Rock Trail, Iron Mountain Trail, Virginia Highlands Horse Trail, Henley Hollow Trail

This slender path leaves from high in the Iron Mountains near Comers Rock Campground to drop down Little Dry Run to reach US 21. It leaves the campground and heads 200 feet to pass a trail junction and then steeply drop along a side ridge to intersect the Virginia Highlands Horse Trail. The path then enters the Little Dry Run Wilderness and becomes a rocky rough treadway that devolves into a hard-to-trace trail while crossing Little Dry Run numerous times. It finally swings into the Dry Run valley and fords Dry Run to end at US 21. Just across the highway is the beginning of the Henley Hollow Trail.

Leave Comers Rock Campground and walk just a short distance to a junction. The Little Dry Run Trail begins here and leaves right, away from the junction. To the extreme left, the Comers Rock Trail climbs a half mile to Comers Rock and a viewing platform. Also to the left, the Iron Mountain Trail gently meanders along the ridgeline to end in 2.0 miles at Hale Lake. The Little Dry Run Trail comes to a sharp switchback at 0.1 mile. Descend steeply on a narrow single-track path and gain occasional views of the mountains to the right. Pick up the nose of a side ridge at 0.4 mile while gaining more views.

Level off in a gap at 0.7 mile. Work around the right side of a knob availing vistas of the Iron Mountains to the right. Once again pick up the spine and climb over another knob to descend steeply again, coming to a trail junction at mile 1.2. To your left, the Virginia Highlands Horse Trail leads 10.8 miles west to Forest Road 16. The VHHT leads right 2.3 miles to US 21. The Little Dry Run Trail continues forward and enters the Little Dry Run Wilderness. Here, the trailbed instantly becomes rocky. Drop steeply on a rough path through dry woods. At mile 1.6, the trail grade moderates and leaves the rocky slope to enter a streamside forest of white pine, beech, and rhododendron. Begin the first of numerous crossings of Little Dry Run. At mile 1.9, enter a sizable flat as the valley widens. In places the trailbed and creek bed merge in a menagerie of snakelike finger streams. Floods sometimes alter

Winter backpacking can be challenging at Mount Rogers. Photo courtesy of U.S. Forest Service.

the course of flow here and wash out the trailbed. Look for occasional yellow blazes on trees for direction. Travel is slow through muddy areas.

When the valley narrows, the trail stays directly along the stream, crossing it often. Look for large white pines and fading hemlocks down here. Make the final stream crossing at mile 3.6. Drift right, away from Little Dry Run and then come to a 90-degree right turn at mile 3.8. The trail dead ahead leads to posted property. Turn right and begin to curve around the knob dividing Little Dry Run and Dry Run. Climb through a pine-oak-hickory woodland to pass a sign marking the Little Dry Run Wilderness. Descend to Dry Run, making a switchback just before coming to the ford of Dry Run. Hikers can expect to get their feet wet in times of higher flow. The trail opens to a grassy area just after the ford at mile 4.4. A Mount Rogers NRA sign is nearby and so is US 21. The parking area for the lower Little Dry Run trailhead and the Henley Hollow Trail is across the paved road. The Henley Hollow Trail leads uphill 1.6 miles to intersect the VHHT.

Access

Lower Access: From exit 70 on I-81 near Wytheville, drive south on US 21 for 13.6 miles to Speedwell. Continue south on US 21 for 2.1 miles to the Henley Hollow trailhead, which will be on the left. The Little Dry Run Trail starts across US 21 from the Henley Hollow parking area.

Upper Access: From exit 70 on I-81 near Wytheville, drive south on US 21 for 17.8 miles to Forest Road 57. Turn right on FR 57 and follow it for 3.6 miles to Comers Rock campground, which will be on your right. The Little Dry Run Trail starts near the bathroom on the west side of the campground.

Mike's Gap Trail

Type:	Foot, horse, bicycle
Length:	2.8 miles
Difficulty:	Moderate
Use:	Low
Condition:	Good
Highlights:	Views, wildlife clearings
Book Map #:	12
USGS Topo:	Cripple Creek
Connections:	Virginia Highlands Horse Trail

This trail is primarily a horse path that climbs along an intermittent feeder stream of Cold Run and travels over Ewing Mountain to drop down into the Jones Creek watershed. Along the way, it passes through Mike's Gap, where the 100-miles-per-hour winds of Hurricane Hugo flattened the forest in 1989. (It is recovering nicely now.) The devastation did open views from Mikes Gap to the south. The trail ends near Jones Branch on obscure VA 690.

The trail starts at the point where Forest Road 4050 and FR 4051 diverge. Park at this divergence and take the right-hand road uphill, past a pole gate with a sign stating, "Foot Travel Welcome." Continue steadily uphill in a mixed forest of tulip trees, maple, and pine. At 0.3 mile, an unmaintained path leaves right. The main trail actually descends a bit, then resumes its climb up the hollow to top out in a saddle and a wildlife clearing at 0.9 mile. A sign in the gap explains Hurricane Hugo's wrath. Leave right, away from the clearing onto an old woods road. At 1.0 mile, pass a spring box and pipe flowing off Ewing Mountain. Keep going uphill on an uncanopied trail to Mikes Gap and a trail junction at 1.5 miles. The Virginia Highlands Horse Trail leaves right 2.3 miles to VA 602 and left 5.0 miles to VA 94. The Mike's Gap Trail continues forward, dropping steeply downhill. Dead ahead are great mountain views before the trail reenters the woods. Keep heading downhill through pine-oak woods to a gap, making a sharp switchback to the left at 2.0 miles, passing by a burned area. Continue downhill to intersect a closed forest road at 2.3 miles. Veer left on the road and pass alongside posted property before bridging Jones Creek on a culvert and coming to a pole gate at mile 2.8. Here the gravel-surfaced VA 690 leads right 1.1 miles to VA 602 near Brush Creek.

Access

Western Access: From exit 70 on I-81 in Wytheville, drive 13.6 miles south on US 21 to Speedwell. In Speedwell, turn left on VA 619 (Saint Peters Road). Stay with 619 for 4.9 miles. (The actual name of 619 changes from Saint Peters to Cripple Creek Road.) Turn right onto VA 602, still named Cripple Creek Road, and follow it for 2.4 miles to Forest Road 4050. Turn left onto signed Forest Road 4050.

Follow FR 4050 0.1 mile to a split in the dirt road. Park here. The Mikes Gap Trail heads up the gated roadbed to the right.

Eastern Access: From exit 80 on I-81 near Fort Chiswell, head south on US 52 for 1.2 miles to VA 94. Turn right on VA 94 and follow it 14.9 miles to VA 602 (Brush Creek Road). There is a convenience store at this turn. Turn right on Brush Creek Road and follow it for 3.2 miles to Forest Road 690 (Snowbird Lane). Turn right on Snowbird Lane and follow it for 1.1 miles to a split in the gravel road. Turn left at the split and come to a metal pole gate. The Mikes Gap Trail starts here. Note that the trail description starts from the western access.

Perkins Knob Spur Trail

Type:	Foot, horse, bicycle
Length:	0.5 mile
Difficulty:	Moderate
Use:	Low
Condition:	Good
Highlights:	Good views, solitude
Book Map #:	13
USGS Topo:	Speedwell
Connections:	Perkins Knob Spur Trail

This wide trail leads a half mile up from the Perkins Knob Trail to Perkins Knob, where there is a wildlife clearing. A grassy clearing along the way avails good vistas of the valleys and mountains to the east.

Leave an attractive gap ringed in white pine and locust to head uphill on a wide grassy roadbed canopied by a deciduous forest of black birch, red maple, and oak. Level off at 0.2 mile and then open to a clearing. Make a "U" turn and resume climbing. Turn around and look east. The mountains appear as numerous as the clarity of the sky allows. Keep climbing back into woods and emerge onto a grassy clearing pocked with rock outcrops. At the very top of this clearing, the 3,852-foot pinnacle of Perkins Knob, there are obscured views to the south into North Carolina.

Access

Perkins Knob Spur Trail is an interior trail. It can be reached by walking 2.1 miles up the Perkins Knob Trail from US 21.

Perkins Knob Trail

Type:	Foot, horse, bicycle
Length:	2.2 miles
Difficulty:	Moderate

Use:	Low
Condition:	Good
Highlights:	Solitude
Book Map #:	13
USGS Topo:	Speedwell
Connections:	Perkins Knob Spur Trail, Iron Mountain Trail

This trail leads up the intimate valley of Perkins Creek, crossing this small stream numerous times before ending up in a pretty gap and a trail junction. From here the Perkins Knob Spur Trail leaves right, while the Perkins Knob Trail continues a short distance farther to intersect the Iron Mountain Trail. The Perkins Knob Trail is seldom traveled by anyone and is a hidden gem of the recreation area's East End. A rewarding loop can be made by combining this trail with the Iron Mountain Trail from Dry Run Gap. Complete the loop with a half-mile walk on US 21.

Leave the grassy clearing alongside US 21 and pass around a pole gate to enter the woods. Immediately make the first of more than a dozen crossings of Perkins Creek. The creek is fairly small and should be easily crossed year-round except when floods occur. Fraser magnolia and tulip trees grow tall in the valley.

Cross Perkins Creek the final time at 1.3 miles. Head uphill through a rich deciduous forest, passing several spring seeps coming down off Perkins Knob. At 2.0 miles, reach a grassy gap at 3,600 feet, surrounded by tall white pines and locust trees. To the right, the Perkins Knob Trail heads uphill to reach the top of Perkins Knob in a half mile. Leave the pretty gap and keep going forward on a narrow track to make a sharp left turn and intersect the Iron Mountain Trail at 2.2 miles, where there are sawn trees that make good benches. From here, it is 0.3 mile right on the IMT to intersect the Divide Trail. To the left, it is 3.6 miles on the IMT to Dry Run Gap.

Access

From exit 70 on I-81 near Wytheville, drive south on US 21 for 13.6 miles to Speedwell. Continue south on US 21 for 3.8 more miles to the Perkins Knob trailhead, which will be on the left, just before a guardrail near a right curve. If you pass a Mount Rogers National Recreation Area sign on the left, you have gone a little too far.

Raven Cliff Trail

Type:	Foot, horse, bicycle
Length:	1.2 miles
Difficulty:	Easy
Use:	Moderate
Condition:	Good

```
..........................................................................
:  Highlights:      Views of Cripple Creek, Raven Cliff Furnace, rock-blasted    :
:                   trailbed                                                      :
:  Book Map #:      12                                                            :
:  USGS Topo:       Cripple Creek                                                 :
:  Connections:     Raven Cliff Furnace Trail, Ewing Mountain Trail               :
..........................................................................
```

This path connects Raven Cliff Recreation Area with Collins Cove Horse Camp. It traces an old railroad grade as it winds through the Cripple Creek gorge near Raven Cliff. The path is very level, as impressive rock-blasting work kept it that way. There is one exception, however, and that is when the trail descends to ford Cripple Creek. There was once a trestle here in the railroad days, and the stone foundations of the trestle stand today.

Leave the parking area and look for a roadbed heading easterly to a pole gate. Pass around the gate and take the upper path leading left, not the one heading downhill over the bridge. That is the Raven Cliff Furnace Trail. Begin to trace the railroad grade, paralleling Cripple Creek, down to the right. Gleaves Knob is to your left. Notice the blasting work done on the rock of Gleaves Knob that made this railroad grade possible. The level trail makes for easy travel and allows views of a field across Cripple Creek. Just before entering a section of blasted rock on both sides of the trail, look right, by Cripple Creek, for the Raven Cliff Furnace, which was used to process ore. Bisect the blasted rock and come to a junction at 0.5 mile. An unmaintained trail leaves right, back toward the furnace, while the Raven Cliff Trail drops left, downhill, to ford Cripple Creek. While making the ford, look for the stone trestles of the former bridge.

Make the ford and enter a flat of sycamore and pine. Negotiate a switchback and gain the railroad grade again. Keep heading downstream along Cripple Creek, coming to a narrow section on a bluff overlooking the water. Leave the railroad grade at 1.1 miles and veer right, downhill, to reach Cove Branch Road. The Collins Cove Horse Camp is 0.1 mile left on Cove Branch Road. The Ewing Mountain Trail leaves from the upper end of the horse camp.

Access

Western Access: From exit 70 on I-81 in Wytheville, drive 13.6 miles south on US 21 to Speedwell. In Speedwell, turn left on VA 619 (Saint Peters Road). Stay with 619 for 6.5 miles. (The actual name of 619 changes from Saint Peters to Cripple Creek to Gleaves Road.) Turn right on Raven Cliff Lane, where there is a sign for Raven Cliff Recreation Area. Follow Raven Cliff Lane for 0.9 mile and dead-end at an auto turnaround. The Raven Cliff Trail starts here.

Eastern Access: In Speedwell, turn left on VA 619 (Saint Peters Road). Stay with 619 for 7.8 miles and turn right on VA 642 (Pope Road). Stay on Pope Road for 0.9 mile, passing Eagle Cliff Furnace, and come to VA 643 (Cove Branch Road).

Turn right on Cove Branch Road and follow it for 0.5 mile, just past the left turn for Collins Cove Horse Camp. The Raven Cliff Trail starts on the right-hand side of the road, just beyond the culvert over Cove Branch. The trail is not signed here.

Raven Cliff Furnace Trail

Type:	Foot only
Length:	0.5 mile
Difficulty:	Easy
Use:	Heavy
Condition:	Good
Highlights:	Old iron ore furnace, views of Raven Cliff
Book Map #:	12
USGS Topo:	Cripple Creek
Connections:	Raven Cliff Trail

This is an easy trail that heads along Cripple Creek down to an old iron ore furnace. Leave the parking area and head down toward Cripple Creek and a wide footbridge. (The Raven Cliff Trail stays forward along the left bank of Cripple Creek.) Span the steel and wood structure and then veer left, paralleling the watercourse downstream on an old railroad grade. Enter a field that curves along with Cripple Creek. Brush begins to crowd the trail before you arrive at the Raven Cliff Furnace at 0.5 mile. The stone ruins stand upwards of 60 feet high and 30 feet wide. The combination of Cripple Creek, the furnace, a fenced field, and Raven Cliff in the background makes this a scenic spot.

Access

From exit 70 on I-81 in Wytheville, drive 13.6 miles south on US 21 to Speedwell. In Speedwell, turn left on VA 619 (Saint Peters Road). Stay with 619 for 6.5 miles. (The actual name of 619 changes from Saint Peters Road to Cripple Creek Road to Gleaves Road.) Turn right on Raven Cliff Lane, where there is a sign for Raven Cliff Recreation Area. Follow Raven Cliff Lane for 0.9 mile and dead-end at an auto turnaround. The Raven Cliff Furnace Trail starts here.

Unaka Trail

Type:	Foot only
Length:	1.0 mile
Difficulty:	Moderate
Use:	Low
Condition:	Good

Highlights:	Old-growth trees
Book Map #:	12
USGS Topo:	Speedwell
Connections:	Little Dry Run Trail, Comers Rock Trail, Iron Mountain Trail

This is a foot-only loop trail that passes by some fine old-growth pine and tulip trees. It is intended as a nature trail for visitors to Comers Rock Recreation Area. The trail connections are with the other trails that emanate from Comers Rock Recreation Area. They are not trail connections in the literal sense. At any rate, hikers on the Unaka Trail will appreciate the beauty on this path. The Unaka Trail first leaves the picnic area and runs downhill along Iron Mountain. Just when you think it can't return within a half mile, it cuts sharply back to the picnic area, crossing the head-waters of Comers Rock Branch. It is in this creek valley where the big trees grow. Finally, the path makes its way past a few rivulets to return to the picnic area.

Start the Unaka Trail on the far-right-hand side of the picnic area, away from the small covered shelter. Take the upper grassy path, passing the sign indicating the Unaka Trail, and begin heading westerly along Iron Mountain in a maple-oak-hickory forest. At 0.3 mile pass through a fern-laden clearing along a rocky, inter-mittent rill. Swing just beside an old-growth tulip tree on trail left. Keep going downhill and make an unexpected right turn. Just a short distance past this turn, at 0.5 mile, the path makes an acute left turn. Begin heading uphill and cross the headwaters of Comers Rock Branch. Switchback to cross the stream again near some contemplation benches.

This is a good spot to look around and take inventory of the grove. Before you imagine a continuous stand of giant trees, you should realize that authentic old-growth woodland is not an agglomeration of evenly aged trees. On the contrary, evenly aged trees are a sign of disturbance. An old-growth forest will have many big trees along with younger trees that grow when they get the chance. A growth opportunity is created when a big tree falls, creating a light gap. Young trees sprout in this light gap, and other trees that are already somewhat grown thrive in the additional sun. At other times in the dark forest, trees gain a foothold on nurse logs. Nurse logs are already dead, fallen, and decaying trees that allow a seedling to gain root; the young trees are then fed by the energy contained within the decaying log. Later, the new trees grow and spread roots around the fallen log. Some time after that, the nurse log returns entirely to the soil, and the newly grown tree looks as if it grew up with legs. Trees are continually growing and dying, as older trees succumb to lightning strikes, disease, or old age, creating a mosaic of trees of all ages.

Large hemlocks appear along the trail. These old-growth giants, suffering from the hemlock wooly adelgid, are scattered about with their furrowed trunks and ever-green needles emanating from stout limbs far up the tree. Pass over a couple of stone bridges spanning tiny spring branches. Begin to look for tall pine trees as well. The needles on these are longer than the hemlocks, but their trunks are every bit as impressive. The climb moderates, and the trail emerges back into the picnic area at 1.0 mile.

Access

From exit 70 on I-81 near Wytheville, drive south on US 21 for 17.8 miles to Forest Road 57, passing through Speedwell. Turn right on FR 57 and follow it for 3.6 miles to Comers Rock Recreation Area. The Unaka Trail starts on the right-hand side of the picnic area.

High Country Trails

Bearpen Trail

Type:	Foot, horse
Length:	1.2 miles
Difficulty:	Moderate
Use:	Moderate
Condition:	Good
Highlights:	Great views, outcrops
Book Map #:	9
USGS Topo:	Trout Dale
Connections:	Scales Trail, Appalachian Trail, Big Wilson Creek Trail

This path traverses the mostly open slopes of Stone Mountain. Along the way are significant vistas of Pine Mountain and much more high country. Leave the Scales Trail near Scales and head south onto an open meadow, where rounded stone outcrops make mini-vista points of their own. The Bearpen Trail then skirts a high-elevation bog and descends in a mix of trees, brush, and meadows while forming the boundary of the Little Wilson Creek Wilderness. The path ends at the junction with the Big Wilson Creek Trail. Bearpen Trail once continued to a gap between First Peak and Second Peak, but the railroad grade the trail followed has devolved into a virtually impassable, muddy mess.

Speaking of bears, the Commonwealth of Virginia is experiencing a growth in its black bear population. In recent years, the Virginia Department of Game and Inland Fisheries estimates the number of bears in the state to be 7,000–9,000.

Start the Bearpen Trail by veering left off the Scales Trail, 0.5 mile from Scales. Ascend among rhododendron while traversing several rills flowing off Stone Mountain to the left. Keep climbing into a maple woodland. Leave the woodland for the open country at 0.2 mile. Continue alongside a wooden fence. There are far-reaching vistas to the west across the valley of East Fork Wilson Creek, including the Virginia Highlands Horse Trail. Begin to swing left, easterly, tracing the orange-blazed wooden poles. Emerge onto a grassy clearing broken with a rounded stone outcrop that resembles a monument. An evergreen forest stands to the right of the grassy flat. At 0.5 mile, span a low wooden bridge that drains a high elevation bog to the left.

Easily cruise through the rest of the meadow before twisting down into a hodgepodge of brush and trees. Pass through a gate. The trail now traces the northern boundary of the Little Wilson Creek Wilderness. Intersect the Appalachian Trail at 0.9 mile. It leads left 6.1 miles to Fairwood Valley and right 10.9 miles to Elk Garden. On the Bearpen Trail, pick up and follow a railroad grade. Keep going forward on the Bearpen Trail, now descending in deep woods. Wind around a muddy part of the grade that is hemmed in by a soil berm. Rejoin the grade before intersecting the Big Wilson Creek Trail at 1.2 miles. From here the Big Wilson Trail leads right 0.8 mile to the Kabel Trail and 2.1 miles to Seed Orchard Road Trail at Grayson Highlands State Park. A sign here states, "Deep Mud, Travel Not Recommended." This is the abandoned portion of the Bearpen Trail. It makes a very muddy track to a gap between First Peak and Second Peak. Do not proceed farther on the Bearpen Trail. To reach the First Peak Trail, take the Big Wilson Creek Trail to the Kabel Trail, which then intersects the First Peak Trail.

Access

The Bearpen Trail is an interior trail. It can be reached by traveling 0.5 mile on the Scales Trail from Scales.

Big Wilson Creek Trail

Type:	Foot, horse
Length:	2.1 miles
Difficulty:	Difficult
Use:	Low
Condition:	Good
Highlights:	Connects high country with lower Big Wilson Creek
Book Map #:	9
USGS Topo:	Trout Dale
Connections:	Bearpen Trail, Kabel Trail, Upchurch Road Trail

This path starts on the southeast slope of Stone Mountain and then drops 800 feet down to noisy Big Wilson Creek, which is making its own descent out of the high country. On the way down, it enters Grayson Highlands State Park. After a ford of Big Wilson Creek, the trail follows this crashing stream to Wilburn Branch. A final climb along Wilburn Branch brings the trail traveler to the Upchurch Road Trail.

Start the Big Wilson Creek Trail by leaving the Bearpen Trail and entering the Little Wilson Creek Wilderness. Stairstep down a rib ridge of Stone Mountain through northern hardwoods interspersed with red spruce. At 0.8 mile, intersect the Kabel Trail, which leads left 2.1 miles to meet the Hightree Rock and First Peak trails.

Beyond the junction with the Kabel Trail, the Big Wilson Creek Trail descends steeply on a wide, dirt track divided by many wooden and stone water bars. Come alongside a rhododendron thicket shading a small stream that feeds Big Wilson Creek. Pick up a roadbed and soon abruptly turn right to cross the small stream, leaving the Little Wilson Creek Wilderness.

Pick up another woods road and turn left, continuing downhill, now far above the tumbling creek. Come along a fence line and then reach another woods road at 1.6 miles. The roar of Big Wilson Creek is nearby. Turn left on this woods road to soon reach Big Wilson Creek. Ford the watercourse, colored tan from vegetational decay. Follow Big Wilson Creek downstream to reach a clearing at mile 1.9. Now ascend along Wilburn Branch, which is off to the left. Reach the Upchurch Road Trail at mile 2.1, just north of where it fords Big Wilburn Branch. The Big Wilson Creek Trail ends here. On the Upchurch Road Trail, it is 1.1 miles left down to VA 742 and 1.8 miles right, up to the Seed Orchard Road Trail.

Access

The Big Wilson Creek Trail is an interior trail. It can be reached by traveling from Scales 0.5 miles on the Scales Trail, then 1.2 miles on the Bearpen Trail.

Cliffside Trail

Type:	Foot only
Length:	1.5 miles
Difficulty:	Difficult
Use:	Low
Condition:	Good to fair
Highlights:	Direct access to Mount Rogers high country from Fairwood Valley
Book Map #:	4, 5
USGS Topo:	Whitetop Mountain
Connections:	Lewis Fork Trail

The Cliffside Trail does in 1.5 miles what the Lewis Fork Trail does in 4.2 miles, and that is climb up the side of Pine Mountain. This trail is steep, especially the last half mile, but it does offer direct access for hikers wishing to reach the high country without delay. The Cliffside Trail starts one mile from Fairwood Valley along Lewis Fork. It continues up the dark, shady Lewis Fork valley and then leaves the streambed, wasting no time in heading directly up the north slope of Pine Mountain and ending at some meadows on Pine Mountain.

Hike one mile up the Lewis Fork Trail from Fairwood Valley and reach the Cliffside Trail. It leaves right, up a very straight logging grade. Rhododendron lines the trail. Yellow birch and maple tower overhead. Lewis Fork lies off to the right. Pass a feeder stream on a culvert at 0.2 mile. Keep heading up the valley; then veer left away from Lewis Fork at 0.5 mile. Rhododendron then diminishes. The lavender-blazed path climbs sharply and then comes to the Lewis Fork Trail at 0.9 mile, as that trail snakes up the mountain instead of taking the direct route. Bisect the wide Lewis Fork Trail and keep heading uphill on an old woods road.

At 1.1 miles, turn left, leave the old woods road, and climb directly up the mountain. The trail clambers over an extremely rocky, extremely steep section. Keep climbing steeply and come to a gate. Pass a wide old cherry tree and maintain the lung-challenging ascent, reaching the final junction with the Lewis Fork Trail at mile 1.5. From here, it is 0.1 mile left to the Pine Mountain Trail and 0.3 mile left to the Crest Trail on the Lewis Fork Trail.

Access

The Cliffside Trail is an interior trail. It can be accessed by hiking up the Lewis Fork Trail for 1.0 mile from Fairwood Valley and VA 603.

Crest Trail

Type:	Foot, horse, bicycle
Length:	3.4 miles
Difficulty:	Moderate
Use:	High
Condition:	Excellent
Highlights:	Fantastic views, pony-sighting areas, numerous trail connections
Book Map #:	9
USGS Topo:	Trout Dale, Whitetop Mountain
Connections:	Scales Trail, Appalachian Trail, Virginia Highlands Horse Trail, First Peak Trail, Lewis Fork Trail, Pine Mountain Trail, Rhododendron Gap Trail

This wide, road-like trail offers nearly continuous vistas as it courses the top of Pine Mountain. It starts at Scales to climb through open country, broken by occasional groves of evergreen and deciduous trees. Wild ponies, which live in the recreation area year-round, are often seen in this stretch of the high country. The Crest Trail breaks out above 5,000 feet, offering even more views before making an ascent to reach Rhododendron Gap. From here, the trail makes a downward course, drifting in and out of Fraser fir groves. It switchbacks down to Cabin Ridge, looking out at the hulking mass of Mount Rogers, before intersecting the Virginia Highlands Horse Trail.

The gravel-surfaced Crest Trail heads west out of Scales and climbs along a wooden fence through open land. Look back down to Scales and the First Peak Trail across the gap. Sporadic cherry, red spruce, and hawthorn trees dot the surrounding fields. Briefly level off, enjoying great views of Wilburn Ridge. At 0.4 mile, the brush and trees close in, though the trail is more open than not. Gain the crest of the ridge at 0.7 mile for wide-ranging vistas. Swing around the headwaters of Big Wilson Creek to the left, with an outcrop to the right. Look right, across a field, for a fence line at 0.8 mile. The white blaze of the Appalachian Trail is on the fence. Here, the AT meets the Pine Mountain Trail, which has come 1.9 miles from Rhododendron Gap.

Undulate, heading more up than down, passing through occasional evergreen and hardwood banks of trees. At mile 1.5, on the right, is a fenced-in spring. Just past the spring is the junction with the Lewis Fork Trail, which has come 5.6 miles from Fairwood Valley and VA 603. Keep going forward on the Crest Trail, now breaking 5,000 feet. Pockets of beech and birch are mixed with frequent clearings. Fraser fir becomes more common as well. Open country ahead reveals Wilburn Ridge and the massive outcrops by Rhododendron Gap. To the left are views into the Big Wilson Creek drainage.

Mount Rogers National Recreation Area high country.

At mile 2.0, the path begins to climb toward Rhododendron Gap. It switchbacks through open areas bordered by a fence, alternating with dense thickets of rhododendron topped with mountain ash trees. Look back down at the portion of the Crest Trail just traveled. At mile 2.6, intersect the Appalachian Trail at Rhododendron Gap. The AT leads left 7.0 miles to Scales and right just a few feet to intersect the Pine Mountain Trail and 5.0 miles beyond to Elk Garden.

The Crest Trail continues uphill, leaving Rhododendron Gap and entering scattered fir trees, brush, and grass. Reach the Rhododendron Gap Trail at mile 2.8. The Rhododendron Gap Trail leads left 1.4 miles to Grayson Highlands State Park. Keep going forward on the Crest Trail, traversing open country with views of Brier Ridge, Mount Rogers, and down the Cabin Creek watershed. Clear a gate at mile 3.0. Descend on a rocky, sometimes muddy trail with Mount Rogers as a backdrop. Intersect the Virginia Highlands Horse Trail at mile 3.4. The Crest Trail ends here. At this point, the VHHT leads right 4.0 miles to Elk Garden and left 5.3 miles to Scales.

Access

From exit 45 on I-81 near Marion, drive 6.0 miles south on VA 16, passing the Jennings Visitor Center. Stay on VA 16 for 11.0 miles to VA 603 (Fairwood Road) in Troutdale. Turn right on VA 603 and follow it for 2.7 miles to Forest Road 613. (FR 613 is a rough, high-clearance-vehicle road and not recommended for low-slung passenger vehicles.) Turn left on FR 613 and follow it 4.0 miles to Scales. The Crest Trail starts on the west side of the corral, to the right of where 613 enters Scales.

Elk Garden Trail

Type:	Foot, horse, bicycle
Length:	1.5 miles
Difficulty:	Moderate
Use:	Low
Condition:	Excellent
Highlights:	Cross-country ski trail, sugar maple tapping area
Book Map #:	5
USGS Topo:	Whitetop Mountain
Connections:	Appalachian Trail, Virginia Highlands Horse Trail

This trail follows the route of old VA 600, abandoned decades ago, along Davis Ridge up to Elk Garden, a saddle on Balsam Mountain. It winds up the ridgeline via wide switchbacks and passes an area rich with sugar maples, where the sap, or "sugar water," is tapped for making molasses and other products that are featured in an early spring maple festival in the nearby Whitetop community. The path is primarily used by equestrians but also enjoys popularity as a cross-country ski trail since it is on the north slope of Balsam Mountain.

Start the Elk Garden Trail at 3,800 feet and pass around a metal vehicle-barrier post. Begin to head up Davis Ridge in a thick forest mixed with upland species such as Fraser fir and oak. Pass through clearings on the right at 0.3 mile and 0.4 mile. Maintain a continual but moderate ascent, passing occasional "No Horses" signs, placed as an attempt to keep equestrians from cutting the numerous switchbacks.

At mile 1.2, pass a sign explaining the sugar maple tapping area. There are tubes attached to the trees, and the sap is collected in common tanks. Metal buckets were once used, but efficiency has overruled nostalgia. Pass one of these syrup collection tanks at mile 1.4, just before traversing a gate and emerging onto the clearing at Elk Garden and the end of the Elk Garden Trail. From here, the Appalachian Trail leaves right to reach Damascus after 23.0 miles, and left, across VA 600, to reach Fairwood Valley after 17.0 miles. The Virginia Highlands Horse Trail leaves also left to reach Fairwood Valley after 12.9 miles.

Access

From the Little Red Caboose in Damascus, drive 11.0 miles east on US 58. Here, US 58 curves right; continue forward, now on VA 603 (Konnarock Road). Stay on 603 for 2.6 miles to VA 600 (Whitetop Road). Turn right on VA 600 and follow it for 1.8 miles to the lower end of the Elk Garden Trail, which will be on the right. The upper end of the Elk Garden Trail can be reached by driving 3.3 miles farther on VA 600 past the lower trailhead to the actual Elk Garden area and trailhead.

First Peak Trail

Type:	Foot, horse
Length:	3.2 miles
Difficulty:	Moderate
Use:	Heavy on first section of trail, moderate thereafter
Condition:	Good
Highlights:	Views, varied forests
Book Map #:	8, 9
USGS Topo:	Trout Dale
Connections:	Virginia Highlands Horse Trail, Appalachian Trail, Scales Trail, Crest Trail, Third Peak Trail, Jackie Streets Trail, Hightree Rock Trail, Kabel Trail

The First Peak Trail climbs out of Scales and rambles over a series of knobs, starting on Stone Mountain and ending on the far east end of Pine Mountain. The trail starts high and stays high, with no excessive elevation changes. Begin in the open meadows of Scales and climb to a wide vista on Stone Mountain. Then undulate southeasterly in a patchwork of clearings and woods to end in a flat and an intersection with the Kabel and Hightree Rock trails.

Start the trail by leaving Scales from the east end of the corral. Begin to ascend the west side of Stone Mountain on a wide path with many rock waterbars. Stay on the trail to keep the adjacent meadow grassy. The meadow is slowly being overtaken by hawthorn and blueberry bushes. Gain a view left down into the Opossum Creek valley. Clear a bank of trees at 0.3 mile and stay with the orange-blazed posts. Top out on Stone Mountain at 0.7 mile. The views are tremendous here, especially to the west. Occasional rock outcrops and a border of spruce trees make the meadow even more picturesque. Many hikers enjoy the view here and then turn back. The old closed portion of the First Peak Trail comes in here. Keep going forward and intersect the Third Peak Trail at 0.8 mile. It leads left to reach Forest Road 613 in 1.7 miles.

Keep descending into a heavily wooded area, passing through a gate. Yellow birch, mountain maple, red spruce, and sugar maple abound here. Reach a gap and climb into a more oak-heavy woodland. The forest here has a warmer, southwestern exposure that allows the oaks to grow. Begin to descend, bypassing the pinnacle of Third Peak and reaching another gap at mile 1.6. Enter the Little Wilson Creek Wilderness. Climb amid trees and brush to crest out on Second Peak in a small clearing at mile 1.8.

Once again, drop into thick woods on a rocky track, broken by occasional tiny clearings. Reach a gap in a clearing at mile 2.4. Here, the Jackie Streets Trail leads left 2.5 miles to VA 739. To the right, a trail sign states, "Deep Mud, Travel Not Recommended." This is an abandoned portion of the Bearpen Trail and is slated to be closed. Do not take this terribly muddy, old railroad grade! The First Peak Trail leads forward out of the clearing. Soon climb over wooded First Peak. At mile 3.0, pick up a logging railroad grade, turning left to reach a flat and a trail junction at mile 3.2. The First Peak Trail ends here. To the left, the Hightree Rock Trail leads 4.7 miles down to VA 739. To the right, the Kabel Trail leads 2.1 miles to intersect the Big Wilson Creek Trail.

Access

From exit 45 on I-81 near Marion, drive 6.0 miles south on VA 16, passing the Jennings Visitor Center. Stay on VA 16 for 11.0 miles to VA 603 (Fairwood Road) in Troutdale. Turn right on VA 603 and follow it for 2.7 miles to Forest Road 613. (FR 613 is a rough, high-clearance-vehicle road and not recommended for low-slung passenger vehicles.) Turn left on FR 613 and follow it 4.0 miles to Scales. The First Peak Trail starts on the east side of the corral at Scales, to the left of where 613 reaches Scales.

Grassy Branch Trail

Type:	Foot, horse
Length:	3.2 miles
Difficulty:	Moderate
Use:	Low
Condition:	Fair to good
Highlights:	Wilderness trail, solitude
Book Map #:	4, 5
USGS Topo:	Trout Dale, Whitetop Mountain
Connections:	None

The Grassy Branch Trail passes through former pasture and farmland, now forested, to reach VA 600. It follows an old logging grade amid the formerly settled country to make a pleasant forest cruise along the lower north slope of Elk Garden Ridge. Many old woods roads spur off the main trail, but the primary path is evident. Having no official trail connections keeps the use of Grassy Branch Trail low. Toward the end, the path leaves the grade to ascend sharply to reach VA 600. Beyond Grassy Branch, the popular bridle path enters the northern portion of the Lewis Fork Wilderness.

Leave VA 603 and pass around a pole vehicle barrier in an upland hardwood forest of beech, yellow birch, and oak. The wide, blue-blazed path soon passes a clearing and then picks up an old logging grade easterly. Pass an old homesite on the left just before crossing a wide feeder stream of Big Laurel Creek at 0.4 mile.

Keep going easterly and come to Grassy Branch at 0.8 mile; then enter the Lewis Fork Wilderness. Notice the many trailside buckeye trees and Fraser magnolia trees. The path settles down around the 3,700-foot level and then gently ascends an arm of Elk Garden Ridge. The mountainside is much more sloped here than it was earlier. Begin to swing into the valley of Charlies Branch, which soon becomes audible. Cross many tributaries of Charlies Branch between mile 2.2 and mile 2.5. Shortly after the stream crossings, the trail leaves the logging grade and ascends steeply on a single-track path, switchbacking up the mountainside to reach VA 600 at mile 3.2.

Access

Northern Access: From exit 45 on I-81 in Marion, head south on VA 16 for 6.0 miles, passing the Jennings Visitor Center. Continue south on VA 16 for 11.0 miles to VA 603 (Fairwood Valley Road) in Troutdale. Turn right on VA 603 and follow it 6.8 miles to the trailhead, which is on the left.

Southern Access: From the Little Red Caboose in Damascus, drive 11.0 miles east on US 58. Here, US 58 curves right; continue forward, now on VA 603 (Konnarock Road). Stay on 603 for 2.6 miles to VA 600 (Whitetop Road). Follow VA 600 for 3.8 miles to the trailhead, which is on the left.

Helton Creek Spur Trail

Type:	Foot, horse
Length:	1.3 miles
Difficulty:	Moderate
Use:	Low
Condition:	Fair
Highlights:	Solitude, good loop connector, good views
Book Map #:	5
USGS Topo:	Whitetop Mountain
Connections:	Helton Creek Trail, Virginia Highlands Horse Trail

This spur path is helpful in creating loops for hikers and equestrians using the Helton Creek and Virginia Highlands Horse trails. It leaves Helton Creek and traverses a northern hardwood forest to open up on the lower reaches of Balsam Mountain in the Lewis Fork Wilderness. Here, views abound of the mountains to the south. Be aware that this trail can be very muddy. Consider alternate paths during or after wet periods.

Trail users must travel 1.0 mile of the Helton Creek Trail to reach the lower Helton Creek Spur Trail. Leave the junction with the Helton Creek Trail and veer left across an often muddy flat to then cross Helton Creek, which can be dry-footed most times of the year. Climb away from Helton Creek through a forest of beech, birch, maple, and rhododendron.

At 0.4 mile, many spring branches trickle across the trail. Steadily ascend and enter the Lewis Fork Wilderness at 0.8 mile. Continue southwesterly along the lower reaches of Balsam Mountain to pass through a gate at 1.1 miles. Enter open country, broken by occasional stands of trees. Keep heading uphill and intersect the Virginia Highlands Horse Trail at 1.3 miles. To the left, it is 0.3 miles to Elk Garden. To the right, it is 9.0 miles to Scales.

Access

Helton Creek Spur Trail is an interior trail. It can be reached either by traveling 1.0 mile from the lower end of the Helton Creek Trail or by heading east from Elk Garden on the Virginia Highlands Horse Trail for 0.3 mile.

Helton Creek Trail

Type:	Foot, horse
Length:	3.1 miles
Difficulty:	Moderate
Use:	Low

Condition:	Fair
Highlights:	Beaver ponds, fruit trees, old homesite, views
Book Map #:	5
USGS Topo:	Whitetop Mountain
Connections:	Sugar Maple Trail, Helton Creek Spur Trail, Virginia High lands Horse Trail

This trail has many faces. It starts out as a roadbed through old farmlands and passes near some beaver ponds on Helton Creek and then enters a northern hardwood forest to climb the slopes of Brier Ridge, reaching the Lewis Fork Wilderness. It then swings around the upper reaches of Helton Creek to intersect the Virginia Highlands Horse Trail on Balsam Mountain. The views are wide along lower Helton Creek. Anglers sometimes use this path to vie for trout in Helton Creek. Cows may be grazing in the lower portions of the Helton Creek valley. A word of warning: Some sections of this trail can be very muddy. Consider avoiding this trail during wet periods.

Start the path by passing around a pole gate to trace an old roadbed through an open valley broken with some tree stands, including apple trees. At 0.1 mile, pass through a wooden gate and intersect the Sugar Maple Trail. It leads right and connects to the upper end of the Helton Creek Trail after 2.2 miles. The Helton Creek Trail stays forward. Bluff Mountain is visible to the left across the valley. Watch for cattle trails leading away from the proper path, which stays on the old roadbed. At 0.4 mile, pass through another gate to continue through mixed pasture and woodland. Ahead is a good view of the high country on Balsam Mountain. Look for stone steps leading right to a flat, where a home once stood. At 0.8 mile, pass through another gate and enter beech, birch, and maple woods, coming to a trail junction at 1.0 mile. The Helton Creek Spur Trail leads left across Helton Creek and climbs 1.3 miles to the Virginia Highlands Horse Trail.

The Helton Creek Trail stays right and heads uphill. Leave Helton Creek and keep going easterly, winding up the slopes of Brier Ridge on an old roadbed. The forest floor has grass and ferns in many spots. Enter the Lewis Fork Wilderness at mile 1.5. Make a couple of wide switchbacks uphill to intersect the Sugar Maple Trail at mile 2.1. The Sugar Maple Trail leads forward then loops back down to lower Helton Creek. The Helton Creek Trail leaves left, briefly downhill.

The trail and mountainside are rocky in places here on the west slope of Brier Ridge. The trail passes by many spring branches that feed Helton Creek and then crosses the upper reach of Helton Creek at 2.6 miles. Continue uphill for another half mile to intersect the Virginia Highlands Horse Trail. From here it is 1.0 mile left to Elk Garden and 8.3 miles right to Rhododendron Gap.

Access

From the Little Red Caboose in Damascus, drive east on US 58 for 20.3 miles to VA 783 (Helton Creek Lane). Turn left on VA 783 and follow it 1.3 miles to dead-end at a metal pole gate. The Helton Creek Trail starts on the far side of the metal gate.

Hightree Rock Trail

Type:	Foot, horse
Length:	4.7 miles
Difficulty:	Moderate to difficult
Use:	Low
Condition:	Good
Highlights:	Vista from Hightree Rock, solitude
Book Map #:	8, 9
USGS Topo:	Trout Dale
Connections:	Kabel Trail, First Peak Trail

This is an underused trail. It starts out as a woods road and climbs up Rocky Hollow and then follows an old railroad grade into Little Wilson Creek Wilderness and Hightree Rock. From the rock, there is a wide view of mountains and farmland east of the high country. Beyond the outcrop, the path swings around the headwaters of Little Wilson Creek. (I refer here to the more easterly one; there are two Little Wilson Creeks in close proximity in this area.) Finally, the Hightree Rock Trail leaves the railroad grade and makes a steep dash for the south side of First Peak and a junction with the Kabel and First Peak trails.

This trail description starts at VA 739. Leave gravel-surfaced VA 739 and head west up a gravel road through a former field growing up in locust, sumac, and tulip trees. The gravel road quickly deteriorates and becomes rocky as the roadbed leaves the clearing and enters full-fledged woods beyond a wooden and wire fence. Overhead are maple and white pine. A shallow rill flows over the trail before the trail splits at 0.3 mile. There is a cabin to the immediate right and a "No Horses" sign. Turn left here, heading up the rhododendron-lined woods road. Ascend straight up Rocky Hollow with a fence line on the right and the stream of Rocky Hollow on the left. Veer left and cross the stream of Rocky Hollow, now heading south on a level course, to swing around a small knob to the right. Old woods roads and trails spur off the trail, but the main path is evident.

Enter the Mill Creek valley to cross Mill Creek at mile 1.6. An old abandoned shack lies just on the far side of Mill Creek. The trailbed narrows and forms the boundary of Little Wilson Creek Wilderness to the right. The path fully enters the wilderness at mile 2.0. Keep heading up in viney woods, ascending toward Hightree Rock, along a decaying fence line. At mile 2.8, come to Hightree Rock on the left.

There is a trailside flat here. Just beyond the flat, it is a short few steps to High-tree Rock. From the outcrop, there is the hamlet of Grant below, along with many Christmas tree plantations and mountains to the east.

From here, the Hightree Rock Trail continues along the grade to swing south-westerly into the headwaters of Little Wilson Creek. Cross a perennial stream at mile 4.0. An old road leads left down this tributary of Little Wilson Creek. The Hightree Rock Trail jumps a small hill and continues forward for 0.1 mile to leave the grade for good. Climb sharply to the right, on a single-track path. Switchback in northern hardwoods interspersed with a few spruce trees and come to a trail junction at mile 4.7. The Hightree Rock Trail ends here. The Kabel Trail leads forward 2.1 miles to meet the Big Wilson Creek Trail. The First Peak Trail leads right 3.2 miles to Scales.

Access

From exit 45 on I-81 near Marion, drive 6.0 miles south on VA 16, passing the Jennings Visitor Center. Stay on VA 16 for 11.0 miles to VA 603 (Fairwood Road) in Troutdale. Turn right on VA 603 and follow it for 1.2 miles to VA 739 (Rocky Hollow Road). Turn left on Rocky Hollow Road and drive 1.8 miles, looking for Hidden Hollow Road on the right and High Crest Lane on the left. The Hightree Rock trailhead is 0.5 mile beyond these roads on the right. The trail is an unmarked gravel road leading into a former field growing up with trees. The trailhead is not marked. Turn right off 739; then park beside the gravel road, once on national forest property.

Jackie Streets Trail

Type:	Foot, horse
Length:	2.5 miles
Difficulty:	Moderate
Use:	Low
Condition:	Good
Highlights:	Many views, meadows
Book Map #:	8, 9
USGS Topo:	Trout Dale
Connections:	First Peak Trail

The Jackie Streets Trail is a little-used path. It starts at over 3,400 feet and leads up from VA 739 to a clearing in a saddle on the First Peak Trail. Along the way, it passes pastureland with wide views. Later, it skirts the edge of Shapiro Meadows, a larger pasture with more vistas. Finally, it enters the woods and the Little Wilson Creek Wilderness, climbing into northern hardwoods and eventually a spruce forest before ending at a grassy gap between First Peak and Second Peak.

Start the trail by leaving the grassy clearing by VA 739 and passing around the metal pole gate. Follow a woods road into a rhododendron patch. Soon bisect private property with a barn and a cabin. Clear a metal stock gate, leaving the private property. Open into a meadow at a sharp right turn at 0.2 mile. Walk to the top of the meadow on the left and behold a huge vista of lands to the north and east.

The forest road winds in and out of pastureland. Shapiro Meadows is uphill to the right. Pass a spring flowing into a huge truck tire at 0.6 mile. Leave the forest road on a sharp curve to the right at 1.0 mile. The upper end of Shapiro Meadows, with grand vistas, is up the forest road a short distance. The Jackie Streets Trail continues forward and passes through the metal stock gate. Swing around the head of Rocky Hollow. The trailbed soon narrows, and the Jackie Streets Trail makes a steady climb through rocky woodland. Pass a wide, rocky tributary of Mill Creek; then enter the Wilson Creek Wilderness at mile 1.7. Northern hardwoods predominate in the forest.

Stay on a single-track path overlain on a woods road. Tall red spruce trees become common. Pass a spring branch flowing off Second Peak at mile 2.4. Open into a small field growing up with bushes and locust trees, reaching the First Peak Trail at mile 2.5. From here it is 0.8 mile left to reach the Kabel and Hightree Rock trails. It is 2.4 miles right to Scales.

Access

From exit 45 on I-81 near Marion, drive 6.0 miles south on VA 16, passing the Jennings Visitor Center. Stay on VA 16 for 11.0 miles to VA 603 (Fairwood Road) in Troutdale. Turn right on VA 603 and follow it for 1.2 miles to VA 739 (Rocky Hollow Road). Turn left on Rocky Hollow Road and drive 1.0 mile. Looking for a grassy clearing behind an old stone wall on the right of the road. A house sits across the road from this clearing. In the back of the clearing, visible from the road, is a metal pole gate. Park on the edge of the clearing. Do not block the pole gate at the back of the clearing.

Kabel Trail

Type:	Foot, horse
Length:	2.1 miles
Difficulty:	Easy
Use:	Low
Condition:	Good
Highlights:	Wilderness trail, solitude
Book Map #:	9
USGS Topo:	Trout Dale
Connections:	Hightree Rock Trail, First Peak Trail, Big Wilson Creek Trail

This path is a hidden gem of the Mount Rogers high country. It has no views, and it doesn't lead to any particular feature; therefore, it doesn't see the traffic other trails do. Offering solitude, it is a pleasure to travel and has that everywhere-you-look beauty. The path starts at the junction with the First Peak and Hightree Rock trails on the east end of Pine Mountain. From there it leads up to Bearpen Ridge and then around to Little Wilson Creek to meet the Big Wilson Creek Trail. It uses an old logging railroad grade for much of its length, making it a user-friendly proposition.

Start the Kabel Trail by heading southwesterly away from the junction with the Hightree Rock and First Peak trails. Follow a single-track treadway through tall hardwoods with an open understory. Sporadic red spruce and rhododendron round out the vegetational variety. At 0.2 mile, cross a small spring branch. Pass an abandoned side trail leading left, downhill, at 0.4 mile; then pick up a logging grade. Moderately ascend to make Bearpen Ridge. Begin to curve northerly through a mountainside flat. Keep going north in maple-oak woods. The bulk of First Peak stands to the right.

At mile 1.1, cross the first of many streamlets feeding Little Wilson Creek. Yellow birch and beech loom over grass and ferns among the gray boulders. The logging grade splits at mile 1.4. Follow the left, lower grade. By 1.6 miles, the Kabel Trail leaves the second grade and dives left, downhill. Make a rocky, rapid descent to enter a level clearing and Little Wilson Creek at mile 1.8. Cross the creek and climb a small hill to pick up another logging grade. Swing around a rib ridge of Stone Mountain and reach a trail junction at mile 2.1. The Kabel Trail ends here. To the left, the Big Wilson Creek Trail descends 1.3 miles to ford Big Wilson Creek and intersect the Seed Orchard Road Trail in Grayson Highlands State Park. To the right, the Big Wilson Creek Trail climbs the slope of Stone Mountain 0.8 mile to intersect the Bearpen Trail.

Access

The Kabel Trail is an interior trail. It can be reached by traveling 3.2 miles on the First Peak Trail or 4.7 miles on the Hightree Rock Trail.

Lewis Fork Spur Trail

Type:	Foot only
Length:	0.4 mile
Difficulty:	Moderate
Use:	Moderate
Condition:	Good
Highlights:	Connects Lewis Fork and Mount Rogers trails
Book Map #:	5
USGS Topo:	Whitetop Mountain
Connections:	Lewis Fork Trail, Mount Rogers Trail

This trail increases the options for hikers traversing the trails from the Fairwood Valley area. It connects the Lewis Fork Trail on its way to the top of Pine Mountain to the Mount Rogers Trail atop Elk Ridge. Leave the Lewis Fork Trail at 3.4 miles, as it makes a sharp switchback, and begin the Lewis Fork Spur Trail. Follow an old logging grade north for 0.1 mile; then the blue-blazed trail abruptly leads left, uphill, through beech and maple sprinkled with red spruce. Keep climbing on a single-track path to top out on a flat atop Elk Ridge. Turn sharply left and intersect the Mount Rogers Trail at 0.4 mile. From here, the Mount Rogers Trail leads left 2.0 miles to the Appalachian Trail near Deep Gap and right 2.0 miles to Grindstone Campground.

Access

The Lewis Fork Spur Trail is an interior trail. It can be reached by hiking 3.4 miles on the Lewis Fork Trail from Fairwood Valley or 2.0 miles on the Mount Rogers Trail from Grindstone Campground.

Lewis Fork Trail

Type:	Foot, horse
Length:	5.5 miles
Difficulty:	Moderate to difficult
Use:	Moderate
Condition:	Good
Highlights:	Views up top, gentle climb
Book Map #:	4, 5
USGS Topo:	Whitetop Mountain
Connections:	Fairwood Valley Trail, Cliffside Trail, Old Orchard Trail, Lewis Fork Spur Trail, Pine Mountain Trail, Crest Trail

This trail leaves Fairwood Valley and enters the Lewis Fork Wilderness, where it gently but consistently climbs the slope of Pine Mountain, Mount Rogers and Elk Ridge to reach the high country atop Pine Mountain. The difficulty is not in the steepness, but in the length of the climb, which is nearly the entire path. It follows an old logging grade most of the way as it transitions from field to northern hardwood forest to field again. The trail is never hard to follow and the only confusing part is the beginning, where there are two trailheads.

The equestrian trailhead spurs off the Fairwood Valley Trail and crosses VA 603. It passes around a gate before emerging onto a field, meeting the Lewis Fork hiker trail, which starts at VA 603 and courses through the field to meet the equestrian trail. The two trails merge and then come to a gate and an information board at 0.2 mile. Pass through a gate and enter the Lewis Fork Wilderness. Span Lewis Fork on a wide plank bridge suitable for hikers and horses.

Sun-dappled Lewis Fork Trail.

Trace a logging grade in a forest cathedral of yellow birch and maple. Rosebay rhododendron flanks the trail. Noisy Lewis Fork lies off to the right, unseen but always audible. Pass a couple of diminishing clearings on the left before intersecting the Cliffside Trail at 1.0 mile. The Cliffside Trail leaves right and heads 1.5 steep miles to intersect the Lewis Fork Trail in the high country. The Lewis Fork Trail veers left up a feeder branch and ascends at a much gentler clip.

The blue-blazed path picks up a southeasterly direction while traversing rocky woods. Reach the junction with the Old Orchard Trail at mile 1.6. The Old Orchard Trail leads left 0.3 mile to the Appalachian Trail and the Old Orchard trail shelter. The Lewis Fork Trail switchbacks right and picks up the grade the Old Orchard Trail has been following. The climb along Pine Mountain remains steady. Cross a branch of Lewis Fork; then intersect the Cliffside Trail at mile 2.6 as Cliffside trail continues to take the direct route up Pine Mountain. Red spruce trees begin to appear and gain in number as the elevation increases. Hemlocks decrease in number. Hemlocks have pliable, flat needles with white stripes underneath them, whereas red spruce have stiff, entirely green, squared-off needles.

The Lewis Fork Trail crosses Lewis Fork at mile 2.9. The remains of an old bridge abutment are evident. Look upstream for a small, attractive waterfall. The trail briefly steepens before resuming its moderate grade. Beyond here, the track crosses many small, shallow, wide spring branches flowing off Mount Rogers above. Intersect the Lewis Fork Spur Trail on a sharp switchback at mile 3.4. The spur trail leaves right and climbs 0.4 mile to reach the Mount Rogers Trail on Elk Ridge.

Begin to swing beneath the bulk of Mount Rogers. Enter an area rife with rhododendron and pass the headwaters of Lewis Fork, disguised as a series of spring seeps that flow across the trail. The logging grade peters out in the rhododendron, and the path now undulates through rocky woods. In these woods, northern red squirrels—or "boomers," as they are often called—will scold you as you pass them. At mile 5.0, clear a gate. Ascend to meet the Cliffside Trail in the edge of a field at mile 5.2. The Cliffside Trail drops steeply left to intersect the Lewis Fork Trail in 1.5 miles. The Lewis Fork Trail proceeds up a meadow broken with bushes and occasional fir and spruce trees. Intersect the Pine Mountain Trail at mile 5.3. It leads left 0.9 mile to the Appalachian Trail and right 1.0 mile to the AT at Rhododendron Gap. Stay in mostly open country, leaving the Lewis Fork Wilderness and reaching the Crest Trail at mile 5.5. The Lewis Fork Trail ends here. From this junction, the Crest Trail leads left 1.5 miles to Scales and right 1.1 mile to Rhododendron Gap.

Access

From exit 45 on I-81 near Marion, drive 6.0 miles south on VA 16, passing the Jennings Visitor Center. Stay on VA 16 for 11.0 miles to VA 603 (Fairwood Road) in Trout Dale. Turn right on VA 603 and follow it for 4.6 miles to the equestrian trailhead and 4.8 miles to the hiker trailhead.

Little Wilson Creek Trail

Type:	Foot only
Length:	1.6 miles
Difficulty:	Moderate to difficult
Use:	Low
Condition:	Fair to good
Highlights:	Wilderness hiking, solitude, trout fishing
Book Map #:	9
USGS Topo:	Trout Dale
Connections:	None

This lesser-used path makes an obscure start and then enters the more obscure Little Wilson Creek valley, where attractive cascades crash down a heavily wooded valley. True to form, the path peters out in a hodgepodge of grassy glades, rhododendron thickets, and hawthorn groves. Anglers and solitude seekers will enjoy this valley walk.

This narrative starts at the first gate on VA 817. Begin hiking up the now-rough, rocky road past a clearing and then an old cabin. Big Wilson Creek lies to the left. Pass a couple of more clearings; then squeeze between large boulders. At 0.3 mile, the trail splits. An unmaintained horse trail leaves left to cross Big Wilson Creek. The Little Wilson Creek Trail leaves right, passing signs indicating the Little Wilson Creek Wilderness and trout fishing regulations. Virginia's trout streams have three kinds of trout in them: brook, rainbow, and brown. The only native trout is the brook trout, which is technically not a trout but a char from Arctic waters, forced south by the last Ice Age. During the logging days at the beginning of the last century, many of the Old Dominion's streams became warm and silted, unfit for the finicky brook trout. Some early naturalists and lumber companies noticed the absence of the char and so restocked many streams with rainbows, natives of the West, and later brown trout that were brought from Germany and Scotland. They were brought into the mountain streams by rail, mule, and foot, expanding their range through the years. Now, the rainbow is king in the Mount Rogers area and the native brook has been pushed back into remote headwater streams high in the mountains. In retrospect, it would have been best to restock these streams with the native brook trout. However, 600 miles of these are seasonal streams that are stocked only in winter, when the waters are cool enough for trout to survive. In addition to cool water, trout need clean water with minimal sedimentation. Stream sedimentation smothers both trout eggs and aquatic insects upon which the trout feed.

Keep going forward on the Little Wilson Creek Trail, which veers right to enter the Little Wilson Creek watershed. The single-track path curves along the right bank of Little Wilson Creek in rhododendron and mountain laurel, with an overstory of oak.

Pick up an old roadbed at 0.6 mile. The rocky route widens and rises well above the creek, which falls in many small cascades over large boulders. At 1.0 mile, the path comes to the stream, then leaves the roadbed, and climbs steeply up and to the right. At mile 1.4, pass a large, cabin-sized boulder to the right of the trail.

At mile 1.6, the Little Wilson Creek Trail peters out near a roadbed running parallel to a mountainside glade. It is possible, however, to reach the Kabel Trail, which crosses Little Wilson Creek a very rough half mile upstream. This last section is extremely challenging and should be attempted only by experienced off-trail hikers. The key to meeting the Kabel Trail is to stay as close to the east bank of Little Wilson Creek without getting caught up in the extensive rhododendron thickets that grow profusely along the streamside. To avoid those entanglements, bushwhackers should make their way northwest through grassy glades, hawthorn copses, and some rhododendron thickets, while crossing several feeder branches of Wilson Creek and keeping Little Wilson Creek within earshot.

Access

From the Little Red Caboose in Damascus, drive east on US 58 for 29.0 miles to VA 817 (Briar Run Road). Turn left on VA 817 and follow it 1.2 miles to a metal pole gate. Beyond this gate, the road may or may not be open, but if the road is open, it is a rough four-wheel-drive trek 0.3 mile to the upper trailhead. Passenger vehicles should stop at the first gate.

Mount Rogers Spur Trail

Type:	Foot only
Length:	0.5 mile
Difficulty:	Moderate
Use:	High
Condition:	Good
Highlights:	Highest point in Virginia, views, spruce-fir forest
Book Map #:	5
USGS Topo:	Whitetop Mountain
Connections:	Appalachian Trail

This path leads from a high point in the Mount Rogers high country to the highest point in the state of Virginia. It offers views in its first half and then enters a dense spruce-fir forest to top out on a rock outcrop that is 5,729 feet in elevation. There are no views at the high point, as the outcrop is encircled by dense evergreens.

Leave the Appalachian Trail and walk northwest through a field broken by cherry, spruce, Fraser fir, and mountain ash trees. Pine Mountain, with its outcrops and open fields, is visible to the right. Behind you lies most of the high country. At 0.3 mile, enter thick woods of red spruce and Fraser fir. The primary way to distinguish the two trees is by their needles. Fraser fir trees are flat, fragrant, and friendly, meaning they are wider on one side than the other, smell strongly of evergreen,

Hiker near the actual Mount Rogers.

and are pliable to the touch. Fraser fir is the only native southern fir, growing in the mountains of Virginia, North Carolina, and Tennessee. The needles of red spruce are squared off, have a milder smell, and are stiff to the touch. They grow mostly in New England and Canada but range southward down the spine of the Appalachians into Tennessee.

Keep ascending on a sometimes muddy path through sunlight-blocking woods. Climb sharply just before reaching the rocky summit of the mountain. At 0.5 mile, look on the rock outcrop for a survey marker indicating the actual high point of Mount Rogers, elevation 5,729 feet.

Access

The Mount Rogers Spur Trail is an interior trail. It can be reached by hiking north 3.8 miles on the Appalachian Trail from Elk Garden.

Mount Rogers Trail

Type:	Foot only
Length:	4.0 miles
Difficulty:	Difficult
Use:	High
Condition:	Good
Highlights:	Numerous forest environments, relic old-growth woods
Book Map #:	5
USGS Topo:	Whitetop Mountain
Connections:	Flat Top Trail, Lewis Fork Spur Trail, Appalachian Trail

This trail is popular with hikers headed for the highest point in the state and with campers staying at Grindstone campground. The path starts at a gap between Fox Creek and Big Laurel Creek valleys and then heads south in a mixed upland hardwood forest. A few switchbacks take hikers higher into a very attractive northern hardwood forest on Elk Ridge, where there are nearly pure stands of beech. The footpath then ascends the north slope of Mount Rogers, where red spruce and finally Fraser fir come to prominence as the trail exceeds the 5,000-foot level. It ends just above Deep Gap at the Appalachian Trail, leaving hikers 2.3 more miles to walk before reaching the actual summit of Mount Rogers.

Leave Fairwood Valley Road on a plank walkway flanked by rhododendron. Continue south into a mixed upland hardwood forest of maple, Fraser magnolia, and oak. At 0.2 mile, intersect the Mount Rogers campground access trail, coming 0.3 mile from Grindstone Campground. (This access trail leaves from near the Opossum Loop, passes through rhododendron, and spans several small streams via railroad-tie footbridges before meeting the Mount Rogers Trail.) Enter the Lewis Fork Wilderness. Start to switchback up the north side of Elk Ridge. Cross five small streamlets on little railroad-tie bridges. The blue-blazed footpath begins to switchback up the north slope of Elk Ridge. Make the final switchback and reach the spine of Elk Ridge. Walk beneath a classic northern hardwood forest of yellow birch, beech, cherry, and sugar maple to intersect the Lewis Fork Spur Trail at mile 2.0. The Lewis Fork Spur Trail leaves left 0.3 mile to intersect the Lewis Fork Trail. Keep heading up the spine of Elk Ridge and gently ascend beneath a nearly pure stand of beech trees over a light understory. At mile 2.5, leave the flat of Elk Ridge and veer to the northwest side of Mount Rogers. Begin climbing, passing a large outcrop on the left and tracing an old woods road. Climb beneath relic old-growth yellow birch and cherry trees mixed with younger red spruce and Fraser fir. When this area was logged, these trees were deemed unsuitable as timber, probably because they appeared misshapen in one way or another. Now they have survived to grow to this day.

A common trailside plant here is the hobblebush, also known as witch-hobble. It has big, roundish, heart-shaped leaves that are finely toothed along their edges. Witch-hobble sometimes forms nearly impenetrable thickets. Mountain people would break off limbs of this bush and put them over their doorways to ward off witches. Nowadays, hikers notice this high-elevation plant as one of the first to show its autumn colors, often by early August.

The single-track trail stays nearly level through rocky woods. There are occasional views of the Iron Mountains to the north. Cross a shallow, rocky rill at 3.2 miles. Climb for another half-mile before topping out and starting a moderate downgrade to meet the Appalachian Trail at 4.0 miles. The Mount Rogers Trail ends here. The AT leads 2.1 miles right to Elk Garden and 1.8 miles left to the Mount Rogers Spur Trail, which reaches the actual summit of Mount Rogers.

Access

From exit 45 on I-81 near Marion, drive 6.0 miles south on VA 16, passing the Jennings Visitor Center. Stay on VA 16 for 11.0 miles to VA 603 (Fairwood Road) in Troutdale. Turn right on VA 603 and follow it for 5.6 miles to the trailhead, on the left just past the Grayson-Smyth county line. Hikers should park on the north side of the road just before reaching the county line on the right. A second access trail reaches the main Mount Rogers Trail from Grindstone Campground.

Old Orchard Spur Trail

Type:	Foot, horse
Length:	1.7 miles
Difficulty:	Moderate
Use:	Low
Condition:	Fair to poor
Highlights:	Good loop trail
Book Map #:	8

USGS Topo: Trout Dale, Whitetop Mountain
Connections: Old Orchard Trail, Virginia Highlands Horse Trail

Using a combination of newer trail and old roads, the Old Orchard Spur Trail travels the lower slope of Pine Mountain, providing a connection and loop possibilities for equestrians in the Fox Creek area. It starts 1.1 miles from Fairwood Valley on the Old Orchard Trail and runs along the 3,800-foot level of Pine Mountain on a fairly narrow and often muddy track. It crosses a few shallow feeder streams and then passes an abandoned trail before taking a sharp turn to the north on an old roadbed. The trail remains in poor shape as it runs along a rib ridge of Pine Mountain, finally dropping sharply to reach the Virginia Highlands Horse Trail near Fox Creek.

Start the Old Orchard Spur Trail by heading eastward away from the Old Orchard Trail on a narrow, often muddy track. The path is either level or slopes slightly downhill among a mixed forest of northern and southern hardwoods. Leave the Lewis Fork Wilderness at 0.1 mile. Cross a couple of wide, shallow spring branches. At 0.8 mile, a closed trail comes in from the right as the mountainside levels out.

Come to a "T" intersection at 1.0 mile. Another closed trail comes in from the right. The Old Orchard Spur Trail turns left and joins an old roadbed. The path is much wider now as it rolls north over a rib ridge. Descend off the roadbed at mile 1.2, passing yet another closed trail. The rate of descent sharpens as the path switchbacks down toward Fairwood Valley. Pass a fourth closed trail before leveling out and reaching the Virginia Highlands Horse Trail at mile 1.7. From here, the VHHT leads left 0.1 mile to Fox Creek Horse Camp and right 3.5 miles to Scales and the high country.

Access

The Old Orchard Spur Trail is an interior trail. It can be reached by taking the Old Orchard Trail for 1.1 miles from Fairwood Valley or by taking the Virginia Highlands Horse Trail 0.1 mile from Fairwood Valley near Fox Creek Horse Camp.

Old Orchard Trail

Type:	Foot, horse
Length:	1.7 miles
Difficulty:	Moderate
Use:	Low
Condition:	Fair to good
Highlights:	Good loop trail
Book Map #:	8, 4
USGS Topo:	Whitetop Mountain
Connections:	Fairwood Valley Trail, Appalachian Trail, Old Orchard Spur Trail, Lewis Fork Trail

This trail connects the Fairwood Valley with the Old Orchard area on the lower north slope of Pine Mountain. It uses an old grade for nearly its entire length, first passing through a meadow and then winding up the side of Pine Mountain via wide turns. Once in the Old Orchard area, the path nears the Old Orchard trail shelter and then descends to intersect the Lewis Fork Trail. Its connections with other bridle paths make it a viable part of any Fairwood Valley loop ride.

The Old Orchard Trail actually starts at the junction with the Fairwood Valley Trail, which runs alongside VA 603 (Fairwood Valley Road). This junction is a half mile north of Fox Creek Horse Camp. Trail travelers can simply pick up the Old Orchard Trail as it crosses Fairwood Valley Road, just a few yards after its beginning. From the junction with the Fairwood Valley Trail, the Old Orchard Trail heads south a few yards and crosses VA 603. Keep going south, skirting the wooded edge of a field that is growing up in locust and ferns. Look back for a good view of Hurricane Mountain.

At 0.2 mile, come to a sharp left turn beside a small stream. Enter the woods and begin to gently angle up the slope of Pine Mountain. The forest here has northern species such as beech and birch but also tulip trees and Fraser magnolia. Soil berms provide erosion control. Enter the Lewis Fork Wilderness at 0.4 mile, maintaining a moderate climb. Intersect the Appalachian Trail at 0.7 mile, which connects Fairwood Valley to the Old Orchard area.

Come to the Old Orchard Spur Trail at mile 1.1. It leaves left and heads 1.7 miles to intersect the Virginia Highlands Horse Trail. The Old Orchard Trail continues forward as a wide, rocky, and sometimes muddy trailbed. The woods level out as it nears the Old Orchard area. Intersect the Appalachian Trail once again at mile 1.4. The AT leads left 100 yards to the Old Orchard trail shelter. The Old Orchard Trail continues forward through a young forest of multi-trunked red maples that have invaded the lower part of a clearing. Descend to reach the Lewis Fork Trail at mile 1.7. The Lewis Fork Trail leads left 3.9 miles to the Crest Trail and right 1.6 miles to Fairwood Valley.

Access

From exit 45 on I-81 near Marion, drive 6.0 miles south on VA 16, passing the Jennings Visitor Center. Stay on VA 16 for 11.0 miles to VA 603 (Fairwood Road) in Troutdale. Turn right on VA 603 and follow it for 4.3 miles. The Old Orchard Trail starts just beyond the old Fairwood Valley Picnic Area.

Pine Mountain Trail

Type:	Foot only
Length:	1.9 miles
Difficulty:	Moderate
Use:	High

Condition:	Good
Highlights:	Blooming rhododendron, views
Book Map #:	5, 8
USGS Topo:	Whitetop Mountain
Connections:	Appalachian Trail, Crest Trail, Lewis Fork Trail

On average, the Pine Mountain Trail may be one of the highest trails in the Mount Rogers high country. Formerly the route of the Appalachian Trail, the Pine Mountain Trail traces the western shoulder of Pine Mountain from near Scales to Rhododendron Gap. Along the way, it passes through northern hardwood and spruce forests and open meadows, as well as by tall outcrops and major rhododendron thickets. The lowest elevation is just under 4,800 feet and the highest is 5,400 feet.

Begin the Pine Mountain Trail after hiking 1.3 miles on the Appalachian Trail to reach the Pine Mountain Trail. Enter a spruce–beech–yellow birch woodland accentuated by gray boulders. The single-track trail heads southwest along the border of the Lewis Fork Wilderness, which lies to the right. Come to the first of many small clearings, clearing a stile. Continue in and out of small meadows with moderate, occasional, uphill grades. At 0.5 mile, reach a large, open meadow with great views of Wilburn Ridge and Mount Rogers dead ahead. The rest of Pine Mountain lies before you.

Cross a tiny stream before intersecting the Lewis Fork Trail at 0.9 mile. There is a fenced-in spring to the left. From this junction, the Lewis Fork Trail leads left 0.2 mile to intersect the Crest Trail and right 0.1 mile to intersect the Cliffside Trail and then, 5.3 miles farther, to reach VA 603 in Fairwood Valley.

Keep going forward on the blue-blazed Pine Mountain Trail, ascending into forest. There is a wooden fence to the left. Spruce trees join the mix of field and forest. At mile 1.2, the trail twists and turns through rhododendron and rock. The brush canopy lowers, availing views. There are more views in occasional clearing and outcrops. The scenery keeps improving, and the trail keeps climbing. Trailside boulders avail even more vista opportunities. Make sporadic sharp climbs up rock faces and beside low-slung rhododendron to intersect the Appalachian Trail at mile 1.9. The Pine Mountain Trail ends here. There is a very large outcrop to the right of this intersection that begs to be climbed. On the AT, it is 5.0 miles right to Elk Garden and 7.0 miles left to Scales.

Access

The Pine Mountain Trail is an interior trail. It can be reached by hiking the Appalachian Trail 1.3 miles north from Scales or by hiking 5.0 miles north on the AT from Elk Garden.

Rhododendron Gap Trail

Type:	Foot, horse, bicycle
Length:	1.4 miles
Difficulty:	Moderate
Use:	Moderate to high
Condition:	Good to fair
Highlights:	Immense vistas, numerous trail connections
Book Map #:	5
USGS Topo:	Whitetop Mountain
Connections:	Springs Trail, Rhododendron Trail, Appalachian Trail, Virginia Highlands Horse Trail, Wilburn Ridge Trail, Crest Trail

The Rhododendron Gap Trail does not actually reach Rhododendron Gap but does come within 0.2 mile of it. It connects the Grayson Highlands State Park Rhododendron Trail with the Crest Trail, which in turn reaches Rhododendron Gap. The Rhododendron Gap Trail traverses some spectacular mountain scenery along the southwest slope of Wilburn Ridge. The views are nearly constant and are framed by grassy meadows, huge boulders, and windswept trees. In early June, the rhododendron blooms in profusion and is a sight to see. The Rhododendron Gap Trail starts around 5,000 feet at the border with Grayson Highlands State Park. It traverses federal land and moderately climbs in scenic high country, making numerous trail connections along the way.

Start the Rhododendron Gap Trail by leaving the state park from the Rhododendron Trail and climbing a fence stile. From the fence stile, the Rhododendron Gap Trail lies between the Appalachian Trail and the Virginia Highlands Horse Trail. Begin to ascend an open slope dotted with Fraser fir trees. The valley of Quebec Creek lies to the right. At 0.1 mile, leave the roadbed that the trail has been following and keep rising. Here, the unsigned Springs Trail begins and follows the roadbed. At 0.5 mile, come to an outcrop, where wind-stunted bushes grow in pockets. The trail winds amid the outcrop and becomes rocky and rutted. Intersect the AT at 0.8 mile. Continue forward and shortly intersect the Wilburn Ridge Trail. It leaves right 0.5 mile toward Rhododendron Gap and left 0.5 mile to intersect the AT. Keep heading north over the grassy area and look west over the Cabin Creek valley to wooded Cabin Ridge. The dark mantle of Mount Rogers lies in the distance.

Climb onto a rocky slope vegetated with berry bushes and Fraser fir. A rock outcrop of Wilburn Ridge lies above to the right. Level off; then come to the Crest Trail at mile 1.4. The Rhododendron Gap Trail ends here. From this junction, to the left, it is 0.6 mile on the Crest Trail to the Virginia Highlands Horse Trail. To the right, it is 0.2 mile on the Crest Trail to the actual Rhododendron Gap.

View from Rhododendron Gap. Photo by Jeff Patrick.

Access

The Rhododendron Gap Trail is an interior trail. It can be reached by hiking 0.8 mile on the Rhododendron Trail from Grayson Highlands State Park or 2.8 miles on the Crest Trail from Scales.

Scales Trail

Type:	Foot, horse, bicycle
Length:	1.3 miles
Difficulty:	Moderate
Use:	High
Condition:	Good
Highlights:	Views, numerous trail connections
Book Map #:	8, 9
USGS Topo:	Trout Dale
Connections:	Crest Trail, Appalachian Trail, Virginia Highlands Horse Trail, First Peak Trail, Bearpen Trail, Wilson Creek Trail, Seed Orchard Road Trail

The Scales Trail connects the mountain gap area known as Scales (so named because cattle were historically corralled and weighed there after they spent the summer in the pastures of the high country) with Wilson Creek. It starts with good views and keeps them most of the way, while occasionally entering and exiting woodland. The path skirts the Little Wilson Creek Wilderness before crossing the East Fork of Big Wilson Creek and ending at the boundary of Grayson Highlands State Park, where it meets the Wilson Creek and Seed Orchard Road trails.

Start the Scales Trail on the far end of the corral at Scales, opposite where Forest Road 613 enters Scales. Follow an old roadbed downhill through a mix of field, brush, and trees. There are good views of Wilburn Ridge dead ahead—and all around, for that matter. Enter an occasional bank of cherry, hawthorn, and red maple trees.

At 0.5 mile, intersect the Bearpen Trail. It leaves left 1.2 miles to meet the Big Wilson Creek Trail. Continue descending at a moderate grade through rhododendron. East Fork of Big Wilson Creek lies off to the right. Spring branches cross the trail from atop Stone Mountain. The old roadbed keeps passing in and out of woods. At 0.8 mile, come along a fence line and the Little Wilson Creek Wilderness.

At mile 1.0, drop off the roadbed and get a view of the state park seed orchard on the left. Keep descending to reach the Appalachian Trail at mile 1.2. The AT leads left 7.2 miles to Fox Creek trailhead in Fairwood Valley and right 9.8 miles to Elk Garden. Soon come to a crossing of East Fork of Big Wilson Creek. If the water is high, hikers can use the AT footbridge to cross the stream. At mile 1.2, the Scales Trail ends just before coming to Big Wilson Creek. To the left, the Seed Orchard Road leads 0.7 mile to meet the state park Horse Trail and the Upchurch Road Trail; to the right, the Wilson Creek Trail leads 0.7 mile to join the Virginia Highlands Horse Trail.

Access

From exit 45 on I-81 near Marion, drive 6.0 miles south on VA 16, passing the Jennings Visitor Center. Stay on VA 16 for 11.0 miles to VA 603 (Fairwood Road) in Troutdale. Turn right on VA 603 and follow it for 2.7 miles to Forest Road 613. (FR 613 is a rough, high-clearance-vehicle road and is not recommended for low-slung passenger vehicles.) Turn left on FR 613 and follow it 4.0 miles to dead-end at Scales.

Springs Trail

Type:	Foot
Length:	0.5 mile
Difficulty:	Easy
Use:	Medium
Condition:	Good
Highlights:	Views, springs, campsite
Book Map #:	5
USGS Topo:	Trout Dale
Connections:	Rhododendron Gap Trail

The unsigned Springs Trail follows an old road grade along the southeast side of Wilburn Ridge before dead-ending in a half mile. Leave the Rhododendron Gap Trail 0.1 miles from its beginning. Here the Crest Trail leaves uphill to the left, and the Springs Trail begins. Trace a level grade on an open hillside mixed with spruce and hawthorn. The south end of Wilburn Ridge is clearly visible across Quebec Branch. Shortly enter a thicket of beech and yellow birch before reopening onto grassy country, where springs flow across the path, giving the trail its name. Large rock outcrops thrust forth from the meadows. Cross two streams before the trail ends at a rocky campsite shaded by yellow birch and maple.

Access

The Springs Trail is an interior trail. It can be accessed by following the Rhododendron Gap Trail 0.1 mile from its beginning near Grayson Highlands State Park.

Sugar Maple Trail

Type:	Foot, horse
Length:	2.2 miles
Difficulty:	Moderate
Use:	Low
Condition:	Good
Highlights:	Views, aspen trees, solitude, maple tree growing out from washtub
Book Map #:	5
USGS Topo:	Whitetop Mountain
Connections:	Helton Creek Trail

The Sugar Maple Trail is a little-used jewel of a path that can be part of a loop hike with the busier Helton Creek Trail. It starts in the Helton Creek valley to climb through pastureland past some uncommon aspen trees. The trail keeps ascending at a moderate but steady clip via numerous switchbacks, up the west side of Brier Ridge to enter the Lewis Fork Wilderness. It then swings north to a high point and makes a slight descent to once again intersect the Helton Creek Trail.

Leave the lower junction with the Helton Creek Trail and climb through mountainside pasture. Look on trail right for a red maple tree growing out of an old washtub. The maple has almost filled the entire tub. At 0.1 mile, look left for a dense stand of bigtooth aspen trees, rare in this part of the world. Enjoy mountain views before diving into a rhododendron thicket, only to emerge at a wire gate. Do not pass through the gate. Instead, turn sharply right and climb steadily alongside a fence on trail left. Notice the conifers mixed in with the sugar maple, beech, birch, and other components of the northern hardwood forest, broken by occasional clear areas.

At 0.4 mile, pass though a wooden gate and keep climbing. A side trail just before the gate leads forward to a field being overcome by locust trees and blackberries. Beyond the gate, come alongside a meadow to the left and then a sign indicating the Lewis Fork Wilderness. (Notice piles of rocks indicating formerly farmed land. To make the soil easier to till, homesteaders unearthed these rocks years ago and left them in piles beside their fields.) Begin a series of switchbacks that work up the side of Brier Ridge. Top out at mile 1.7 in rocky woods and then gently descend, making one last switchback to the left before intersecting the Helton Creek Trail at 2.2 miles. From here, the Helton Creek Trail leads right 1.0 mile to the Virginia Highlands Horse Trail and forward 2.0 miles down to the lower Helton Creek and Sugar Maple trailhead.

Access

From the Little Red Caboose in Damascus, drive east on US 58 for 20.3 miles to VA 783 (Helton Creek Lane). Turn left on VA 783 and follow it 1.3 miles to dead-end at a metal pole gate. Walk the Helton Creek Trail, which starts at the metal gate, for 0.1 mile to a wooden gate. The Sugar Maple Trail starts on the far side of the wooden gate.

Switchback Trail

Type:	Foot, horse, bicycle
Length:	1.2 miles
Difficulty:	Moderate
Use:	Moderate
Condition:	Good
Highlights:	Connector path to Virginia Highlands Horse Trail
Book Map #:	8
USGS Topo:	Trout Dale
Connections:	Virginia Highlands Horse Trail

The Switchback Trail connects the lower part of Forest Road 613 with the Virginia Highlands Horse Trail. It leaves Forest Road 613 and follows a railroad grade a short distance and then winds up a ridgeline to a knob and a flat, coming to a second intersection with FR 613. It then makes a southwesterly course for the Virginia Highlands Horse Trail. The path is primarily used as part of a loop by equestrians out of Fairwood Valley.

Leave FR 613 and follow a railroad grade a short distance. This grade was used by logging trains to negotiate the sharp turn in the railroad that FR 613 now follows. First, the train would climb a mountain. Then, instead of negotiating a sharp turn, the train would head away from the main track on a short spur line, continuing up the mountain with the rear of the train now in front and the former front of the train now in the rear—a "switch back." Locomotives were positioned at either end of the train while climbing from Fairwood Valley up to Scales.

Follow the railroad grade away from 613 and work around a fence line, quickly returning to the grade and climbing along a small streamlet to the left. At 0.1 mile, leave the railroad grade and enter deep woods. Keep heading uphill through mixed hardwoods interspersed with large boulders. Make a few switchbacks in rocky woodland; then top out on a knob.

Slightly descend to a mountain flat and cross Forest Road 613 at 0.9 mile. Resume a moderate climb through maple–chestnut oak–magnolia woods on a single-track path. Begin to descend just before reaching the Virginia Highlands Horse Trail at 1.2 miles. From here, the VHHT leads left 1.1 miles to Scales and right 2.5 miles down to Fairwood Valley and the Fox Creek Horse Camp.

Access

From exit 45 on I-81 near Marion, drive 6.0 miles south on VA 16, passing the Jennings Visitor Center. Stay on VA 16 for 11.0 miles to VA 603, Fairwood Road, in Troutdale. Turn right on VA 603 and follow it for 2.7 miles to Forest Road 613. (FR 613 is a rough, high-clearance-vehicle road not recommended for low-slung passenger vehicles.) Turn left on FR 613 and follow it 1.2 miles to the Switchback Trail, which will be on the left.

Third Peak Trail

Type:	Foot, horse, bicycle
Length:	1.7 miles
Difficulty:	Moderate to difficult
Condition:	Fair to good
Highlights:	Views at top
Book Map #:	8
USGS Topo:	Trout Dale
Connections:	First Peak Trail

This trail begins on an old railroad grade and then climbs up the valley of Solomon Branch, never too near the creek, and works its way into the high country to a saddle between Stone Mountain and Third Peak. Parts of the trail can be muddy after rainy periods. The path follows the railroad grade just a short distance before winding up the valley, where the forest transitions from maple-oak to yellow birch–beech–red spruce woods. Finally, it enters open country and gains views from nearly 4,900 feet.

Leave Forest Road 613 and pass a few boulders on a nearly level railroad grade. Continue along a fence line and come to a trail junction at 0.2 mile. Ahead, the grade dead-ends. To the left, an unmaintained bridle path leads down Solomon

Branch. The Third Peak Trail leads right, away from the railroad grade and uphill. Begin a southward course up the valley of Solomon Branch. The stream is never in sight or heard. A series of switchbacks takes trail travelers steadily up toward Stone Mountain. Cross an intermittent streambed at 0.5 mile. Maintain a constant upgrade.

Pass through an old, decrepit gate and fence line at mile 1.1. The course is nearly level here on an old woods road. Leave the woods road at mile 1.4. Make a final climb through spruce, cherry, and yellow birch on a rocky, rooty, and sometimes muddy track. Clear a stock gate and enter a meadow. Just ahead, at mile 1.7, is the intersection with the First Peak Trail. From here the First Peak Trail leads right 0.8 mile to Scales and left 2.4 miles to the Hightree Rock and Kabel trails.

Access

From exit 45 on I-81 near Marion, drive 6.0 miles south on VA 16, passing the Jennings Visitor Center. Stay on VA 16 for 11.0 miles to VA 603 (Fairwood Road) in Troutdale. Turn right on VA 603 and follow it for 2.7 miles to Forest Road 613. (FR 613 is a rough, high-clearance-vehicle road not recommended for low-slung passenger vehicles.) Turn left on FR 613 and follow it 2.8 miles to the Third Peak Trail, which is on the left and unsigned. It starts by several large boulders.

Whispering Waters Trail

Type:	Foot only
Length:	0.6 mile
Difficulty:	Easy
Use:	Moderate
Condition:	Very good
Highlights:	Interpretive tree-identification signs
Book Map #:	4
USGS Topo:	Whitetop Mountain
Connections:	None

This trail is mostly used by Grindstone campground visitors. It makes a loop along Grindstone Branch. There are many interpretive tree-identification signs along the way as it heads up the rocky, heavily wooded valley. Leave the campground picnic parking area and walk a rock-lined path past the campground amphitheater. Come to a trail junction. Stay left and enter a hardwood forest of birch, beech, and cherry with occasional Fraser magnolias. Head upstream through the valley to bridge Grindstone Branch. Pick up an old woods road and pass through the rocky woodland. Descend to the creek again, crossing it on a bridge made of several logs lain together. Pass along the rear of the amphitheater to complete the loop, backtracking a few steps to the parking area.

Access

From exit 45 on I-81 near Marion, drive 6.0 miles south on VA 16, passing the Jennings Visitor Center. Stay on VA 16 for 11.0 miles to VA 603 (Fairwood Valley Road) in Troutdale. Turn right on VA 603 and follow it for 6.0 miles to Grindstone Campground. Pass the entrance station at Grindstone Campground and stay right, heading to the picnic area. The Grindstone Trail starts near the upper end of the picnic parking area.

Wilburn Ridge Trail

Type:	Foot only
Length:	1.0 mile
Difficulty:	Moderate
Use:	High
Condition:	Good
Highlights:	Great views, unusual trail topography
Book Map #:	5
USGS Topo:	Whitetop Mountain
Connections:	Appalachian Trail, Rhododendron Gap Trail

This is one of the most scenic trails in a long list of scenic trails in the Mount Rogers high country. It diverges from the Appalachian Trail on Wilburn Ridge and makes

Wilburn Trail offers backpackers a scenic trek.

a detour around, over, and through high rock outcrops that burst forth from the windswept meadows of Wilburn Ridge. It climbs amid rhododendron, over boulders, along long rock faces, and steeply down to grassy swaths where the views are only exceeded by the stone towers above them. In short, don't bypass this trail. However, hikers with full backpacks may have a tough time navigating some tight and steep sections.

Leave the Appalachian Trail 5.5 miles from Elk Garden. The Wilburn Ridge Trail diverges right in a compact rhododendron thicket. Wind up on a very rocky path and come alongside a rock wall. Tunnel beneath mountain ash trees and switchback to the first outcrop at 0.1 mile. Views from the top of this hard, erosion-resistant rhyolite, a volcanic rock similar to granite, are far reaching. Drop off the outcrop steeply on boulder jumbles. Stay with the blue blazes and, at 0.5 mile, emerge onto a more level grassy flat. Soon cross the Rhododendron Gap Trail. The AT is farther to the left in the same meadow. The Wilburn Ridge Trail continues forward toward another, more brushy outcrop. Reach and ascend the outcrop, where Fraser firs cling to the thin soil and potholes hold water in wet times. The views are nothing short of awesome: Mount Rogers, Haw Orchard Mountain, and much more. Leave the outcrop and descend through another meadow to intersect the AT at 1.0 mile. From here it is 0.8 mile left back to the first junction with the Wilburn Ridge Trail and 10.3 miles right to Fox Creek trailhead and VA 603.

Access

The Wilburn Ridge Trail is an interior trail. It can be reached by hiking 5.5 miles north on the Appalachian Trail from Elk Garden or 0.8 mile on the Rhododendron Trail from Massie Gap at Grayson Highlands State Park and then 0.3 mile southbound on the Appalachian Trail.

Wilson Creek Trail

Type:	Foot, horse, bicycle
Length:	0.7 mile
Difficulty:	Moderate
Use:	Moderate
Condition:	Good
Highlights:	Views, blueberries and blackberries in season
Book Map #:	9
USGS Topo:	Trout Dale
Connections:	Virginia Highlands Horse Trail, Appalachian Trail, Scales Trail, Seed Orchard Road Trail

The Wilson Creek Trail is a relatively short connector path that uses an old high-country road. It leads from the confluence of East Fork Big Wilson Creek and Big

Wilson Creek up along the East Fork to intersect the Virginia Highlands Horse Trail. Just as on many trails in the open high country, blueberries and blackberries are abundant in season, usually from late July through late August.

Start the Wilson Creek Trail by leaving the Scales Trail and the Seed Orchard Road Trail to ascend along East Fork Wilson Creek. Span a small stream via culvert and come to the Appalachian Trail at 0.1 mile. It leaves left to reach Elk Garden in 9.7 miles and right 7.3 miles to reach Fairwood Valley. Keep going forward, passing a fence line. There is field uphill to the left. Level out and gain views of Pine Mountain.

At 0.3 mile, cross a major feeder stream of East Fork Big Wilson Creek. The trail increases its ascent in a meadow with phenomenal views of Wilburn Ridge and lots of berries along the trail. Keep climbing to intersect the Virginia Highlands Horse Trail at 0.7 mile. The VHHT leads right 0.6 miles to Scales and left 8.7 miles to Elk Garden.

Access

The Wilson Creek Trail is an interior trail. It can be reached by traveling 0.6 miles south on the Virginia Highlands Horse Trail from Scales or by traveling 1.3 miles on the Scales Trail from Scales.

Trails of Grayson Highlands State Park

Appalachian Spur Trail

Type:	Foot only
Length:	0.8 mile
Difficulty:	Moderate
Use:	High
Condition:	Good
Highlights:	Meadows, views, Appalachian Trail access
Book Map #:	9
USGS Topo:	Whitetop Mountain
Connections:	State park Horse Trail, Appalachian Trail

This trail provides quick access to the Appalachian Trail and the Mount Rogers high country. Along the way it offers some serious warm-up views of things to come. Leave the Overnight Backpacker Parking Area and bisect a rhododendron tunnel to emerge onto a field. After this, pass alternating field and forest to reach a rock outcrop atop Wilburn Ridge and the AT.

Start the trail by crossing a boardwalk to a stream flowing beneath rhododendron. Soon come to a gate. Pass through the gate to enter a small meadow. At 0.1 mile, intersect the state park Horse Trail. Veer right, staying with the blue blazes, and enter northern hardwood forest mixed with spruce. Keep ascending and open to a clearing at 0.3 mile. There are good views to the right of Haw Orchard Mountain and mountain lands to the southeast.

Alternate with field and forest before opening into a significant clearing with widespread views to the east. Crest out on Wilburn Ridge at 0.8 mile to intersect the Appalachian Trail. From here it is 2.7 miles left to Rhododendron Gap and 9.3 miles right to Fairwood Valley.

High country ponies enchant hikers.

Access

To reach Grayson Highlands State Park from the Little Red Caboose in Damascus, drive east on US 58 for 26.0 miles to the park entrance, which will be on the left. This trail starts at the Overnight Backpacker Parking Area. Head up the main park road and turn right on the campground road. After the right turn, immediately look left for the Overnight Backpacker Parking Area.

Big Pinnacle Trail

Type:	Foot only
Length:	0.5 mile
Difficulty:	Moderate to difficult
Use:	High
Condition:	Excellent
Highlights:	360-degree views from atop Big Pinnacle
Book Map #:	9
USGS Topo:	Trout Dale
Connections:	Rhododendron Gap Trail, Cabin Creek Trail, Horse Trail, Twin Pinnacles Trail

Great views await hikers of this short but steep trail. It leads from Massie Gap through rocky woods to a craggy outcrop on Haw Orchard Mountain. From atop this outcrop, there are 360-degree views of the Virginia Highlands, also including mountain lands of Tennessee and North Carolina. Leave Massie Gap and enter a northern hardwood forest, primarily yellow birch mixed with spruce. Wind up the slope of Haw Orchard Mountain and pass alongside an outcrop at 0.2 mile. Keep ascending and arrive at the base of Big Pinnacle at 0.4 mile. Climb steeply up a rocky path, where stone steps make the trail more foot-friendly. Soon intersect the Twin Pinnacles Trail. At this point, follow the yellow blazes right, uphill, and emerge onto the rock outcrop of the Big Pinnacle, the park's highest point at 5,048 feet. Look out on the mountainous country around this state park. Keep following the path to another pinnacle to your left. A trail leaves this second pinnacle and makes a mini-loop, returning to the junction with the Twin Pinnacles Trail.

Access

The Big Pinnacle Trail starts on the south side of Massie Gap, just a few feet on the visitor center access road beyond the turnoff for the stables.

Cabin Creek Trail

Type:	Foot only
Length:	1.9 miles
Difficulty:	Moderate
Use:	Moderate to high
Condition:	Excellent
Highlights:	Numerous waterfalls and cascades
Book Map #:	5
USGS Topo:	Whitetop Mountain
Connections:	Rhododendron Trail, Horse Trail, Big Pinnacle Trail

This trail leads from open Massie Gap through thick rhododendron down to Cabin Creek, where there are three significant waterfalls and many smaller cascades. It then picks up an old railroad grade and returns to Massie Gap on a pleasant, nearly level course.

Start the hike at Massie Gap and follow a grassy path along the road to the stables. Shortly, the Rhododendron Gap Trail leaves right, and the Cabin Creek Trail continues forward across the meadow broken by a few red spruce trees. At 0.2 mile, intersect the state park Horse Trail. From here it is 0.5 mile left to the park stables and 1.0 mile right to the park campground. The Cabin Creek Trail enters a hodgepodge of brush, meadow, and trees. This is the vicinity of the homesite of Lee Massey, who lived here a century ago. Soon enter a dark rhododendron tunnel and cross a feeder stream of Cabin Creek. At 0.3 mile, come to the loop portion of the trail. Stay left and step over the feeder stream twice more in succession while dropping steeply.

Begin to head toward Cabin Creek. Reach this stream, named for a hunting shack once astride the watercourse, at 0.6 mile. The trail heads upstream along the right bank of Cabin Creek, passing a trail shelter. Soon come to a waterfall. This is a 35-foot double-chute cascade bisected by a large boulder. Climb steeply to the head of the falls to see a 25-foot single-chute cascade. Keep heading up the intimate valley, passing a sign indicating the elevation as 4,280 feet.

At 1.1 miles, the trail splits again. Forward, upstream, a narrow side trail zigzags a short distance for a view of another waterfall, a stairstep cascade. Return to the main trail and pick up a nearly level railroad grade left over from the lumbering era. Return toward Massie Gap, coming alongside a fence line. The railroad grade splits; stay with the lower grade and come to the beginning of the loop. Backtrack 0.3 mile to Massie Gap, reaching the trailhead at 1.9 miles.

Access

This trail starts at Massie Gap, near the road leading to the park stables.

Horse Trail

Type:	Foot, horse
Length:	1.7 miles
Difficulty:	Moderate
Use:	High
Condition:	Good, but muddy in spots
Highlights:	Meadows, views, connects park stables to high country
Book Map #:	9
USGS Topo:	Trout Dale
Connections:	Cabin Creek Trail, Rhododendron Trail, Virginia Highlands Horse Connector Trail, Appalachian Spur Trail, Wilson Trail, Upchurch Road Trail, Seed Orchard Road Trail

The Horse Trail is heavily used by horseback riders to connect the parks stables and equestrian campground with the east side of the state park and the Virginia Highlands Horse Trail on national forest land. Hikers also use the path that offers numerous connections to other trails throughout the highlands. It starts at the park stables and leads east to the meadow at Massie Gap and a host of trail connections. Beyond the gap, it enters a second meadow, while paralleling the park road along Wilburn Ridge that leads to the main campground. There are other connections near the campground. The trail then dips into the Big Wilson Creek valley to end at the junction with the Seed Orchard Road Trail and the Upchurch Road Trail.

Start the Horse Trail by leaving the park stables and tracing the orange-blazed wide path uphill beneath a canopy of yellow birch. At 0.5 mile, intersect the Cabin Creek Trail. It leaves left downhill 0.4 mile to Cabin Creek. The Horse Trail continues uphill through meadows, brush, and trees. Come along a fence line and intersect the Rhododendron Trail at Massie Gap. The Rhododendron Trail leads left up to the federal national recreation area and numerous other trails. Pass through a gate and intersect the Virginia Highlands Horse Connector Trail. This trail is important for equestrians. It leads left 0.9 mile to meet the Virginia Highlands Horse Trail. The Horse Trail veers right to enter a meadow. Pass through two gates and enter a second meadow dotted with trees ranging from hickory to hawthorn. Notice how the tops of the trees "flag" east, a result of the strong winds up here. The Appalachian Spur Trail crosses the Horse Trail here and leads left 0.7 mile to intersect the AT. Leave the meadow at 1.2 miles and pass through a gate. Generally stay parallel with the campground road, pass through another gate, cross a service road, and come to a picnic area complete with hitching posts at mile 1.5. Here, a short side trail leads directly to the park Country Store. The main park campground is nearby to the right.

The Horse Trail continues beyond the picnic area and begins to descend to a junction at 1.7 miles. From here, the Upchurch Road Trail leads right 2.9 miles to Mill Creek Road. To the left, the Seed Orchard Road Trail leads 0.7 mile to intersect the Scales Trail and the Big Wilson Trail.

Access

The Horse Trail starts near the park stables but also can be accessed at Massie Gap.

Listening Rock Trail

Type:	Foot only
Length:	1.6 miles
Difficulty:	Moderate
Use:	Low
Condition:	Good
Highlights:	High country forest, good views, big boulders, solitude
Book Map #:	9
USGS Topo:	Park
Connections:	None

This is the forgotten trail of the Grayson Highlands—and for no reason. It starts off with a great vista from Buzzard Rock and then descends off the south slope of Haw Orchard Mountain through a jumble of huge, gray boulders cloaked in spruce. The path then leads to Listening Rock, an overhanging outcrop with wonderful views, so named because farmers listened here for the bells of their cows in the surrounding lands to locate them. This outcrop was also known as Wildcat Rock. From Listening Rock, the trail loops back toward the park visitor center.

Start the hike by stepping out to the Buzzard Rock Overlook, where the lands of North Carolina can be seen. Head a bit to the right, away from the visitor center, and pick up the yellow-blazed Listening Rock Trail. Pass between two large boulders and come to a similar vista. Drop right, twisting and turning among the boulders. Spruce, rhododendron, and yellow birch shadow the rocks.

Cross over an old roadbed just before reaching a flat at 0.4 mile. Look for hickory and buckeye trees here. At 0.6 mile the trail splits. Head right and take the stone steps up to Listening Rock. This overhanging outcrop offers great views to the west. A wind-sculpted red spruce grows out of the outcrop. Notice the Christmas tree orchards below. Return to the main trail and continue the loop. Soon ascend, heading back up the slope of Haw Orchard Mountain, reaching the lower visitor center parking area at mile 1.6.

Access

This trail starts at the far end of the visitor center picnic area, near the Buzzard Rock Overlook.

Rhododendron Trail

Type:	Foot only
Length:	0.8 mile
Difficulty:	Moderate
Use:	Moderate to high
Condition:	Good
Highlights:	Vistas, meadows, numerous trail connections
Book Map #:	9
USGS Topo:	Whitetop Mountain
Connections:	Rhododendron Gap Trail, Cabin Creek Trail, state park Horse Trail, Appalachian Trail, Virginia Highlands Horse Connector Trail, Virginia Highlands Horse Trail

This trail is essentially the beginning of the Rhododendron Gap Trail, which technically starts once the Rhododendron Trail leaves Grayson Highlands State Park, and heads north from the state park boundary and continues toward Rhododendron Gap. On the Mount Rogers high country map, this is shown as the Rhododendron Gap Trail but is referred to at the state park as the Rhododendron Trail.

Names aside, this pathway leaves Massie Gap and climbs the open slopes of Wilburn Ridge. It then merges with the Virginia Highlands Horse Connector Trail, also a state park trail, and swings around the headwaters of Quebec Branch, where

Sullivan Swamp is located. Sullivan Swamp is actually a high elevation bog, featuring many plants found much farther north. After rounding Sullivan Swamp, the Rhododendron Trail diverges from the horse connector trail to reach a fence stile and the federal Mount Rogers National Recreation Area, where it becomes the Rhododendron Gap Trail.

Leave the Massie Gap parking area and follow the grassy, mown swath north toward a fence line. The Cabin Creek Trail diverges left. Meet the state park Horse Trail on the far side of the grassy gap. This bridle path leaves left 0.5 mile to reach the park stables and right 1.0 mile to the park campground. Pass through a gate and begin to climb through the open slopes of Wilburn Ridge on a grassy trail with wooden water bars that minimize erosion. Look back at the Pinnacles on the far side of Massie Gap. At 0.3 mile, merge with the Virginia Highlands Horse Connector Trail, which has also come from Massie Gap. The two paths share the same wide, rocky treadway, meeting the Appalachian Trail at 0.4 mile. From here, the AT leaves left to soon meet the Rhododendron Trail and leaves right 2.1 miles to the Wise trail shelter. The views of the surrounding mountains are widespread.

Swing around the headwaters of Quebec Branch off to the right. Sullivan Swamp, a trove of biodiversity that includes numerous types of cranberries, lies in the brush of the headwaters. The Rhododendron Trail and the horse connector trail diverge. The Rhododendron Trail leaves left on a grassy path just before coming to a fence stile and the federal lands of the national recreation area at 0.8 mile. Here, it meets the Appalachian Trail. Both paths cross the stile, and here the Rhododendron Trail ends. The AT continues forward to Elk Garden after 6.6 miles. The Virginia Highlands Horse Trail leaves left to reach Elk Garden in 5.8 miles and right to reach Scales in 3.5 miles. The Rhododendron Gap Trail lies between the AT and VHHT and heads uphill to reach Rhododendron Gap in 1.6 miles via a short section of the Crest Trail.

Access

The Rhododendron Trail starts at the Massie Gap Parking Area.

Rock House Ridge Trail

Type:	Foot only
Length:	1.2 miles
Difficulty:	Moderate
Use:	Low
Condition:	Good
Highlights:	Rock shelter, views, old homesteads
Book Map #:	9
USGS Topo:	Trout Dale
Connections:	None

Beauty near and far at Mount Rogers National Recreation Area.

This path packs a lot into a short loop trail. Start by passing a large overhanging rock, once used as shelter by Indians, giving the trail its name. Then drop down through rich woods to a grassy clearing with far-reaching mountain views. Curve around back toward the picnic area, passing historic buildings along the way.

Leave the picnic parking area and immediately pass by the rock house, an overhanging rock under which shelter can be found; then tunnel though a rhododendron thicket. Leave the rhododendron and descend a ridgeline in an oak forest with scattered spruce trees. At 0.6 mile, enter a grassy area broken with locust and hawthorn trees. From here, hikers can look to the southeast toward the hamlets of Mill Creek and Rugby.

Reenter the woods and continue descending a rock-lined trail. At 0.9 mile, emerge onto a service road and begin ascending along a small stream branch and fence line. At mile 1.1, to the right, is a clearing with several historic buildings on it. Take the side trip to learn about each of these old structures. Return to the service road and soon come to the picnic parking area, veering left to return to the original trailhead.

Access

The Rock House Ridge Trail starts at the lower end of the state park picnic area.

Seed Orchard Road Trail

Type:	Foot, horse, bicycle
Length:	0.7 mile
Difficulty:	Easy
Use:	Moderate
Condition:	Good
Highlights:	High country views, Fraser fir seed orchard
Book Map #:	9
USGS Topo:	Trout Dale
Connections:	Horse Trail, Seed Orchard Road Trail, Scales Trail, Wilson Creek Trail

This old woods road traces an old railroad bed along the upper reaches of Big Wilson Creek. It starts at 4,300 feet and heads north to reach the Fraser fir seed orchard, which nearby Christmas tree growers use to start tree plantations. The path then opens to wide views before coming to Big Wilson Creek and federal land. On the far side of the creek, it meets the Scales Trail and the Wilson Creek Trail.

Start the Seed Orchard Trail in a northern hardwood forest with a grassy understory. Keep a level course. The roar of Big Wilson Creek is to the right. At 0.1 mile, the Wilson Trail leaves right to reach Big Wilson Creek and doubles back downstream to intersect the Upchurch Road Trail. Keep going forward and descend to pass a yellow metal gate at 0.2 mile. Soon cross Quebec Branch. Stay with the light blue blazes of Seed Orchard Road, and the canopy opens overhead. Reach the Fraser fir seed orchard on the left at 0.5 mile. There are wide views of the mountains all around. Cross a metal gate and continue forward, reaching Big Wilson Creek at 0.7 mile. On the far side of the creek are the Wilson Creek and Scales trails. The Scales Trail heads 1.3 miles up to Scales. The Wilson Creek Trail leads left 0.7 miles to the Virginia Highlands Horse Trail.

Access

The Seed Orchard Road Trail is an interior trail. It can be reached by taking the Horse Trail for 0.2 mile. Or it can be reached by taking the Scales Trail 1.3 miles down from Scales.

Stampers Branch Trail

Type:	Foot only
Length:	1.7 miles
Difficulty:	Moderate
Use:	Moderate

Condition:	Excellent
Highlights:	Diverse forest, loop possibilities
Book Map #:	9
USGS Topo:	Trout Dale
Connections:	Horse Trail, Wilson Creek Trail, Twin Pinnacles Trail

The Stampers Branch Trail links not only the campground and the visitor center but also the highest peaks of the state park and the lower ridges. Start on Haw Orchard Mountain and drop down to the headwaters of Stampers Branch, crossing Wilburn Branch, too, before gently climbing the shoulder of Wilburn Ridge. Along the way, the surrounding woodlands change from northern hardwoods mixed with spruce to an oak forest. It is most easily hiked from high to low and can be combined with the Horse Trail and Big Pinnacle and Twin Pinnacles trails to form a loop.

The yellow-blazed trail starts behind the visitor center. Wide, windswept yellow birch and maple share the trailside with red spruce. Descend along the east slope of Haw Orchard Mountain to cross the main park road at 0.7 mile. Reenter the woods, swinging past the headwaters of Stampers Branch and then a small trail shelter. Tunnel beneath rhododendron to Wilburn Branch, which can be crossed on a plank bridge at mile 1.1. Look upstream for a small cascade.

The trail picks up an old road grade and gently ascends in oak woods, leveling off just before coming to the campground amphitheater. Beyond the amphitheater are the Country Store and the trail's end. To complete a loop back to the Visitor Center, cross the campground road to the orange-blazed Horse Trail. Take the Horse Trail west, left, and proceed to Massie Gap. Once at Massie Gap, take the Big Pinnacle Trail to the Twin Pinnacles Trail back to the Visitor Center.

Access

The upper Stampers Branch Trail starts behind the Visitor Center. The lower Stampers Branch Trail starts by the Country Store near the main campground.

Twin Pinnacles Trail

Type:	Foot only
Length:	1.6 miles
Difficulty:	Moderate
Use:	High
Condition:	Good
Highlights:	Forest and meadows, 360-degree views, interpretive loop trail
Book Map #:	9
USGS Topo:	Whitetop Mountain
Connections:	Big Pinnacle Trail, Stampers Branch Trail

This path accesses the highest point in the state park. Along the way it passes several interesting environments, capping off with a fine view from Little Pinnacle; it then makes an encore at Big Pinnacle before looping back to the visitor center. An interpretive brochure from the park visitor center will help hikers to further appreciate the beauty of these Virginia Highlands.

Leave the park visitor center on a gravel path. At 0.1 mile, the trail splits; veer left and enter a cleared area. Soon enter woods of spruce and yellow birch. Keep an eye to the left of the trail for a yellow birch growing on top of a large rock. The tree's roots grasp the peak of the rock. The path emerges onto another clearing and then comes to a trail shelter. At 0.4 mile, reach Little Pinnacle. The views are wide and numerous. This area was once covered with spruce and fir trees, but it was logged and then burned over, exposing the rocks. It will eventually become forested again, but for now, enjoy the views.

Drop away from Little Pinnacle through a rocky area dotted with flagged spruce trees. Grassy Massie Gap is below. Hit a forested flat and climb a bit, passing a trail shelter. Reach the Big Pinnacle Trail. It is a short but steep walk to the Big Pinnacle. Grab more vistas; then return to the Twin Pinnacles Trail. Begin to loop around the northeast end of Haw Orchard Mountain on a rock-lined path. Undulate through a northern hardwood forest, broken with occasional clearings. Pass a small trail shelter at mile 1.3. Complete the loop and backtrack a short distance, reaching the visitor center at mile 1.6.

Access

This trail starts behind the park visitor center.

Upchurch Road Trail

Type:	Foot, horse, bicycle
Length:	2.9 miles
Difficulty:	Moderate
Use:	Moderate
Condition:	Good
Highlights:	Access trail for angling Big Wilson Creek
Book Map #:	9
USGS Topo:	Trout Dale
Connections:	Big Wilson Creek Trail, Wilson Trail, Horse Trail, Seed Orchard Road Trail

This trail traces an old road that in turn traces an old railroad grade up the valley of Big Wilson Creek. It starts in new woodland, transitioning from pastureland and passing occasional remnant clearings along Big Spring Ridge before coming to Wilburn Branch. The path then continues northwest on the lower reaches of

Wilburn Ridge, switchbacking to near the state park campground, and finally intersects the Seed Orchard Road Trail and the state park Horse Trail.

Start the Upchurch Road Trail by passing around a metal pole gate and descending to a feeder branch of Big Wilson Creek. To the left, a roadbed leads uphill through the creekside meadow to reach the state park picnic area. Pass along an old fence line. Locust, fire cherry, and other trees are invading the former pastureland. Come near a couple of power-line poles before the trail splits at 0.5 mile. An old road leads right, downhill, to cross Big Wilson Creek and reach VA 817. The Upchurch Road Trail keeps leading forward in black birch and rhododendron. At mile 1.1, descend past an old homesite just before crossing Wilburn Branch. Just a few feet past the stream crossing, the unsigned Big Wilson Creek Trail leads right, across Big Wilson Creek 2.1 miles up to the Bearpen Trail on Stone Mountain.

The Upchurch Road Trail briefly climbs along Wilburn Branch before ascending steeply to turn sharply right and make a nearly level passage at the 3,800-foot level of Wilburn Ridge. Catch occasional glimpses of noisy Big Wilson Creek through rhododendron. At mile 2.0, the trail makes an acute left turn. One hundred feet ahead, the trail seemingly dead-ends at a waterfall and pool on Big Wilson Creek. Climb away from Big Wilson Creek to make a sharp right turn, once again heading up Big Wilson Creek valley. Intersect the Wilson Trail at mile 2.5. It leads right a short distance down to Big Wilson Creek and left 0.7 mile back to the state park campground.

Keep going forward on the Upchurch Road Trail through beech woods with a grassy understory. Come to a trail junction at mile 2.9. The Horse Trail leads acutely left 1.7 miles to the state park horse stable. The Upchurch Road Trail ends here. The railroad grade now becomes the Seed Orchard Road Trail, which leads forward 0.7 mile past the state park Fraser fir seed orchard and then intersects the Scales Trail and Big Wilson Trail.

Access

From the Little Red Caboose in Damascus, drive east on US 58 for 28.0 miles to VA 742 (Mill Creek Lane). Turn left on VA 742 and follow it for 1.5 miles to a dead end and a state park sign. The Upchurch Road Trail starts behind the sign. Check with the state park before parking at this trailhead.

Virginia Highlands Horse Connector Trail

Type:	Foot, horse
Length:	0.9 mile
Difficulty:	Moderate
Use:	Moderate to high
Condition:	Fair to good

The state park provides this trail for equestrians to access the Virginia Highlands Horse Trail. Equestrians can then make a loop, using this trail, the VHHT, and the Horse Trail. This connector trail leaves the Horse Trail at Massie Gap and winds up to an open flat to intersect the Rhododendron Trail. The two share the same tread-way for a distance until diverging just as they reach the federal Mount Rogers high country, which is part of the national recreation area located within the Jefferson National Forest.

Start the Virginia Highlands Horse Connector Trail by leaving the Horse Trail near Massie Gap. Pass through a gate and then wind up a northern hardwood forest of beech, birch, and red spruce. Make two switchbacks to come along a fence in open country of Wilburn Ridge. Intersect the Rhododendron Trail, coming 0.3 mile from Massie Gap. The two trails merge and then intersect the Appalachian Trail at 0.4 mile. Here, the AT heads left 0.6 mile before leaving the state park and right 2.1 miles to Wise trail shelter.

Swing around the headwaters of Quebec Branch, where the botanically rich Sullivan Swamp lies. At 0.8 mile, the two paths diverge. The Rhododendron Trail leaves left toward a fence stile, and the connector trail splits right and passes by a spring before coming to a gate and the end of the trail at 1.0 mile. On the far side of the gate lie federal land and the Virginia Highlands Horse Trail. The VHHT leads left 5.9 miles to Elk Garden and right 3.4 miles to Scales. Just to the left is the Rhododendron Gap Trail, which leads right 1.4 miles to the Crest Trail.

Access

The Virginia Highlands Horse Connector Trail can be reached by foot by crossing Massie Gap on the Rhododendron Gap Trail, or by traveling 0.5 mile from the park stables on the Horse Trail.

Wilson Trail

Type:	Foot only
Length:	1.8 miles
Difficulty:	Moderate
Use:	High

Condition:	Good
Highlights:	Waterfalls, rock outcrops, trout fishing
Book Map #:	9
USGS Topo:	Trout Dale
Connections:	Stampers Branch Trail, Horse Trail, Upchurch Road Trail, Seed Orchard Road Trail

The Wilson Trail is one of the finest trails in the state park. It leaves the park campground and drops through a beech forest down to the waters of Wilson Creek, a high country valley where tannin-colored waters crash over huge boulders. The trail then twists and turns among rock outcrops and profuse growths of rhododendron. It finally leaves the creek to make a moderate climb back to the campground.

Start the Wilson Creek Trail near the campground entrance. Enter thick woods and soon cross a park service road. Begin steadily descending through a beech and birch forest with mountain maple as an understory. At 0.3 mile, cross an old railroad bed, the Upchurch Road Trail, which is now used by equestrians, hikers, and bikers.

At 0.5 mile, pass an angler's trail that drops down to the stream. Continue forward in rocky woods, soon passing a small trail shelter. Reach Wilson Creek at 0.7 mile. Begin ascending along the streamside, where the path courses through rhododendron and around rock outcrops, with short side paths extending to the creek. The rocky trail continues to the top of a narrow, chute-like cascade at mile 1.1. Shortly afterward, pass a second trail shelter. Beyond this, an angler's path continues along the creek, but the Wilson Creek Trail turns uphill to the left, away from the creek. Begin a moderate ascent and come to the old railroad grade and turn left, sharing the grade with the Seed Orchard Road Trail. Keep along the grade and stay right as the grade splits. Pass the yellow metal gate and keep climbing. The Horse Trail splits right at mile 1.7. Keep heading forward on the gravel path and emerge near the Country Store and the campground at mile 1.8.

Access

The Wilson Creek Trail starts near the main campground entrance gate, by the Country Store.

Suggested Trail Loops

Hiking Loops

What follows are suggested loop hikes in each of the major divisions of the recreation area. To find the trailhead, simply check the first trail listed in the "Trails Used" information and refer to the description of that trail in the preceding text. The "difficulty" indicated is for average hikers; "length" refers to the mileage of the trail portions in the loop; and "highlights" indicates what is of interest along the way.

Hikers can use all the following loops. Bikers and equestrians need to check trail restrictions before they tackle the hiking loops.

West Side

Feathercamp Loop

Trails Used:	Beech Grove Trail, Iron Mountain Trail, Feathercamp Trail, Appalachian Trail
Difficulty:	Moderate
Length:	6.7 miles
Highlights:	Varied forests

This loop leaves the Whitetop Laurel Valley on the Beech Grove Trail up to the crest of the Iron Mountains. The loop then cruises the ridgeline to Feathercamp Branch and descends down the intimate stream valley to intersect the Appalachian Trail. Take the AT back to the Beech Grove Trail and return to the parking area. Along the way, enjoy streamside woods and open pine-oak stands atop Feathercamp Ridge. None of the climbs are overly steep or long.

Rush-Sawmill Loop

Trails Used:	Rush Trail, Sawmill Trail, Bushwacker Trail, Iron Mountain Trail
Difficulty:	Moderate
Length:	5.0 miles
Highlights:	Trail shelter, wildlife clearings, some views

This loop starts on Iron Mountain and drops down to Rush Creek to intersect the Sawmill Trail. The Sawmill Trail then climbs up to offer views of the South Fork Holston River valley before dropping to Sandy Flats. At Sandy Flats, briefly pick up the Bushwacker Trail and pass by the Sandy Flats trail shelter. Finally, follow the Iron Mountain Trail a short distance to complete the loop. The loop is not long, but there are some short, steep sections.

Central Area

Rowland Falls Loop

Trails Used:	Rowland Creek Trail, Old 84 Trail, Jerry's Creek Trail
Difficulty:	Moderate to difficult
Length:	11.8 miles
Highlights:	Waterfall, some views, solitude

Climb up the attractive Rowland Creek Valley to even more attractive Rowland Falls. Crest out at the Old 84 Trail and make a high country traverse in the shadow of Double Top and Round Knob to Jerry Creek, where the path takes you down quickly and then moderates before completing the loop. The climb up Rowland Creek valley is steady but never too steep.

Comers Creek Falls Loop

Trails Used:	Comers Creek Falls Trail, Appalachian Trail, Iron Mountain Trail
Difficulty:	Moderate
Length:	8.0 miles
Highlights:	Waterfall, good views

Start out on the Comers Creek Falls Trail and make a short side trip to Comers Creek Falls. Backtrack just a bit and take the Appalachian Trail along the north slope of Hurricane Mountain to intersect the Iron Mountain Trail. Head east on the Iron Mountain Trail to gain views of the Mount Rogers high country before returning to Comers Creek. The elevation changes are moderate as the trail stays high on Hurricane Mountain for most of its length.

Far East

Perkins Knob Loop

Trails Used:	Perkins Knob Trail, Perkins Knob Spur Trail, Iron Mountain Trail
Difficulty:	Moderate
Length:	7.3 miles
Highlights:	Views, solitude

This loop starts by ascending along seldom-walked Perkins Creek to make the Perkins Knob Spur Trail. Take this little side trip to gain good views. Backtrack; then intersect the Iron Mountain Trail and walk in classic pine-oak woods before coming out on US 21. Make a short half-mile walk down US 21 to complete the loop. In all likelihood, you won't see anyone else on this underappreciated section of the recreation area.

Little Dry Run Loop

Trails Used:	Little Dry Run Trail, Virginia Highlands Horse Trail, Henley Hollow Trail
Difficulty:	Moderate to difficult
Length:	8.3 miles
Highlights:	Little Dry Run Wilderness, wildlife clearings, waterfall

This trail heads up the valley of Little Dry Run on a rough path that crosses the stream numerous times, ultimately to intersect the Virginia Highlands Horse Trail. Take the VHHT downhill, passing many wildlife clearings; then cross US 21. Past US 21, the VHHT climbs toward Horse Heaven before intersecting the Henley Hollow Trail. Drop down this single-track path past a few small falls set in an intimate valley. The trail can be challenging because of its numerous ups and downs.

High Country

First Peak Loop

Trails Used:	First Peak Trail, Kabel Trail, Big Wilson Creek Trail, Bearpen Trail, Scales Trail
Difficulty:	Moderate
Length:	7.8 miles
Highlights:	Views, meadows

This loop starts high and stays high. Leave Scales to make the crest of Stone Mountain and enjoy wide views. Undulate over Third, Second, and First peaks to intersect the Kabel Trail. Swing past Little Wilson Creek; then intersect the Big Wilson Creek Trail. Climb a bit to the Bearpen Trail. Once on the Bearpen Trail, there are more views. Complete the loop on the Scales Trail.

Mount Rogers high country offers many scenes such as this.

Wilburn Ridge Loop

Trails Used:	Rhododendron Trail, Rhododendron Gap Trail, Crest Trail, Appalachian Trail, Wilburn Ridge Trail, Appalachian Trail
Difficulty:	Moderate
Length:	5.2 miles
Highlights:	Views, wild ponies, rock scrambling

Leave Grayson Highlands State Park at Massie Gap and ascend on the Rhododendron Trail. Enter federal land and take the Rhododendron Gap Trail for great views to the Crest Trail. Turn right on the Crest Trail and follow it a short distance to Rhododendron Gap. Pick up the Appalachian Trail and follow it along Wilburn Ridge to the Wilburn Ridge Trail. Do a little rock scrambling in between vistas; then return to the state park via the Appalachian Trail.

Biking Loops

West Side

Sandy Flats Loop

Trails Used:	Forest Road 90, Bushwacker Trail, Iron Mountain Trail, Feathercamp Ridge Trail, Sawmill Trail, Rush Trail, Iron Mountain Trail, Forest Road 90
Difficulty:	Moderate to difficult
Length:	7.9 miles
Highlights:	Many ups and downs

This loop leaves Forest Road 90 and climbs to the Bushwacker Trail, which in turn leads to Sandy Flats. From here take the Iron Mountain Trail west to the Feathercamp Ridge Trail and make a steep decline to the Sawmill Trail. Once on the Sawmill Trail, gain a few views before dropping down to Rush Creek. Climb away from Rush Creek on the Rush Trail to reach Forest Road 90. Then take this gravel road down to the point of origin. The numerous trail intersections will inspire you to make some loops of your own.

Grosses Mountain Loop

Trails Used:	Straight Branch Trail, Forest Road 837, Shaw Gap Trail, Iron Mountain Trail, VA 600
Difficulty:	Moderate
Length:	10.7 miles
Highlights:	Variety of trail conditions

This loop leaves VA 600 and climbs up the Straight Branch Trail to a gap. It then makes an extended descent past Beartree Campground and down Forest Road 837 to the Shaw Gap Trail. Climb up to the crest of Grosses Mountain and pick up the Iron Mountain Trail for some great single-track pedaling before passing the Straight Branch trail shelter. Emerge onto VA 600 and make a lightning descent back to the Straight Branch Trail. There are no really long climbs. The loop is on paved, gravel, and single-track trail.

Central Area

Barton Gap Loop

Trails Used:	Barton Gap Trail, Forest Road 643, Comers Creek Trail, Forest Road 84
Difficulty:	Moderate to difficult
Length:	8.1 miles
Highlights:	Waterfall, good views

This loop uses one popular trail and a somewhat traveled forest road, along with a little-used forest road and a little-used trail. Start on the Barton Gap Trail to climb for a bit. Make a longer descent down to Forest Road 643, which is infrequently driven. Take the gravel FR 643 along Barton Branch and the north slope of Bear Ridge to Comers Creek. Just before the ford of Comers Creek, turn right on the Comers Creek Trail and pass through Hurricane Campground to reach Forest Road 84. Make a steady ascent on FR 84 along Hurricane Creek to reach the Barton Gap Trail.

Far East

Middle Creek Loop

Trails Used:	Horne Knob Trail, Virginia Highlands Horse Trail, Forest Road 16
Difficulty:	Moderate
Length:	9.9 miles
Highlights:	Solitude, old-growth trees

This entire loop is infrequently traveled by foot, bike, horse, or auto. Take the Horne Knob Trail a short distance to intersect the Virginia Highlands Horse Trail. Turn right on the VHHT and swing around Horne Knob, continuing east along the north slope of Snake Den Mountain. Drop down to Middle Creek and come to Forest Road 14. Head west on Forest Road 14. Begin to look for old-growth hemlock and oak trees. The gravel road climbs out of Middle Fork to a gap. Finally drop down along Dry Creek to meet the Horne Knob Trail. The trails are in great shape here, making for a pleasant ride.

Dry Run Gap Loop

Trails Used:	Dry Run Gap Trail, Iron Mountain Trail, Divide Trail, Forest Road 14
Difficulty:	Moderate
Length:	8.2 miles
Highlights:	Steep technical drop on Divide Trail

Start this loop by climbing up to Dry Run Gap on a trail that was once part of old US 21. Intersect the Iron Mountain Trail for some good single-track action and a scenic stretch of pathway. Keep your hands at the brakes as you drop down the Divide Trail, the steepest trail described in this guidebook, to reach Forest Road 14. Take Forest Road 14 and appreciate the easy gravel road that returns to Dry Run Gap Trail.

High Country

Rhododendron Gap Loop

Trails Used:	Crest Trail, Rhododendron Gap Trail, Virginia Highlands Horse Trail
Difficulty:	Moderate to difficult
Length:	8.1 miles
Highlights:	Views, meadows, creek crossings

Head away from Scales on the Crest Trail and immediately gain views of the high country. Make a climb to Rhododendron Gap, passing numerous other paths. Descend a bit past Rhododendron Gap and intersect the Rhododendron Gap Trail. Turn left on the Rhododendron Gap Trail and head through some rocky sections that may require you to walk your bike. The pedaling eases up upon intersecting the wider Virginia Highlands Horse Trail. Take the VHHT down into Big Wilson Creek and more views before climbing back to Scales.

Rock outcrops reach for the sky.

Scales/Wilson Creek Loop

Trails Used:	Scales Trail, Wilson Creek Trail, Virginia Highlands Horse Trail
Difficulty:	Easy
Length:	2.6 miles
Highlights:	Views, stream crossings

Most high country trails are closed to bikes, reducing circuit possibilities. However, this short loop is rewarding. Leave Scales on the Scales Trail and drop down to East Fork Wilson Creek. Cross a small stream feeding East Fork and then East Fork itself to reach the Wilson Creek Trail at Big Wilson Creek. Turn right on the Wilson Creek Trail and climb through open meadows to reach the Virginia Highlands Horse Trail. Return to Scales via the VHHT.

Equestrian Loops

West Side

Chestnut Ridge Loop

Trails Used:	Chestnut Ridge Trail, Iron Mountain Trail, Forest Road 90, Sawmill Trail, Forest Road 615
Difficulty:	Moderate to difficult
Length:	8.6 miles
Highlights:	Creek and ridgeline environments

Start on the little-used Chestnut Ridge Trail and climb up to reach the Iron Mountain Trail at Shaw Gap. Turn right on the Iron Mountain Trail and enjoy some ridgetop riding to reach Forest Road 90. Descend from FR 90 to pick up the Sawmill Trail. Curve down on the Sawmill Trail to reach Rush Creek. Cross Rush Creek and head north on Forest Road 615. This gravel road is rarely traveled. Wind along a dry ridgeline to complete the loop at the headwaters of Mill Creek.

Taylors Valley Loop

Trails Used:	Virginia Creeper Trail, Taylors Valley Trail
Difficulty:	Moderate
Length:	12.5 miles
Highlights:	Whitetop Laurel Creek, solitude on Taylors Valley Trail

This loop follows the Virginia Creeper Trail up along Whitetop Laurel Creek with its many rapids, crossing numerous trestles to reach Creek Junction. Here, riders ford Whitetop Laurel Creek and pick up the Taylors Valley Trail. This path climbs past a homesite and drops down into Taylors Valley. Backtrack a bit on the Creeper Trail to complete the loop.

Central Area

Fox Creek Loop

Trails Used:	Virginia Highlands Horse Trail, Iron Mountain Trail, Flat Top Trail, Fairwood Valley Trail
Difficulty:	Moderate
Length:	7.8 miles
Highlights:	Can make loop directly from Fox Creek Horse Camp

This loop starts and ends at Fox Creek Horse Camp, making it especially convenient for equestrians. Take the Virginia Highlands Horse Trail up Locust Ridge to meet Iron Mountain. Here, the horse trail and Iron Mountain Trail share treadway to reach Flat Top. Descend on the Flat Top Trail to Fairwood Valley and the Fairwood Valley Trail. Cruise down the Fairwood Valley back to Fox Creek Horse Camp.

Seng Mountain Loop

Trails Used:	Rowland Creek Trail, Virginia Highlands Horse Trail, Barton Gap Trail, Forest Road 643
Difficulty:	Moderate
Length:	11.7 miles
Highlights:	Waterfall, solitude

Climb up one of the recreation area's most attractive trails, passing a waterfall, to reach the Virginia Highlands Horse Trail. Take the VHHT down along Hurricane Creek to meet the Barton Gap Trail. Turn left on Forest Road 643 and wind along the north slope of Seng Mountain, passing several small creeks before returning to the Rowland Creek valley.

Far East

Cressy Creek Loop

Trails Used:	Kirk Hollow Trail, Virginia Highlands Horse Trail, Forest Road 16, Horne Knob Trail, Virginia Highlands Horse Trail
Difficulty:	Moderate
Length:	10.8 miles
Highlights:	Solitude, some views, ponds

Start the loop on the nearly forgotten Kirk Hollow Trail to meet the Virginia Highlands Horse Trail. Turn right on the VHHT, pass some ponds, and enjoy views before dropping down to Cressy Creek. Cruise along Cressy Creek via Forest Road 16 to reach the Horne Knob Trail. Make this short cutoff to once again reach the VHHT. Head down the Dry Creek valley and reach the Kirk Hollow Trail. Backtrack a short distance down Kirk Hollow to complete the loop.

Horse Heaven Loop

Trails Used:	East Fork Trail, Virginia Highlands Horse Trail, Forest Road 14, East Fork Trail
Difficulty:	Moderate
Length:	8.5 miles
Highlights:	Starts at Hussy Mountain Horse Camp, views

Leave attractive Hussy Mountain Horse Camp and head east on the East Fork Trail to meet the Virginia Highlands Horse Trail. Climb up to Horse Heaven on the VHHT and enjoy occasional views before dropping back down to East Fork. Take Forest Road 14 just a short distance to pick up the East Fork Trail, which winds beneath large pines of the valley to return to Hussy Mountain Horse Camp.

High Country

Big Wilson Creek Loop

Trails Used:	Horse Trail, Virginia Highlands Horse Connector Trail, Virginia Highlands Horse Trail, Wilson Creek Trail, Seed Orchard Road, Horse Trail
Difficulty:	Moderate
Length:	6.7 miles
Highlights:	Views, meadows, starts at state park horse camp

This loop conveniently starts at Grayson Highlands State Park horse camp and then heads up to meet the Virginia Highlands Horse Trail via the Virginia Highlands Horse Connector Trail. Head northeast through mostly open country in the upper valley of Big Wilson Creek to reach the Big Wilson Creek Trail. Descend on the Big Wilson Creek Trail to reenter the state park via the Seed Orchard Road Trail. Take this trail to the Horse Trail and return along Wilburn Ridge to the horse camp.

Horseback riding is popular at Mount Rogers. Photo courtesy of U.S. Forest Service.

Pine Mountain Loop

Trails Used:	Virginia Highlands Horse Trail, Crest Trail, Lewis Fork Trail, Old Orchard Trail, Old Orchard Spur Trail
Difficulty:	Moderate to difficult
Length:	2.6 miles
Highlights:	Views, diverse forests

This loop climbs away from Fox Creek Horse Camp up to Scales on the Virginia Highlands Horse Trail. Pick up the Crest Trail at Scales and gain wide-ranging vistas before reaching the Lewis Fork Trail. Take the wide Lewis Fork Trail, leaving meadows and spruce-fir forest, down to a northern hardwood forest before meeting the Old Orchard Trail. Take the Old Orchard Trail a short distance to the Old Orchard Spur Trail. A final jaunt on the VHHT takes riders back to Fox Creek Horse Camp.

Other Recreational Opportunities

Fishing Streams and Lakes

Beartree Lake

Lake Acreage:	11 acres
Fishing Pressure:	Heavy
Fishing Quality:	Fair to good
USS Quads:	Konnarock

Beartree Lake is part of the larger Beartree Recreation Area. It is popular and enjoyed by all types of recreationalists. Beartree Lake is a "put-and-take" fishing proposition; this means it is regularly stocked and has no reproducing trout. The primary catch is rainbow trout. The big ones are down deep, and as the summer wears on, the smaller ones join them. If you are looking for a rustic fishing experience, don't come here during the warmer months. Beartree Lake has a swim beach and picnic area that draws large crowds.

Access

A one-mile trail circles the lake and there are handicap-access fishing platforms on the shore. A canoe launch near the picnic area makes for the only boat fishing in the recreation area. No motors are allowed on the lake.

Big Wilson Creek

Stream Size:	Small to medium
Fishing Pressure:	Light
Fishing Quality:	Excellent
USGS Quads:	Whitetop Mountain, Trout Dale

This is a high-gradient plunge/pool stream, with numerous house-sized boulders in it. Big Wilson has a brown tint due to tannin from vegetational decay in the Mount

Rogers high country from which it flows. Parts of the stream are bordered by or wholly within Grayson Highlands State Park. It offers put-and-take rainbow trout fishing on the lower end. The feeder streams have brook trout. The most important tributaries are Little Wilson Creek, Wilburn Branch, and Quebec Branch. These are wilderness streams that don't receive stocking. All are special-regulation, 9-inch-minimum streams, at which only single-hook artificial lures can be used.

Access

A number of trails access Big Wilson Creek, including the Wilson Trail and Upchurch Road Trail in Grayson Highlands State Park and the Big Wilson Creek Trail, Wilson Creek Trail, and the Appalachian Trail in the recreation area. Road access to Big Wilson Creek and Little Wilson Creek is via VA 817. Upper Little Wilson Creek can be accessed via the Little Wilson Creek Trail.

Comers Creek

Stream Size:	Small to medium
Fishing Pressure:	Moderate to heavy
Fishing Quality:	Excellent
USGS Quads:	Trout Dale

This is a small to medium fast-moving stream that drains Hurricane Mountain and Bobbys Ridge. The tight valley is heavily forested and thick with rhododendron. Comers Creek is a plunge/pool rivulet that offers both put-and-take and wild rainbow trout fishing. The upper section in the Comers Creek Valley is a little slower moving—a meadow stream. Beaver ponds break the stream in areas here. There are brookies in the headwaters.

Access

VA 650 (Comers Creek Road) avails much easy access. Also, the Comers Creek Trail starts near Forest Road 643 and heads upstream along the west bank for 0.7 mile to the Hurricane Campground, which is a good base camp for fishing the Comers Creek watershed.

Cripple Creek

Stream Size:	Large
Fishing Pressure:	Moderate to heavy
Fishing Quality:	Good
USS Quads:	Cripple Creek

An approximately 2.0-mile section of Cripple Creek flows through the recreation area. Anglers can vie for smallmouth and redeye bass year-round. Trout are stocked in the winter and spring. The large, clear stream, slightly tinted by agriculture, has many slack pools between rapids and shoals but other areas of fast-moving water. Anglers can walk the grassy banks, broken by wooded portions of streamside. The area is more rugged below Raven Cliff.

Access

The national forest portion of Cripple Creek can be accessed via Raven Cliff Lane from the west and VA 648 from the east, near Collins Cove Horse Camp. However, the central portion, below the actual Raven Cliff, can only be reached by the 1.2-mile Raven Cliff Furnace foot trail. Raven Cliff Campground lies on the west end of the stream.

Dickey Creek

Stream Size: Small
Fishing Pressure: Fairly heavy
Fishing Quality: Good to excellent
USS Quads: Trout Dale, Atkins

This heavily stocked put-and-take stream is the major tributary of South Fork Holston River; it drains Straight Mountain and Bobbys Ridge. It is stocked in spring and fall and is moderately steep with wooded banks and some rhododendron. Raccoon Branch, a full-fledged mountain stream that feeds Dickey Creek, has reproducing rainbow, brookies up high, and trail access.

Access

Dickey Creek can be accessed by VA 16, which runs beside the stream from top to bottom in the recreation area. Raccoon Branch can be accessed via the Virginia Highlands Horse Trail, which traces Raccoon Branch from just above its mouth near Raccoon Branch Campground to its headwaters.

East Fork/West Fork Dry Run

Stream Size: Small streams that rapidly decrease in size
Fishing Pressure: Very light to light
Fishing Quality: Moderate to good
USGS Quads: Speedwell

These lesser-known streams of the "East End" are known more for scenic fishing than for big trout. They offer reproducing rainbow and brook trout. The East Fork meanders beneath majestic white pines. The forest service has installed covered logs and deflectors to create pool habitats and cover. The West Fork, half the size of East Folk, flows along the southern boundary of the Little Dry Run Wilderness as a steeper plunge/pool stream. Fishing can be questionable on West Fork above the large cascade that falls about a mile above the confluence of East Fork and West Fork.

Access

The West Fork can be accessed via the Virginia Highlands Horse Trail. The East Fork can be accessed via Forest Road 14 and the East Fork Trail, which winds up East Fork. Hussy Mountain Horse Camp makes for a good base of operations while fishing here.

Fox Creek

Stream Size:	Small to medium
Fishing Pressure:	Heavy
Fishing Quality:	Good to excellent
USGS Quads:	Whitetop Mountain, Trout Dale

This is a valley stream that offers put-and-take rainbow, with occasional brown trout. There are brook trout primarily above the Appalachian Trail and in the tributaries. It has mixed wooded and grassy banks. The fencing along this stream is for riparian vegetation protection. The forest is attempting to restore shade covering over the stream. Opossum Creek, flowing off Pine Mountain, is an interesting tributary that offers brook trout fishing.

Access

Fox Creek can be accessed by VA 603 or Fairwood Cemetery Road. The Fairwood Valley Trail runs parallel to VA 603, offering trail access in several locations. Opossum Creek can be accessed via Forest Road 613.

Green Cove Creek

Fishing Pressure:	Moderate to heavy
Fishing Quality:	Good
Stream Size:	Small
USGS Quads:	Konnarock, Grayson

A major feeder stream of Whitetop Laurel Creek, this is a special-regulations creek that has a 12-inch-minimum limit from VA 859 downstream to its mouth. There is put-and-take stocking above VA 859. Rainbow and brown fingerlings are stocked, and there are some reproducing rainbow as well as some brown trout.

Access

The mouth of Green Cove Creek can be reached by driving to Creek Junction and walking the Taylors Valley Trail a short distance. The upper portion of the stream can be reached either by the Virginia Creeper Trail or VA 859.

Hale Lake

Lake Acreage:	5 acres
Fishing Pressure:	Heavy after stocking
Fishing Quality:	Fair to good
USS Quads:	Speedwell

This scenic impoundment lies 3,400 feet above sea level. A small foot trail encircling the lake is enjoyed by anglers and sightseers alike. This is a put-and-take body of water. Beneath its clear waters are trout, smallmouth bass, and some bluegill. There are rumored to be a few big brown trout in it as well.

Access

Most anglers fish from the dam, which is just a short walk up the steps from the parking area. The Hale Lake Trail provides anglers the means to reach the rest of the lake.

Hurricane Creek

Stream Size:	Small
Fishing Pressure:	Moderately light, heavier near Hurricane Campground
Fishing Quality:	Good
USGS Quads:	Trout Dale, Whitetop Mountain

This is a feeder stream of Comers Creek that drains Seng Mountain and Hurricane Mountain. It is a rhododendron-lined, rocky Southern Appalachian creek. There are reproducing rainbow below a large fall on the stream and brookies above it.

Access

Forest Road 84 heads up the Hurricane Creek valley, allowing road access, although some portions of the stream can also be reached by the Hurricane Knob

Trail. Hurricane Campground, a good fishing base for this stream, lies near its mouth, where it enters Comers Creek.

Lewis Fork

Stream Size:	Small
Fishing Pressure:	Light to moderate
Fishing Quality:	Good
USGS Quads:	Whitetop Mountain

Flowing off the slopes of Mount Rogers in the Lewis Fork Wilderness, this nifty little trout stream offers scenic angling. Brook trout inhabit the steep pool/fall environment. Anglers here will be seeking an attractive fishing environment that ranges between 3,600 and 4,500 feet in elevation, as well as getting a few fish on the line. Fishing pressure decreases away from VA 603.

Access

Foot power is the only means of reaching this rivulet. The Lewis Fork Trail, starting on VA 603, climbs along the stream banks for a mile. The upper stretches of Lewis Fork can be reached via the Cliffside Trail.

Little Laurel Creek

Stream Size:	Extremely small to small
Fishing Pressure:	Very light
Fishing Quality:	Good
USGS Quads:	Whitetop Mountain

This is a small, rough, rhododendron-laden stream that runs between 3,000 and 4,000 feet in elevation. It is a feeder stream of Whitetop Laurel Creek. The lower half flows along VA 600; then the stream turns east and becomes very tough to fish. There are no roads and only a faint trail to follow, descending into the upper half of the creek. This is a brook trout stream, but be apprised: you earn your trout on this creek.

Access

Little Laurel Creek flows into Whitetop Creek just east of Konnarock. From here VA 600 traces the stream for about a mile. After that, it is a tough pull in a scenic valley that makes for a wild and rugged fishing experience. The Little Laurel Trail leaves from Cherry Tree Camp on Forest Road 84 to drop down into the upper watershed. Be careful on Little Laurel.

New River

Stream Size:	Very large
Fishing Pressure:	Medium
Fishing Quality:	Good
USGS Quads:	Galax, Austinville

The New River is by far the largest fishable body of water in the recreation area. Reputed to be the second-oldest river in the world, the New flows out of North Carolina into Virginia and is bordered on much of its length by the New River Rail Trail State Park. Two dams, Buck and Byllesby, break up the flow of this wide but often rocky river. It is a warm-water fishery where anglers vie for smallmouth bass, catfish, and bream. A native population of walleye adds to the mix. Bank fishing is popular, though anglers can be seen in some areas using rubber rafts or small boats. Be careful fishing below the Byllesby and Buck dams, as the water may rise rapidly.

Access

The New River Rail Trail offers the most consistent access, though there are auto-access areas at Fries, Byllesby Dam, Buck Dam, Ivanhoe, and VA 608.

South Fork Holston River

Stream Size:	Medium to large
Fishing Pressure:	Heavy
Fishing Quality:	Excellent
USS Quads:	Marion, Atkins

The South Fork Holston drains the slopes of Glade Mountain and Iron Mountain. It gathers just below Sugar Grove and then flows through the wooded and pastured land of Rye Valley before flowing through the recreation area for a few miles.

This is a special-regulations trout stream with creel and size limits. The current limits are two fish of a minimum 16 inches in length per day. Only artificial lures are allowed. The banks are mostly wooded in the recreation area, and road access is the norm, except for a section of Barton Branch and the Buller Fish Hatchery—a section is known as "The Gorge." The primary trout are rainbow and brown, though there are some brook trout reputed to be around. There are large pools on the Holston, some of which can harbor big fish due to size and creel limits.

Access

The national forest portion of South Fork Holston can be accessed via VA 670 (South Fork Road). Another road access is via VA 650 at Buller Fish Hatchery.

Anglers can walk up the Holston upstream for about 2.0 miles from the fish hatchery beneath Barton Mountain and Dunford Ridge. This is known as "The Gorge," and its upper section passes through private land. Please respect the landowner's rights so that you will be allowed access in the future.

Straight Branch

Stream Size:	Small
Fishing Pressure:	Heavy
Fishing Quality:	Good
USGS Quads:	Konnarock

The lower half of Straight Branch belies its name. The tumbling creek tortuously winds through a narrow valley, intertwining with US 58 for several miles after it flows out of Beartree Lake. This lower portion is primarily for put-and-take rainbow fishing. Above the lake, it is small and actually straight (for a mountain stream); it harbors mainly rainbow trout and possibly a few brookies.

Access

There are many auto pullouts along US 58. Some areas are so narrow that anglers must be careful while walking along the highway. Forest Road 837 winds along the upper half of the stream, and Beartree campground lies at the top end of the watershed.

Tennessee Laurel Creek

Stream Size:	Small to medium
Fishing Pressure:	Heavy
Fishing Quality:	Good
USGS Quads:	Laurel Bloomery

This tributary stream of Whitetop Laurel Creek flows from Tennessee's Cherokee National Forest into Virginia's Jefferson National Forest and the Mount Rogers National Recreation Area. It is primarily a put-and-take fishery with some reproducing wild rainbow.

Access

Paved Virginia Highway 91 provides easy road access—you can practically fish from your car. Moderate traffic makes a decent experience possible though. The stream and highway both continue into Tennessee, but the creek there falls under Volunteer State regulations.

Whitetop Laurel Creek

Stream Size:	Medium
Fishing Pressure:	Heavy
Fishing Quality:	Excellent
USGS Quads:	Damascus, Konnarock

Whitetop Laurel is the primary fishing stream of the recreation area's west end. It is a special-regulations waterway with both brown and rainbow trout plying its shoals and holes. Brook trout are rumored to be in its headwaters and feeder streams. The size limit is a minimum of 12 inches; only artificial lures can be used; and only six fish can be caught per day. There are several handicap-accessible fishing piers along the stream near Creek Junction.

Access

The stream's east and west ends can be reached by US 58. Between the two ends, the Virginia Creeper Rail Trail follows Whitetop Laurel Creek for nearly 7.0 miles to Creek Junction, the confluence with Green Cove Creek.

Angler on Whitetop Laurel Creek with Virginia Creeper trestle in the background. Photo courtesy of U.S. Forest Service.

Swimming Holes

Mount Rogers Recreation Area may be primarily known for the tall mountains that lay claim to Virginia's highest point, but there is also a fair amount of water running off the slopes of this lofty land. As these streams gather, sooner or later there comes to be just the right spot to cool off during a warm summer day. What follows are descriptions of five good swimming holes that will be calling your name when the sun bears down overhead. Remember: be careful to use good judgment around mountain waters. A long time ago, while trying to show off at a swimming hole in the Smoky Mountains, I made a wild jump off a bluff and hit the rocks before hitting the water. Luckily, I only broke my foot. Be smarter than I was on the front end, and you will be enjoying one of nature's finest moments—swimmin' in a mountain stream.

Cripple Creek

Cripple Creek is a stream that runs east along the northern border of the recreation area; it then enters national forest land at Raven Cliff. Just downstream from Raven Cliff, near the Collins Cove Horse Camp, is a quiet, deep stretch of water between rapids. A footpath leads through a stile from the parking area, down to a grassy spot that has shade or sun options. Beside the pool are some outcrops that stretch into the water. Cove Branch flows into Cripple Creek just above here. The pool is wide and fairly deep. This is public land; however, across the water are some cabins. Please stay on the public land and remember to "pack it in, pack it out."

Access

From Wytheville, drive 11.0 miles south on US 21 to Speedwell. In Speedwell, turn left on VA 619 (Saint Peters Road). Stay with 619 for 7.8 miles—it changes names several times—and turn right on Pope Road (VA 642). Stay on Pope Road for 0.9 mile, passing Eagle Cliff Furnace, and come to Cove Branch Road (VA 643). Turn right on Cove Branch Road and follow it for 0.4 mile. Park at the left turn for Collins Cove Horse Camp. A footpath leads down to Cripple Creek.

Fox Creek

Fairwood Valley is one of the highest valleys in Virginia. It is situated between the Mount Rogers high country and the Iron Mountains. It was timbered over and settled a century ago but is now primarily forest land. Fox Creek bisects the valley, and it is on this creek where one of the highest swimming holes, at 3,200 feet, lies. This hole is often backed up by beaver dams. Beavers have recovered well in this area. The water here has a slight brown tint from the decay of vegetation high in the mountains. Streamside rocks make entry and exit easy. Part of the swimming hole is canopied, but a poolside clearing makes for a good spot to warm up in the sun after a dip.

Access

From exit 45 on I-81 near Marion, drive 6.0 miles south on VA 16, passing the Jennings Visitor Center. Stay on VA 16 for 11.0 miles to VA 603 (Fairwood Road) in Troutdale. Turn right on VA 603 and follow it for 1.2 miles to VA 847 (Ashland Lane). Turn right on Ashland Lane and cross Fox Creek on a bridge. Immediately after crossing Fox Creek, turn left onto a grass and dirt road canopied in trees. Continue up the road 0.1 mile and turn sharply left down to Fox Creek, where there is a clearing.

New River

The New River is a great Appalachian Mountain river, if not one of America's great rivers. It originates in North Carolina and flows north into the commonwealth. It picks up steam and passes along the eastern edge of the recreation area, where two historic power-producing dams slow the waters. VA 737 parallels the river here and provides numerous access points for dropping down to the waterway. Also paralleling the river is the New River Trail, a rail trail offering foot and bicycle access. On the whole, the waters here are warmer than most recreation area streams, making it a more viable option during the shoulder seasons.

Access

From exit 80 on I-81 near Fort Chiswell, head south on US 52 for 1.2 miles to VA 94. Turn right on VA 94 and follow it 13.0 miles to VA 602 (Byllesby Road). Turn left on Byllesby Road and follow it for 3.6 miles down to the New River and Buck Dam Road (VA 737). Turn left and parallel the river for 2.0 miles. There are numerous access points along this stretch.

South Fork Holston River

The South Fork Holston River is a valley stream that flows through the recreation area below Teas to the Buller Fish Hatchery. The water is chilly, as feeder streams flow off down from Brushy Mountain to the north and the Iron Mountains to the south. The swimming hole here is at the confluence of Comers Creek and the Holston. Here, the Holston flows in from the east, and Comers Creek flows in from the south. At this point, there is a large pool with mostly grassy banks, allowing for easy access to the water.

Access

From the Jennings Visitor Center, head south on VA 16 for 3.5 miles to Sugar Grove and VA 601 (Teas Road). Turn right on Teas Road and follow it for 3.4 miles to Teas. Here, stay left as the main road turns into VA 670 (South Fork Road). Follow 670 for 2.2 miles to VA 672 (Slabtown Road). Turn left on Slabtown Road and follow it for 0.2 mile over Comers Creek. Park on the far side of the bridge over Comers Creek, and then take the foot trail a short distance down along Comers Creek to the confluence of Comers Creek and South Fork Holston River.

Whitetop Laurel Creek

Whitetop Laurel Creek has always been a significant stream in these parts. Its valley has been a corridor for travel as long as people have been passing through here. Today, parts of US 58 and the Virginia Creeper Trail use it. It has become important for recreation seekers, whether those pedaling the Creeper Trail, fishing for trout, or cooling off when the summer sun climbs overhead.

There are a few good swimming holes within close proximity on Whitetop Laurel. The first hole lies where Straight Branch flows into Whitetop Laurel Creek near the Beech Grove trailhead parking. There is a sunny gravel beach looking over a slow-moving pool shaded by rhododendron. Downstream is another slow-moving pool where sunbathers can float a raft. Still another pool is just upstream on the Creeper Trail. Take the side path off the Creeper Trail and walk down through rhododendron to a sandy beach that leads into this third (and final) deep pool. On the far side of the pool is a rock wall.

Access

From the Little Red Caboose in Damascus, drive east on US 58 for 4.5 miles to a Virginia Creeper Trail parking area, off US 58 to the right. After parking, walk up the Creeper Trail to just before a small bridge and head toward the creek. The upper swimming hole is just before the second bridge on the right of the trail.

Scenic Drives

Damascus to Volney Scenic Drive

Type:	Paved
Length:	34 miles
Highlights:	Appalachian Trail, Virginia Creeper Rail Trail, trout fishing, views, Grayson Highlands State Park
Amenities:	Stores, restaurants, picnic areas, campgrounds
Access:	This scenic drive starts at the Little Red Caboose in Damascus, 12.0 miles east of exit 17 on I-81.

This scenic drive covers most of the western portion of the recreation area. It starts in Damascus and heads up along Whitetop Laurel Creek and Straight Branch, in the general vicinity of the Virginia Creeper Rail Trail and the Appalachian Trail. It then gains elevation, passing the Whitetop Community and Grayson Highlands State Park, a very worthwhile side trip. It finally descends through mountain and farm country to end in Volney at VA 16.

Leave the Little Red Caboose in Damascus, and pass through the main part of town. Here are bed-and-breakfasts, Mount Rogers Outfitters, restaurants, and the Adventure Damascus bicycle shop and livery. The Virginia Creeper Trail and the Appalachian Trail go right through town. Nearby, anglers may be fishing in Beaver Dam Creek, Tennessee Laurel Creek, Whitetop Laurel Creek, or the South Fork Holston River.

Keep heading east on 58, also known as J. E. B. Stuart Highway (named for the Confederate general) and begin a winding course. First, drive along Whitetop Laurel and then along Straight Branch, where there are small falls. Along the road are many picnic tables and angler road pull-offs. At 8.0 miles, come to Beartree Recreation Area. Here is a lake with a swim beach and fishing, picnic tables, and, farther up, a campground. Numerous trails, many favored by mountain bikers, emanate from this valley.

Stay on 58 as it begins to climb into the high country. The Appalachian Trail crosses at 13.0 miles. At 15.0 miles is the right turn to Green Cove and the upper end of the Virginia Creeper Trail. Enter the Whitetop Community at 3,400 feet. The community hosts a spring Maple Festival, at which molasses and other goodies are enjoyed. To make molasses, local sugar maple trees are tapped for their "sugar water." This is also a big area for growing Fraser fir Christmas trees. Fraser firs occur naturally only at the highest elevations of the Virginia Highlands and have become a desired Christmas tree.

Secluded high mountain farms are scattered off the roadway before reaching Grayson Highlands State Park at 26.0 miles. A left turn here will lead to many opportunities: a quality campground, a picnic area, pioneer homesteads, and hiking and equestrian trails offering many mountain vistas. The berry picking from Massie Gap in early August isn't bad either. Wild ponies may be observed in the open meadows of the mountains. The view from the Twin Pinnacles, about a 1.0-mile walk from the park visitor center, is dandy. Interestingly, there is also a seed orchard for the local Christmas tree farmers.

Begin to descend along Big Wilson Creek, passing Osbournes General Store. Big Wilson Creek is a viable trout stream. At 34.0 miles, end the scenic drive in Volney. US 58 meets VA 16. A left turn on VA 16 leads back to the interstate and the town of Marion. There are attractions along VA 16 as well.

Far East Forest Drive

Type:	Mostly gravel
Length:	25.0 miles
Highlights:	Round leaf birch viewing area, old-growth forest, Hale Lake, Comers Rock, Little Dry Run Wilderness
Amenities:	Campground, picnic area, a few stores
Access:	From exit 45 on I-81 near Marion, take VA 16 east for 9.5 miles to VA 601 (Flat Ridge Road) in Sugar Grove. Turn left on VA 601 and the forest drive starts here.

This forest drive is long on natural beauty, while passing through a few settled areas in between. Near the town Sugar Grove, you can stop at the Round Leaf Birch Viewing Area to see a species of tree that grows only in Smyth County and there only in a few places. Cruise on up Cressy Creek to Dry Creek Road and enjoy the woods. Drop down along Middle Fork and see the big oak and hemlock trees that were spared the logger's ax. Dip into the hamlet of Camp before climbing up the spine of the Iron Mountains to reach Hale Lake. This high-country impoundment has angling and hiking opportunities. Next comes Comers Rock, a natural viewing area that has the best vistas on this side of the recreation area. Finally drop down along US 21, passing the Little Dry Run Wilderness, which has good trails for getting back to the quiet side of Virginia.

Start the drive by leaving VA 16 at VA 601 and passing through a residential area of Sugar Grove. At 1.0 mile, come to the Round Leaf Birch Viewing Area. Park on the left side of the road; the short path to the viewing area is on the right across the road from the parking area. Appreciate the rare tree that gives the viewing area its name. Resume the drive on Flat Ridge Road and pass Cressy Creek, a stocked trout stream. Enter full-fledged forest land and turn left on Forest Road 16 (Dry Creek Road). A pleasant pine-oak woodland lines the trail. Begin descending at 7.0 miles and start to look for big trees. Hemlock and a few oaks stand tall along Middle Creek. Pass the Virginia Highlands Horse Trail and emerge into the Camp community at 10.0 miles. Turn right here on Camp Road (VA 612) and follow it for 0.5 mile to Hale Lake Road (VA 798). Climb into the Iron Mountains to reach VA 672 (Blue Spring Road) at 13.0 miles. Turn left here, now on the spine of the Iron Mountains. Soon intersect Forest Road 57. Stay left on 57 and pass Hale Lake at 15.0 miles. A nice, short loop trail circles the impoundment. Anglers may be seen dipping their lines for trout.

Next comes a side road leading left up to Comers Rock. The side road leads to a short trail that goes up steps to the overlook. Here is an inspiring view of the mountain and farm country of southwest Virginia. Return to FR 57 and drop down to a gap and the Comers Rock Recreation Area. Here is an underused campground and picnic spot. The picnic area has covered tables and an old-fashioned grill and fire pit. The nearby Unaka Trail is a short interpretive trail that loops through attractive mountain country with some big trees. Campers will often have this place to themselves, especially during the week. The Iron Mountain Trail leads from here back to Hale Lake, and the Little Dry Run Trail drops down into the Little Dry Run Wilderness.

Keep driving east on FR 57 and wind along the crest of the mountain to emerge onto US 21 at 20.0 miles. Turn left here and descend 2.0 miles to the Henley Hollow trailhead. From this trailhead, the Henley Hollow Trail climbs up an intimate valley, passing small falls to reach the Virginia Highlands Horse Trail. On the far side of US 21, the Little Dry Run Trail enters the Little Dry Run Wilderness and crisscrosses its namesake stream many times. It is 2.0 more miles down to the small town of Speedwell and the end of the scenic drive. There is a store here for convenience-type supplies. From Speedwell, it is 14.0 miles north on US 21 to Wytheville and I-81.

Hurricane Forest Drive

Type:	Nearly all gravel
Length:	11.0 miles

Highlights: Hurricane Creek, Rowland Creek Falls, Little Laurel Creek,
               Skulls Gap, Skulls Gap Overlook
Amenities: Campground
Access: From exit 45 on I-81 near Marion, take VA 16 east for 15.0
               miles to VA 650, Comers Creek Road. The forest drive starts
               here.

This is a rustic forest drive on a gravel road that winds through the woods. Travelers taking this route should relax and enjoy the beauty all around. Some individual features enhance the experience. Start on Comers Creek Road and quickly descend to Hurricane Creek Campground, a good camping area with trails and some fishing. Cruise up along Hurricane Creek to Hurricane Gap. Pass the side trail to Rowland Creek Falls, one of Mount Rogers's best cascades. Keep heading west along the Iron Mountains to Cherry Tree Gap and the Little Laurel Trail, a highland ramble on a tiny mountain stream. Come to the paved VA 600 and Skulls Gap, where there is a trailhead for the Iron Mountain Trail. Travel VA 600 a short distance to a wide overlook, where the vista ranges west to Big Walker Mountain, nearly to West Virginia.

Start the scenic drive by leaving VA 16 and heading west on VA 650 (Comers Creek Road). This road is paved a short distance, crossing the Appalachian Trail. Descend to Hurricane Campground Road at 1.3 miles and turn left. The road is paved just a short distance to reach Hurricane Campground, a quality camping area. The Hurricane Knob Trail is an interpretive path that makes a loop through numerous forest types. Comers Creek offers trout fishing.

Turn left on Forest Road 84 and ascend along Hurricane Creek, also a trout stream. Pass a few wildlife clearings, fields that offer food for animals. This part of the road also serves as a portion of the Virginia Highlands Horse Trail. Come to Hurricane Gap and keep climbing. Look for the Rowland Creek Trail at mile 6.0, on the right. This path leads 1.7 miles down to a stairstep cascade.

Pass rough Forest Road 828 and cruise along to Cherry Tree Gap at 7.0 miles. The clearing here stands at 4,200 feet and has two very old sugar maple trees. The Little Laurel Trail leaves the far side of the clearing and descends to deep hemlock woods. Stay along the north slope of the Iron Mountains to emerge onto VA 600 at 10.0 miles. Just across the road is Forest Road 204 and the old Skulls Gap Picnic Area. The IMT heads back east across VA 600 to Cherry Tree Gap and 1.2 miles west to the Lum Trail shelter.

Head back out to 600 and drive north (to the right). Go less than a mile to an overlook. There is a large parking area and a trail sign explaining the views in the distance. The Skulls Gap Trail leaves here and heads up a mile to the Iron Mountain Trail.

Marion to Whitetop Scenic Drive

Type:	Paved, some gravel at very end
Length:	35.0 miles
Highlights:	State Fish Hatchery, Jennings Visitor Center, Dickey Knob, Comers Creek Falls, Fairwood Cemetery, Elk Garden, White-top Mountain
Amenities:	Stores, restaurants, picnic areas, campgrounds
Access:	This scenic drive starts at exit 45 on I-81 near Marion.

This scenic drive takes auto tourists from low country to high, with many side attractions along the way. First, leave Marion, which has nearly every type of store, bank, or restaurant. Head east on VA 16 and pass a state fish hatchery where trout are raised. Next come to the Jennings Visitor Center and the national recreation area headquarters, a great information source. Climb up to Iron Mountain; pass near Comers Creek Falls. Pass through Troutdale, Virginia's highest incorporated community, and enter Fairwood Valley. Stop by the cemetery of former loggers and residents of the area. In Fairwood Valley are campgrounds and a picnic area. Many trails spur out of the valley. Climb into the Mount Rogers high country via VA 600 and stop at Elk Garden, where more trails enter a mountainside meadow. Keep climbing up to Whitetop Road, the state's highest road, and wind up the side of Whitetop Mountain, which has its own meadows and the rare Fraser fir–red spruce forest. The views up here will change the mindset of even the most jaded flatlander.

Leave I-81 at Marion and begin the scenic drive. Pass the Marion State Fish Hatchery. It was built in 1930 and has supplied area mountain streams with thousands upon thousands of trout over the decades. It is open to visitors: get a good look at the big one that can't get away. At 6.0 miles is the Jennings Visitor Center. Inside are forest service personnel eager to help you enjoy your stay at the national recreation area. There are also displays that explain the natural and human history of the area. A few miles farther on 16 is the hamlet of Sugar Grove. Hungry travelers will want to stop at the Sugar Grove Diner, which also serves as a bed-and-breakfast. Leave Sugar Grove, and Dickey Knob lies dead ahead. A trail leads to the top and grand views from nearby Raccoon Branch Campground, just off 16. Dickey Creek, also along VA 16, is a quality trout stream.

At 15.0 miles is Comers Creek Road (VA 650). Here begins a scenic, mostly gravel-surfaced forest drive. At 16.0 miles is Homestead Road, just past the Grayson-Smyth county line. A half mile down the road is the Comers Creek Falls Trail, which leads 0.3 mile down to the Appalachian Trail and a short distance farther to Comers Creek Falls, a 15-foot cascade.

At 17 miles lies Troutdale and the right turn to Fairwood Valley Road (VA 603). A century ago, Troutdale was a busy logging community, along with the rest of

Fairwood. Turn right onto Fairwood Valley Road. A couple of miles up is the right turn to Fairwood Cemetery, on Forest Road 4101, the final resting place for many mountain dwellers in this part of the Virginia Highlands. Back on VA 603 is the Fairwood Livery, where horses can be rented for trail rides in the woods and meadows. At 23.0 miles is the Mount Rogers trailhead. Here, a footpath leads toward the highest point in the state, Mount Rogers, at 5,729 feet. Many other trails, including the Appalachian Trail, leave from Fairwood Valley. Soon, you will pass Grindstone Campground, a well-run operation. Pass through a residential area before coming to VA 600. Don't take the first junction with 600 that leaves right, but keep to the left and pass a couple of small stores before coming to the second turn with 600; here, take a left toward Elk Garden, a saddle on Balsam Mountain 5.0 miles away. At Elk Garden is a trailhead and open mountain meadows at 4,500 feet. A walk in the meadows may reveal some of the wild ponies that live year-round in the Mount Rogers high country.

Keep going another mile past Elk Garden to Forest Road 89 (Whitetop Road). This gravel forest road winds up the slopes of Whitetop Mountain, Virginia's second-highest peak. Open meadows offer great vistas of the surrounding mountains, which stretch into North Carolina and Tennessee.

Picnic Areas at Mount Rogers NRA

The national recreation area and state parks have several designated picnic areas for visitors to enjoy. Recreation opportunities are near all picnic areas, enabling you to work off those hamburgers and hot dogs. The following is a list of those picnic areas, along with suggested area activities.

Beartree

The Beartree Picnic Area is part of the larger Beartree Recreation Area. One of the busiest picnic areas at Mount Rogers, it is located near Beartree Lake. There are numerous picnic tables and grills beneath the shade of pine and hardwood trees. There is also a group picnic area that is available on a reservation-only basis.

Auto access for the picnic area is close by. Also nearby is Beartree Lake, which offers a swim beach with changing rooms. A trail circles the lake and offers handicap angler access. There are trout and bass in the lake.

Access

From the Little Red Caboose in Damascus, take US 58 east for 8.2 miles to paved Forest Road 837. Turn left up 837 and follow it for 1.2 miles to the right turn for the beach picnic area.

Comers Rock

The Comers Rock Recreation Area features both a campground and picnic area. It is in the eastern portion of the recreation area, atop Iron Mountain at 3,400 feet. An old-time picnic shelter with a stone grill adds rainy-day possibilities to this already attractive area, located in a gap shaded by an oak forest. It is a quiet getaway for solitude seekers, especially during the week.

The Unaka Trail, which actually starts at the picnic area, offers a short course in the natural history of the area. The Comers Rock Trail takes hikers 0.5 mile to a superlative view of the surrounding mountain and farm country. Anglers can drive to nearby Hale Lake or hike to it on the Iron Mountain Trail. Another nearby destination is the Little Dry Run Wilderness, where Little Dry Run cuts a valley through the mountains.

Access

From exit 70 on I-81 near Wytheville, drive south on US 21 for 17.8 miles to Forest Road 57, passing through Speedwell. Turn right on FR 57 and follow it for 3.6 miles to Comers Rock Recreation Area. The picnic area will be on your left.

Grayson Highlands

Grayson Highlands State Park has a large picnic area spread out on the edge of Big Spring Ridge. There are numerous picnic tables with every combination of sun and shade. It is a cool place, located at an elevation of nearly 4,000 feet. Nearby is the Rock House Ridge Trail, which allows one to explore the area's beauty. Also nearby is a preserved pioneer homestead and other buildings left over from pioneer days. This homestead area is definitely worth a tour.

Access

From the Little Red Caboose in Damascus, take US 58 east for 26.0 miles to Grayson Highlands State Park, which will be on the left. Enter the park, passing the contact station; then stay on the main park road until the right turn for the picnic area.

Raven Cliff

Raven Cliff Recreation Area is a good destination for many reasons, and the picnic area is no exception. With 35 sites, this is the largest picnic locale in the recreation area. The picnic tables are situated on the banks of Cripple Creek, which features a steep rock cliff on the far side of the stream. A potential drawback is the lack of shade.

With the immediate proximity of Cripple Creek, water recreation is a natural attraction of this area. Swimming and tubing are enjoyed in the warmer months, as is angling for smallmouth bass. Cripple Creek is a put-and-take trout stream in late winter and spring. Picnickers should take the short walk to the Raven Cliff Furnace, an iron-ore-processing spot of yesteryear. Raven Cliff Trail, open to hikers, bikers, and equestrians, heads along Cripple Creek to come near Collins Cove Horse Camp.

Access

From Wytheville, drive 11.0 miles south on US 21 to Speedwell. In Speedwell, turn left on VA 619 (Saint Peters Road). Stay with 619 for 6.5 miles to Raven Cliff Lane. (The actual name of 619 changes from Saint Peters to Cripple Creek to Gleaves Road.) Turn right on Raven Cliff Lane, where there is a sign for Raven Cliff Recreation Area. The picnic area is beside Cripple Creek off Raven Cliff Lane.

Places to
Lay Your Head

Mount Rogers Area Campgrounds

Beartree Campground

Nearby town:	Damascus
Open:	Mid-April through October
Individual sites:	73 campsites
Each site has:	Picnic table, lantern post, fire grate, tent pad
Site assignment:	Some first come, first served; some by reservation (877) 444-6777
Registration:	At entrance station
Facilities:	Hot showers, flush toilets, water spigot
Elevation:	3,400 feet

This heavily wooded, secluded campground is located in the upper end of the Straight Fork Valley. The forest here is a mixture of evergreens and hardwoods, complemented by an abundance of rhododendron. Overall, the campground is well maintained and very clean. It is hard to improve on the nearby works of nature that can be explored via trails that literally emanate from the campground. Hikers and mountain bikers can explore the Iron Mountains, while anglers can fish Beartree Lake. This impoundment also has a swim beach for kids and anyone else who wants to take a dip. There is also a canoe launch on this "no motors allowed" lake.

Beartree Campground is divided into two loops, Beaver Flats and Chipmunk Circle. Pass the guard station, drive a bit, and come to the Beaver Flats loop. This loop is situated in a rich forest of white pine, hemlock, and planted fir trees, in addition to an overstory of deciduous trees. The sites are average in size but are completely separated by thickets of rhododendron. Bathhouses, complete with hot showers, are never far from a campsite. Scattered in the loop are some double campsites and a children's play area. There is also an abundance of campground hosts to help you with any needs or problems. The latter half of the loop is a bit hilly, but the campsites themselves have been leveled.

Chipmunk Circle is at the end of Forest Road 837. There are many reserved sites here. These campsites are also well shaded overhead and offer the maximum in privacy in a profusion of rhododendron. The loop is mostly level with a few hilly spots. Overall, the loop is nearly identical to Beaver Flats, except for the reserved sites.

Campers can literally walk or bike directly from their campsite to trails. The Lum Trail leads from Chipmunk Circle up to the Iron Mountain Trail. Depending on their whim, travelers can head west on the IMT to the Shaw Gap Trail and return via FR 837, or keep heading west to the Yancy Trail, which drops down to the campground entrance station. The Beartree Gap Trail leads from Shaw Gap down to Beartree Lake for fishing and swimming opportunities and also continues to the Appalachian Trail. Mountain bikers may want to head east on the IMT to intersect VA 600. Make a hair-raising and fast ride down VA 600 to the Straight Branch Trail, which loops back to the campground. The Beaver Flats Trail is a short nature trail that makes a circuit out of the Beaver Flats camping loop. And this covers just the recreation opportunities by the campground!

Access

From the Little Red Caboose in Damascus, take US 58 east for 8.2 miles to paved Forest Road 837. Turn left up 837 and follow it for 0.7 mile to the campground guardhouse. Continue past the entrance for 3.0 miles to the campground.

Comers Rock Campground

Nearby town:	Wytheville
Open:	Year-round
Individual sites:	6
Each site has:	Picnic table, lantern post, fire grate
Site assignment:	First come, first served; no reservations
Registration:	Self-registration on site
Facilities:	Water spigot in warm months, vault toilet (but bring water just in case)
Elevation:	3,800 feet

This high-country campground lies on the shoulder of Iron Mountain in the lesser-traveled east end of the national recreation area. The campground is named for a nearby outcrop on Iron Mountain, where there are stellar views of the Cripple Creek valley to the north and the Elk Creek valley to the south. But this camping experience is about more than views: It is a quiet experience in an intimate setting. It is about fishing Hale Lake, or maybe taking a walk on the wild side in the Little

Dry Run Wilderness. Comers Rock is for campers who like their campgrounds spare on developed facilities and long on natural attributes.

Drive along the gravel-surfaced Forest Road 57 and dip into the Comers Rock Recreation Area. The small picnic area is to your left. Here is a little shelter, a grill, and picnic tables. Also, here lies the Unaka Trail. To your right is the campground. It slopes off and down to the right in a scattered oak forest, mixed with a few white pines, a few hemlocks, and rhododendron. The campsites are cut into the sloping mountainside.

Pass the pay station and water spigot and begin to climb to the west side of the gap. Campers have to park and then carry their belongings down to some sites. The Iron Mountain Trail, which leads to the Comers Rock Trail and other paths, departs directly from the campground. This year-round campground is lightly used. At any time during the week, you are likely to have this place to yourself. Winter is quiet almost any day of the week. Summer weekends see the most visitors, followed by fall weekends.

It's a rule: All campers who stay here must make the pilgrimage to Comers Rock. You can either walk from the campground, or drive just a short distance west to Forest Road 57A, and finally walk just a short distance up a set of stone steps to the vantage point. The natural outcrop has been enhanced with a platform. Other views around here can be had by foot or horse. Take the Unaka Trail from the campground and loop through high country woods complemented by some big trees, or drop down the Little Dry Run Trail via the Iron Mountain Trail and access the Virginia Highlands Horse Trail and the Little Dry Run Wilderness.

This little 3,400-acre wilderness has ridge and valley country typical of the recreation area but receives much less use than the wildernesses around the Mount Rogers high country. Little Dry Run and West Fork both offer fishing opportunities for small native brook trout. Anglers who want bigger fish to fry can head west on the Iron Mountain Trail or take Forest Road 57 to Hale Lake, a trout pond that allegedly harbors some bigger rainbows. Hale Lake is the most popular feature of this lesser-frequented parcel of the recreation area.

Access

From exit 70 on I-81 near Wytheville, drive south on US 21 for 17.8 miles to Forest Road 57, passing through Speedwell. Turn right on FR 57 and follow it for 3.6 miles to Comers Rock Campground, which will be on your right.

Grayson Highlands Campground

Nearby Town:	Mouth of Wilson
Open:	Mid-April through October
Individual sites:	31 standard sites, 43 water and electric sites, 23 horse stable area sites

Each site has:	Picnic table, lantern post, fire grate, tent pad
Site assignment:	By reservation, with some first come, first served
Registration:	By phone, (800) 933-PARK, or at campground entrance booth
Facilities:	Hot showers, flush toilets, water spigot, coin laundry, pay phone
Parking:	At campsites only
Elevation:	4,250 feet

Grayson Highlands State Park is a gem in the Virginia State Park system. And the campground matches the high standards such a park should have. Located on the shoulder of Wilburn Ridge in the high country just a few miles from Virginia's highest peak, this campground will suit both tent and RV campers seeking cool relief from summer heat. It is also good for a springtime getaway or to view fall's dramatic color show. The state park has trails galore for campers to enjoy vistas from craggy outcrops or waterfalls from tumbling streams. A relaxed atmosphere here nearly guarantees a welcome respite from the stress of day-to-day life.

The camping area is stretched out along three interconnected loops. The right-hand loop descends through a partially wooded area with campsites fairly close together. Some are standard, and others in the right-hand loop have water and electricity. The campsites on the inside of the loop are more wooded. Pass the lower bathhouse. The second loop has the best campsites. They are in oak-maple woods and are spaced farther apart, resulting in ample privacy. The final loop has larger pull-though sites designed for RVs. The upper bathhouse is here. There are many locust and hawthorn trees scattered about a grassy area.

There is also a separate 23-site camping area near the park stables. These gravel sites spur off a paved road on the edge of Baker Ridge. A fully equipped bathhouse is there. Nearby are stables and facilities for riders and their horses.

Campground hosts make for safe and friendly camping areas. Water spigots are scattered near all campsites. A dump station serves RVs. The Country Store, adjacent to the main campground, is open on weekends.

There is no shortage of activities here. Hiking and horse trails abound. The Wilson Trail is adjacent to the campground and drops down to Wilson Creek, where there are numerous cascades and first-rate trout fishing. The Twin Pinnacles Trail and the Big Pinnacle Trail offer rocky views from the park's highest elevation at 5,048 feet. If that is not high enough, the Rhododendron Trail leads to the federal Mount Rogers National Recreation Area and many other connecting paths that wind through the high country. The Cabin Creek Trail leads to high waterfalls. A pioneer homestead area offers a glimpse into life in the Grayson Highlands before there were state parks.

View from high country to low.

Access

From the Little Red Caboose in Damascus, drive east on US 58 for 26.0 miles to the park entrance, which will be on the left.

Grindstone Campground

Nearby town:	Marion
Open:	Late April through October
Individual sites:	91 sites—48 have water and electricity
Each site has:	Picnic table, lantern post, fire grate, tent pad
Site assignment:	Some first come, first served; some by reservation (877) 444-6777
Registration:	Campground host will come by and register you, or you can register by phone
Facilities:	Hot showers, flush toilets, water spigot, pay phone
Parking:	At campsites only
Elevation:	3,600 feet

Grindstone is a well-maintained campground in a northern hardwood forest at the base of the Mount Rogers high country. A large flat at the upper end of Laurel Creek is the setting for this shady, old-time camping area. Mount Rogers lies directly to the south, and the Iron Mountains are to the north. Outdoor enthusiasts can't help but like this place, as there are more than ample trails all around this high valley.

Pass the security-enhancing entrance station and enter the campground. There are two loops open. The far-right-hand road leads to a picnic area, campground amphitheater, and swim area. The Cottontail Loop heads right, uphill, in a deciduous forest. Large rocks are scattered among the campsites. The campsites are adequately separated from one another and are average in size, except for the larger double units. Birch, cherry, and other deciduous trees form a continuous canopy.

The Opossum loop has 21 sites; all are first come, first served. There is more rhododendron in this loop, and the sites are even more widely separated than in the Cottontail Loop. The third loop, Groundhog, is closest to Fairwood Valley Road. It is much like the Cottontail Loop. Overall the campground has a clean, well-kept look to it, and it is a good place to return to from many adventures nearby. In the immediate area is a water play area, where Grindstone Branch has been rocked in. There is also a playground for children. The Whispering Waters Nature Trail, accessed near the campground amphitheater, makes a 0.6-mile loop from near the campground amphitheater.

The adult playground is the surrounding high country, the loftiest in the state. The Mount Rogers Trail is the campground gateway into the Lewis Fork Wilderness, which starts just south of the campground. It's a little over 2,000 feet to the top of Mount Rogers through the wilderness, but the change in flora will amaze you. There is no view from atop Virginia's highest peak, but there are numerous vistas along the way and on connecting trails as well. Also near Grindstone are the Appalachian Trail and the Lewis Fork Trail. The AT winds throughout the high country. Lewis Fork avails trout-fishing opportunities, as does Fox Creek. To the north are the more mountain-biker-friendly Iron Mountains. The Flat Top Trail leads north to Hurricane Mountain, where the Iron Mountain Trail leaves right to make a great loop in combination with the Virginia Highlands Horse Trail and the Fairwood Valley Trail. There are numerous other hiking and biking opportunities, as well as scenic drives to Elk Garden and the crest of Whitetop Mountain.

Access

From exit 45 on I-81 in Marion, head south on VA 16 for 6.0 miles, passing the Jennings Visitor Center. Continue south on VA 16 for 11.0 miles to VA 603 (Fairwood Valley Road) in Troutdale. Turn right on VA 603 and follow it 6.0 miles to Grindstone Campground, which is on the left.

Hurricane Campground

Nearby town:	Marion
Open:	Mid-April through October
Individual sites:	27
Each site has:	Picnic table, fire grate, lantern post, tent pad
Site assignment:	First come, first served; no reservations
Registration:	Self-registration on site
Facilities:	Hot showers, flush toilets, water spigots
Parking:	At campsites only
Elevation:	2,800 feet

This small campground got the big campground makeover. Located in the naturally attractive flat at the confluence of Comers Creek and Hurricane Branch, Hurricane Campground was improved; yet, with only 27 campsites, it doesn't have that "campground city" aura so often felt in bigger camping areas. Start with a paved campground road and paved campsite pull-ins. Add campground hosts to make things safe and secure. Add attractive wood fencing where needed. Keep grassy green spaces open. Construct the campsites with landscaping timbers and elevated tent pads. Space the campsites far apart in the most appealing locations. Add hot showers. In other words, the forest service gave campers what they most desire but still lent the campground a rustic atmosphere that doesn't detract from the natural beauty of the mountain valley. And being at Mount Rogers National Recreation Area ensures that ample outdoor activities are nearby. But your campsite here may inspire you just to relax, Virginia Highlands style.

The campground is laid out along a road that crosses Hurricane Branch and runs along Comers Creek. However, the first few campsites are along Hurricane Branch. Spacious private campsites are set far from the road. On the right-hand side are campsites along Comers Creek. Green space between the campground road and the campsites lets in plenty of light. On the left-hand side is an intermittent stream flowing through rhododendron.

Pass the first fully equipped bathhouse and descend the valley. Campsites have been leveled. Come to a cluster of campsites that are more shaded in a narrow section of the valley. Pass the Comers Creek Trail on your right before the road climbs away from the stream and past a bathhouse and the campground host. More campsites are up the hill. On the whole, these hillside sites are even more private than the ones below. Being attractive has its price: Hurricane can become busy during the summer. Expect it to be full on weekends. Other than those times, sites are generally available.

Hiking, mountain biking, and fishing are the primary activities here. The Hurricane Knob Trail leaves directly from the campground and makes a 1.1-mile loop around Hurricane Knob. The Comers Creek Trail leaves the campground and heads downstream along its namesake creek. Anglers like this path. Comers Creek has put-and-take fishing and wild rainbow trout, with brook trout in the headwaters and feeder streams such as Hurricane Branch. Equestrians and bicyclers can use the Virginia Highlands Horse Trail, which passes right by the campground. The Appalachian Trail is but a half mile up the Dickey Gap Trail, which starts near the junction of Forest Road 84 and the campground entrance road, 84A. From here, you can hike north one mile on the AT to Comers Creek Cascades. And when you return to Hurricane, it won't seem like campground city but instead like a relaxing forest destination.

Access

From exit 45 on I-81 near Marion, head south on VA 16 for 6.0 miles to the Jennings Visitor Center. From the Jennings Visitor Center, continue south on VA 16 for 8.7 miles to VA 650 (Comers Creek Road). Turn right on VA 650 and follow it for 1.4 miles to Forest Road 84 (Hurricane Campground Road). Turn left on Hurricane Campground Road and follow it a short distance to the campground, which will be dead ahead on FR 84A.

Millrace Campground

Nearby town:	Fort Chiswell
Information:	(276) 699-6778; http://www.dcr.virginia.gov/state_parks/new.shtml
Open:	Year-round
Individual sites:	12
Each site has:	Picnic table, fire grate, lantern post, tent pad
Site assignment:	Reservation only, (800) 933-PARK
Registration:	By phone or at park office
Facilities:	Water spigot, vault toilets
Elevation:	1,940 feet

This state park–run campground is in excellent condition and should serve as a model for other campgrounds. Nestled beneath a grove of sycamore and tulip trees, the well-groomed camping area beckons park visitors to come back one day and spend the night. The campground is on the banks of a carved-out side stream, or millrace, of the New River—a location whose rapids provide wonderful background music for campers wishing to pitch their tents here. Be apprised: This is a campground for walk-in tents only. Campers must also transfer their gear from their vehicles to little park-provided wagons, which they can then haul to their chosen sites. Many of the sites are right on the river, but even those that aren't have views of the stream.

The immaculate, gravel-surfaced camping areas are delineated with railroad ties. Within each camping area is a picnic table, fire grate, and lantern post. Gravel paths connect the campsites. A firewood station is nearby. The vault toilets are by the parking area, as is the drinking water. The rest of your "water satisfaction" can be obtained from the New River itself, where you can fish for walleye, bass, and bream, or go swimming, tubing, or canoeing. Land-oriented visitors will want to ply the New River Rail Trail. A livery offers tubes and canoes for rent, as well as bicycles and shuttle service for heading out on the rail trail. Popular runs are from Galax to Foster Falls, or Pulaski to Foster Falls. On summer weekends, the equestrian livery is open for business, enabling you to ride the rail trail atop a horse.

Campers don't have to worry about whether they will get a campsite or not, since camping is by reservation only. Sites are available most weekdays and on off-season weekends. Call well ahead to reserve a site on summer weekends, since there are only 12 campsites.

Access

From exit 24 on I-77 south of Wytheville, take VA 69 (Lead Mine Road) for 0.2 mile east to US 52. Turn left on US 52 (Fort Chiswell Road) and head north for 1.5 miles to VA 608 (Foster Falls Road). Turn right on 608 and follow it for 1.8 miles to VA 623 (Orphanage Drive). Turn left on Orphanage Drive and shortly enter Foster Falls State Park, part of the New River Rail Trail State Park. The Millrace Campground is on the left as you enter the park.

Raccoon Branch Campground

Nearby town:	Marion
Open:	Mid-April through December
Individual sites:	20—10 have electricity
Each site has:	Picnic table, lantern post
Site assignment:	First come, first served; no reservations
Registration:	Self-registration on site
Facilities:	Water spigot, flush toilets May - October; vault toilet only November–April
Elevation:	2,800 feet

Raccoon Branch Campground is the first stop for many visitors to Mount Rogers National Recreation Area. Campers who stay here can enjoy recreational activities directly from their campsite or they can hop in their vehicles and get to many other locales rather quickly. But don't hurry, as forest drives here can be nearly as pleasant as your destination. Access is a big drawing card at Raccoon Branch, although some may consider the road too close to the campground—cars can be heard and seen. The small size of the campground, with a good mix of sun and shade, makes for a pleasing experience, whether you are roasting hot dogs over the fire, fishing Raccoon Branch, or hiking up to Dickey Knob.

Drive into the campground on a paved road. Dickey Creek flows off to your right. The camping area is a classic loop laid out in a partially wooded flat of pine and oak with a few hemlocks. There are campsites on the inside and outside of the loop. The first couple of sites are inside the loop. More desirable streamside sites lie outside the loop. Just past campsite #4, the Dickey Knob Trail starts its climb to great views.

The next few campsites are open to sun and are grassy. Campsite #8 is shaded and adjacent to the bridge over Dickey Creek. The electric sites start with #10. The upper part of the loop swings closer to VA 16. The sites here are large and open but offer little in the way of privacy. Farther on, inside of the loop, are campsites shaded by rhododendron and hemlock. Of special note is campsite #19, a handicap-accessible site under white pines.

Water spigots can be found throughout the campground, including at all electric sites. Two bathhouses adequately serve campers. Remember to bring your own water during the off-season. Ample campsites will be available during the shoulder seasons and most weekdays. Peak summer weekends can be busy with tent campers and vehicle campers. Hunters will occupy the campground in late fall and early winter.

If exploring the woods is your bag, come here. The Raccoon Branch Nature Trail makes a short loop across Dickey Creek from the campground. Trails emerge directly from the campground. The Dickey Knob Trail makes a 900-foot climb in 2.3 miles to a great view of the recreation area. Equestrians, hikers, and mountain bikers can go for miles in either direction on the Virginia Highlands Horse Trail. Westward travelers can follow the path along Raccoon Branch to fish for trout. Roadside anglers can trace Dickey Creek up- or downstream along VA 16.

Hop in your vehicle for a scenic drive—you have already been on one since Marion. Continue south to Trout Dale on 16. Then head east on VA 603 (Fairwood Road). From here, you can drive to Elk Garden and the Mount Rogers high country via VA 600. Bring your map with you, as divergent temptations are many, such as the drive to Whitetop Mountain or a walk along the Appalachian Trail. On your way in to Raccoon Branch, stop at the Jennings Visitor Center and explore more possibilities.

Or you can return to Sugar Grove and then head west to the South Fork Holston River, where you can fish "The Gorge" for bigger trout, maybe visiting the Buller Fish Hatchery or swimming in the deep hole where Barton Branch flows into the Holston. Whatever you do, stay for a while; Marion is nearby for supply runs.

Access

From exit 45 on I-81 in Marion, head south on VA 16 for 6.0 miles, passing the Jennings Visitor Center. Raccoon Branch Campground is 5.7 miles beyond the visitor center on VA 16, on your right.

Raven Cliff Campground

Nearby town:	Wytheville
Open:	Year-round
Individual sites:	20
Each site has:	Picnic table, fire grate, lantern post, tent pad
Site assignment:	First come, first served; no reservations
Registration:	Self-registration on site
Facilities:	Water spigot, vault toilets
Elevation:	2,150 feet

The forest service did well in purchasing this slice of the Cripple Creek Valley. Here, bluffs border one side of the large watercourse, while on the other side a partially forested hill rises to overlook the bluffs across the way. A little site work in developing the campground, picnic area, and trails has made the setting more user-friendly. Now, visitors can camp in a quiet campground at the end of a gravel road, and fish, swim, hike, or mountain bike year-round.

Turn onto Raven Cliff Lane and settle into the Cripple Creek Valley. Cripple Creek lies off to your right. A grassy picnic area runs alongside the water. Turn left into the campground and look for a site. The campground is laid out along a gravel lane with an auto turnaround at the end. Campsites are built into the side of Gleaves Knob looking on a bluff across Cripple Creek. Overhead is a forest of hemlock, white pine, and assorted maples and oaks. Campsites are higher on the right, up the hill, and lower on the left, down the hill. All sites have been leveled. Now it is a question of finding the right site to fit your desire for sun or shade.

The campsites are well dispersed from one another, resulting in more than adequate campsite privacy. Campsite #9 is of special note. Steps lead down to an extremely shady hemlock forest that is especially nice on a warm day. Beyond this are campsite restrooms for each sex. Here also is the pump well, which is closed in winter. Past this, the sites are more open. They use tent pads, steps, and other wooden borders to ensure that no one is sleeping or camping at an angle. There is also one double site for large parties. Campsite #20 is at the end of the auto turnaround and offers maximum solitude.

The campground is open year-round and sites are always available during cooler weather. Sites are generally available at all times except summer holiday weekends. Although the campground is not directly on the creek, it does offer winter views and quick access to the water. Anglers and swimmers both enjoy the water here. There is smallmouth bass fishing year-round and trout fishing during winter and spring. Swimmers can enjoy some of the slower quiet areas near the picnic area. Sunbathers will also like the spot. Hikers can take the short walk downstream and across the creek (via footbridge) to the Raven Cliff Furnace on the Raven Cliff

Furnace Trail. Walk in a pleasant, grassy floodplain to the tall stone structure where iron ore was processed from about 1880 to 1905. The ruins of Eagle Furnace and Noble Furnace are also nearby. Such furnaces needed three things to operate: iron to process, limestone to mix with the iron ore, and wood to heat the mixture. They were often located along streams to harness waterpower, which was used to power blowers to fan the furnaces.

Access

From Wytheville, drive 11.0 miles south on US 21 to Speedwell. In Speedwell, turn left on VA 619 (Saint Peters Road). Stay with 619 for 6.5 miles to Raven Cliff Lane. (The actual name of 619 changes from Saint Peters to Cripple Creek to Gleaves Road.) Turn right on Raven Cliff Lane, where there is a sign for Raven Cliff Recreation Area. Follow Raven Cliff Lane for 0.7 mile and come to the campground, which will be on your left.

Horse Camps

Mount Rogers has three camps exclusively for equestrians. These primitive camps are larger in size per campsite than other campgrounds and have hitching posts that accommodate riders. Equestrian trails also emanate from these camps, which makes horseback riding at Mount Rogers that much more convenient. Campers will also find that these areas offer other recreational opportunities as well.

Collins Cove Horse Camp

Nearby town:	Wytheville
Open:	Year-round
Individual sites:	8
Each site has:	Picnic table, fire grate, hitching post
Site assignment:	First come, first served; no reservations
Registration:	Self-registration on site
Facilities:	Pump well in warm months, vault toilets
Elevation:	2,200 feet

This camp has ample room for several horse parties and the trucks, RVs, and horse trailers that accompany them. As you drive up the dirt road into the campground, a lush field lies off to your left beyond a fence. Beyond an open grassy hollow, there are a few campsites strung out in a flat backed against a hill. The campsites are very widely dispersed, as horse camps should be. Climb up to the next flat, and there are six campsites dispersed in a large grassy clearing. Here, too, are the vault toilets and water pump.

The Ewing Trail leaves from the rear of the campground. This path connects to the master equestrian path of Mount Rogers, the Virginia Highlands Horse Trail. The Raven Cliff Trail extends for 1.2 miles, heading upstream along Cripple Creek to access Raven Cliff Recreation Area and Raven Cliff Furnace.

Campsite at Collins Cove Campground.

Just across the road from the campground entrance is the Cripple Creek swimming hole. If you don't feel like dipping, you can always drop your line in the water for smallmouth bass year-round or trout in the winter and springtime.

Access

From Wytheville, drive 11.0 miles south on US 21 to Speedwell. In Speedwell, turn left on VA 619 (Saint Peters Road). Stay with 619 for 7.8 miles—it changes names several times—and turn right on Pope Road (VA 642). Stay on Pope Road for 0.9 mile, passing Eagle Cliff Furnace, and come to Cole Branch Road (VA 643). Turn right on Cole Branch Road and follow it for 0.4 mile to the left turn for Collins Cove Horse Camp. Wooden fences line the road to the camp.

Fox Creek Horse Camp

Nearby town:	Marion
Open:	Year-round
Individual sites:	10
Each site has:	Picnic table, fire grate, hitching post
Site assignment:	First come, first served; no reservations
Registration:	Self-registration on site
Facilities:	Pump well in warm months, vault toilets
Elevation:	3,500 feet

This roadside camp has many trails covering varied terrain emanating directly from it. The Mount Rogers high country and the Lewis Fork Wilderness are nearby, and the trails of Iron Mountain are easy to get to as well. The campground itself, however, is no raging beauty and can become a mud hole after rainy periods. It also lies directly alongside VA 603, which makes for a potentially noisy and less than rustic experience. Thus, Fox Creek Horse Camp is good for those who value convenient trail access over a good camping site.

Turn off VA 603 onto VA 741 and immediately turn left into the lower camping area, a field bordered by VA 603 on the left and Fox Creek on the right. Fox Creek has wooded banks and a fence along it. On either side of the gravel campground road are six campsites. The ones by the creek are more desirable.

The upper camping area is on the far side of Fox Creek. Head up VA 741 just a short distance and come to campsites on both sides of the road. The camping area to the left is up a hill on a flat. There are a few sites by an unnamed feeder stream heading into Fox Creek. These are the most desirable sites.

Access

From exit 45 on I-81 near Marion, drive 6.0 miles south on VA 16, passing the Jennings Visitor Center. Stay on VA 16 for 11.0 miles to VA 603 (Fairwood Road) in Trout Dale. From the village of Trout Dale, head west on VA 603 (Fairwood Valley Road) for 4.0 miles. The campground will be on your right.

Hussy Mountain Horse Camp

Nearby town:	Wytheville
Open:	Year-round
Individual sites:	6
Each site has:	Picnic table, fire grate, hitching post
Site assignment:	First come, first served; no reservations
Registration:	Self-registration on site
Facilities:	Pump well in warm months, vault toilets
Elevation:	2,900 feet

This smaller camp is set in the heavily wooded valley of East Fork. Hussy Mountain is in the lesser-used east end of the recreation area. Drop down from Forest Road 14 and immediately enter the first part of the horse camp. Here are three sites bordered by a wooden fence. They lie very near West Fork. Cross East Fork on a bridge and come to the second camping area. This has two sites and is bordered by woods. Just past here is one more wooded and secluded campsite before the campground road rises to a turnaround along a side stream. The area up here is not level, but it is large. Overall, the sites aren't as large as at the other two camps, but the immediate scenery is the best. Also, Hussy Mountain has newer "SST" toilets—that stands for "sweet smelling technology."

Equestrians have ample opportunities to saddle up here. The East Fork Trail passes right through the camp and can be used to reach the Virginia Highlands Horse Trail, which heads up to Horse Heaven. Another loop possibility uses the Divide and Dry Run Gap trails, with the bulk of the loop being on the Iron Mountain Trail.

Access

From exit 70 at I-81 near Wytheville, take US 21 south through Wytheville. Drive 16.8 miles to Forest Road 14, passing through Speedwell. Turn left on Forest Road 14 and follow it 2.0 miles to the horse camp, which will be on the right.

Cabins

Cabins offer a fun lodging possibility at Mount Rogers. This way, you can enjoy the outdoor activities of your choice and then retire to a mountain cabin. Choose from two different cabins: Blue Springs Gap Cabin and Sunrise Cabin. They offer different levels of amenities but both can be reserved by calling 877-444-6777 or online at www.recreation.gov. Call for rates.

Blue Spring Gap Cabin

This cabin is near Hale Lake and offers good views from the mountaintop location. The 900-square foot cabin has a large wraparound porch. It has three bedrooms and can accommodate eight people. There is electricity, a flush toilet, stove, and refrigerator but no shower or drinking water. A fireplace provides heat.

Access
From Exit 45 on I-81, take VA 16 south for 10.0 miles to VA 695. Turn left onto VA 695, and after 1.0 mile, turn left onto VA 614. After 4.0 miles, turn right onto VA 612. After 5.0 miles, turn right onto gravel-surfaced VA 798. After about 3.0 miles, you will reach the top of the mountain and a "T" intersection. Turn right onto VA 672. After about 0.3 mile, take the first road to the right, which leads to the cabin. The total distance from I-81 is 24.0 miles.

Sunrise Cabin

The Sunrise Cabin is the newer of the two getaways. This four-bedroom cabin of 2,500 square feet is a little more civilized. Located in the eastern end of the recreation area, it has water, electricity, and a refrigerator. It also has a big fireplace, a large yard, and a big porch with great views. The capacity is eight people. Situated near the New River, it offers water- and land-based recreation.

Access

From exit 80 on I-81, drive east on US 52 for 1.0 mile. Turn right and go south on VA 94 for 12.0 miles until you intersect the Virginia Highlands Horse Trail. Turn right onto a gravel road called Cha Cha Ridge that is also the Virginia Highlands Horse Trail. Look carefully for the VHHT sign. If you reach VA 602, you have gone too far. About 0.3 mile down Cha-Cha Ridge, bear right onto the Virginia Highlands Horse Trail with its orange diamond marker. A short distance later, turn left onto a grassy lane. After about 100 yards, the gate for the Sunrise Cabin is on the right. Do not use the gravel road past the trailer homes. The total travel distance from I-81 is 14.0 miles.

These cabins are managed by the forest service and can be reserved. The rental season is from April 1 through November 30. These facilities have a "pack-it-in, pack-it-out" policy. After reserving a cabin, you will receive a reference guide that will help you in your stay. The forest service recommends making reservations; the cabins can be reserved during a given calendar year, starting on the first work day of that year. Full payment is due within 14 calendar days of making a reservation, either by check or money order.

Bed-and-Breakfasts, Cottages, and Hostels

Apple Tree B & B

115 East Laurel Avenue
Damascus, VA 24236
(276) 475-5261 or (800) 231-7676
www.AppleTreeBnB.com

This bed-and-breakfast offers two places to stay, a 1904 Victorian mansion or "The Cottage," which offers a view from Red Hill. Both are in the town of Damascus.

Augusta's Appalachian Inn

125 East Laurel Avenue
Damascus, VA 24236
(276) 475-3565

Located in the heart of Damascus, this inn is set in the 1902 former Catron home. The owners are fine people who care for the inn and the town—and will care for you.

Buchanan Inn At Green Cove Station

41261 Green Cove Road
Damascus, VA 24236
(276) 388-3367
www.thebuchananinn.com

This is an old home near the Green Cove Station, part of the Virginia Creeper Trail, at the foot of Whitetop Mountain

Creeper Cottages

128 West Laurel Avenue
Damascus, VA 24236
(276) 623-0059
www.creepercottage.com

These are restored cottages directly adjacent to the Virginia Creeper Trail and beside Laurel Creek in Damascus.

The Davis Bourne Inn

119 Journeys End
Independence, VA 24348
(276) 773-9384
www.davisbourneinn.com

Built in 1864, this grand home is located in the historic district of Independence, Virginia.

Fox Hill Inn

8568 Troutdale Highway
Troutdale, VA 24378
(800) 874-3313
www.bbonline.com/va/foxhill

This bed-and-breakfast is located near the Mount Rogers high country and offers mountain views.

Mount Rogers Outfitters Hostel

110 Laurel Avenue
Damascus, VA 24236
(276) 475-5416
www.mtrogersoutfitters.com

This hostel is located in the heart of Damascus, across the street and in close proximity to the Appalachian Trail, post office, Laundromat, and food. Safe long-term parking is available. No hostel reservations during through-hiker season, March–June. For other seasons and shuttle reservations, please call ahead.

The Place Hostel

Corner of Legion Street and Bank Avenue
Damascus, VA 24236
(276) 475-3441

This hostel is run by the Methodist Church. It is just off Laurel Avenue in Damascus and is used by Appalachian Trail through-hikers and Virginia Creeper Trail users. A small donation is requested.

South Fork Vacation Rental & Boarding Stable

P.O. Box 1153
Damascus, VA 24236
(276) 475-5052
nmorton9@hotmail.com

Located on the Creeper Trail, this operation offers house rentals and boarding stables.

Volunteering

Jefferson National Forest, which manages the Mount Rogers National Recreation Area, can always use some extra help. Volunteer work is a rewarding way to give back to the places you love, and groups as well as individuals are encouraged to get involved. Mount Rogers needs help primarily in the following areas:

Trail maintenance
Backcountry patrol
Bike trail patrol
Horse trail patrol
Horse camp hosting
Campground hosting

Other volunteer work positions are available. The recreation area volunteer supervisor will be glad to provide specific information. The phone number is (276) 783-5196, or (800) 628-7202.

Mount Rogers Area Towns

The following is a quick overview of towns surrounding the recreation area. Each description will give you a feel for what the town is like and what services to expect.

Abingdon

Located on the western terminus of the Virginia Creeper Trail, Abington is often a jumping-off point for those coming to the recreation area. It is located off exits 17 and 19 on Interstate 81. Abington is the seat of Washington County, Virginia, where the western edge of the recreation area is located. It has a little fewer than 10,000 residents and since it's located on the interstate, it's the nearest city with a hospital, big box stores, and everything else imaginable.

Damascus

Damascus is a small town of 900 people. It was named by a developer who planned to turn the former Mocks Mill into an iron refinery like Damascus, Syria. The iron industry attempt failed, and later Damascus became oriented toward the lumber industry, following the Virginia Creeper Railroad, which passed through it. The lumber industry was short-lived. Today, however, the town is coming back, and downtown storefronts are now filling with shops and more, because of an increase in visitors to Mount Rogers.

There are several eateries and a rather small store where groceries can be purchased. The town includes ATMs and a laundromat. For the outdoor enthusiast, Damascus boasts a trail shop, Mount Rogers Outfitters, which has all the equipment to be found in a larger town. The Adventure Damascus bike shop sells and rents mountain bikes and offers a shuttle service. Blue Blaze Bike Shuttle rents bikes and offers shuttles. The only lodgings are bed and breakfasts.

Galax

Galax is at the far east end of the area. It is 10 miles from I-77, close to North Carolina. It is at the south end of the New River Rail Trail. This city has full-service grocery stores, banks, hotels, motels, and megastores. Galax has a historic downtown area and boasts of being the world capital of old-time mountain music.

Trail Days Parade in Damascus.

Marion

Marion is situated on I-81, 45 miles north of the Tennessee state line. It is a town of 7,000, and the primary gateway for the recreation area. It is named after the Swamp Fox of the American Revolution, Francis Marion. Incorporated in 1849, Marion is the birthplace of the soft drink Mountain Dew. In the town are full-service grocery stores, a discount superstore, and most conveniences found in any small city. There are numerous homespun and chain dining options. There are also many banks and ATM machines as well as a hospital.

Wytheville

Wytheville is at the junction of I-77 and I-81 and serves the far eastern portion of Mount Rogers NRA. It is named after a signer of the Declaration of Independence, George Wythe. There are 9,000 residents who enjoy all the services of a town of its size: banks, ATMs, and full-service grocery stores. There are fast-food restaurants as well as locally owned eateries. There is a regional hospital here. Since Wytheville is at the junction of two interstates, hotels and motels are abundant.

Outfitters

Adventure Damascus Bicycle Shop and Tour Company

128 West Laurel Avenue
Damascus, Virginia 24236
(888) 595-BIKE
www.adventuredamascus.com

This is a full service bike shop offering sales, rentals, and repairs. They also provide shuttles service for mountain bikers, hikers, and cross-country skiers. Guided rides are also available.

The Bike Station

US 58 at VA 91
Damascus, VA 24236
(276) 475-3629
www.thebike-station.com

Conveniently located in Damascus, this business rents bikes, including tandems, and offers shuttle services on the Creeper Trail

Blue Blaze Bike & Shuttle Service

P. O. Box 982
Damascus, Virginia 24236
(276) 475-5095 or (800) 475-5095
www.blueblaze.naxs.com

Blue Blaze offers bike rentals and repair, shuttles to all trails, and scheduled weekend departures. Guided rides and full-moon night rides are also available.

JC's Outdoors

425 Douglas Drive
Damascus, VA 24236
(866) 475-5727
jcsoutdoors.com

JC's is located directly on the Virginia Creeper Trail and offers shuttles with scheduled departures. Call ahead for departure times.

Mt. Rogers Outfitters

110 Laurel Avenue
P.O. Box 546
Damascus, Virginia 24236
(276) 475-5416 or (877) 475-5416

Owned by locals, this store has been business for a long time, serving Appalachian trail hikers and area outdoor enthusiasts. They have a wide array of backpacking equipment and offer hiker shuttle service.

New River Adventures

1007 North 4th Street
Wytheville, Virginia 24236
(276) 228-8311
www.newriveradventures.com

This business provides bike rentals and shuttle services for the New River Rail Trail and the eastern recreation area. It has an outpost at Foster Falls, directly on the New River Rail Trail.

New River Riders Bike Shoppe

208 East Stuart Street
Galax, Virginia 24333
(276) 236-5900
Toll free (877) 510-2572

This outfit rents bikes. They are located at the Galax end of the New River Rail Trail.

Contact List

Grayson Highlands State Park

Route 2, Box 141
Mouth of Wilson, VA 24363
www.dcr.virginia.gov/state_parks/gra.shtml
(276) 579-7092

Jefferson National Forest

5162 Valleypointe Parkway
Roanoke, VA 24019
(540) 265-5100
www.fs.fed.us/r8/gwj/

Mount Rogers National Recreation Area Headquarters

USDA Forest Service
Route 1, Box 303
Marion, VA 24354
(276) 783-5196
(800) 628-7202
www.fs.fed.us/r8/gwj/mr/

New River Rail Trail State Park

176 Orphanage Drive
Foster Falls, VA 24360
(276) 699-6778
http://www.dcr.virginia.gov/state_parks/new.shtml

Mount Rogers National Recreation Area Guidebook was designed and typeset on a Macintosh OS 10.4 computer system using InDesign software. The body text is set in 10/13 Goudy and display type is set in Antique Olive Std. This book was designed and typeset by Stephanie Thompson and manufactured by Thomson-Shore, Inc.